Swimming for Freedom is a must-read for a[...] in a sport or had a setback in life. Tera's journ[...] [...]omeback story of someone who persevered in faith through impossible odds.

—JOSH DAVIS, THREE-TIME OLYMPIC GOLD MEDALIST

Swimming for Freedom shows how God can heal with just a mustard seed of faith. Tera's story is proof that you can find so much more freedom in what he has planned for your life than what you have planned. Tera's daily sacrifice to press into God's voice will challenge you to do the same and find the freedom and healing God has for your life.

—BETHANY GALAT, SILVER MEDALIST
AT 2017 WORLD AQUATICS CHAMPIONSHIPS

Tera's perseverance and ultimate redemption is a tale to be shared. How much pain can a human endure, even when they have a competitive fire off the charts like hers? In her honor, I dedicated my morning swim set to Tera the Terror! I'm fifty-five years old, and the pain I felt was nothing compared to what she experienced. Thinking of her helped me through the worst parts. Bravo, Tera, for capturing the essence of your unique and incredible journey into words.

—MIKE KOLEBER, OWNER OF NITRO SWIMMING

Athletes do amazing things when they want to reach their goals. Tera is one of those athletes and has the heart and mind of a champion. Despite her injury, she made all of us proud.

—STEVE BULTMAN, FORMER US OLYMPIC COACH,
HEAD COACH, TEXAS A&M UNIVERSITY

From the very first page of *Swimming for Freedom*, I was hooked and deeply inspired. I couldn't put the book down. While reading about Tera's riveting tales of struggle and triumph, I wondered how I, too, would have responded. I highly encourage you to get two copies of this book: one for you and one for the person in your life who might be going through a personal hell. The reading experience of her story is like a good friend counseling you to never give up.

—JOSH FOLIART, FOUNDER OF MULTIPLi GLOBAL

Tera is one of the most competitive athletes I have ever seen. I was one of the few who got to coach Tera before her injury, and her potential was limitless. Even though her potential fell prey to undiagnosed injuries, she overcame those setbacks and turned them into a story of triumph that will inspire the world.

—RANDY REESE, FORMER US OLYMPIC COACH

Swimming for Freedom

A True
Story
of
Faith,
Hope,
and
Victory

TERA BRADHAM

FOREWORD BY
Annie Grevers
NCAA Champion and former member
of the U.S. National Swimming Team

BroadStreet
P U B L I S H I N G

BroadStreet Publishing® Group, LLC
Savage, Minnesota, USA
BroadStreetPublishing.com

Swimming for Freedom: A True Story of Faith, Hope, and Victory
Copyright © 2020 by Tera Bradham

978-1-4245-5892-6 (softcover)
978-1-4245-5893-3 (e-book)

Stock or custom editions of BroadStreet Publishing titles may be purchased in bulk for educational, business, ministry, fundraising, or sales promotional use. For information, please email info@broadstreetpublishing.com.

Cover Photo: Elements of Light Photography MT

Literary agent: Julie Gwinn of the Seymour Agency
Cover and interior by Garborg Design at GarborgDesign.com

Printed in the United States of America

20 21 22 23 24 5 4 3 2 1

To my Lord and Savior,
Jesus Christ, through
whom the impossible
is just a prayer away.

Contents

It is my pleasure to tell you about the miraculous signs
and wonders that the Most High God has performed for me.
How great are his signs,
how mighty his wonders!
His kingdom is an eternal kingdom;
his dominion endures from generation to generation.
Daniel 4:2-3

Foreword

When I started working for *Swimming World Magazine* in 2014, I envisioned myself as a full-time feature writer. I wanted nothing more than the job description I was presented, which included overseeing the college internship program.

I sat across from my new boss and future colleague as they described the freshly contrived internship program. It sounded like a disaster. One employee was attempting to edit for and send feedback to over thirty inexperienced college writers while also posting their own stories to *Swimming World*'s online platform. I tried not to shudder at the prospect of taking the wheel of such an out-of-control vehicle.

The majority of my job became editing for and corresponding with college interns, most of whom were college swimmers. In order to apply for the internship, applicants had to submit a writing sample. I read through the samples and took notes on each entry as they came in. Rarely did any blow me away. These were student athletes after all, which meant their priorities were school, sport, and then this potential extracurricular, unpaid internship. I graded each entry on a spreadsheet, and one name stood out from the get-go: "Tera Bradham. Texas A&M. A++++." I loved her writing style. You knew a big heart pumped out such passionate words.

Tera was accepted to the program, and as I became better acquainted with her, I began to see her gritty nature in full light. She swam the hardest events in the collegiate lineup and was in the midst of a comeback from a nearly decade-long agonizing bicep/shoulder injury. Oh, not to mention she was also getting her master's while swimming at a Division I school.

I was a D-I swimmer and national champion breaststroker for the University of Arizona. I'm married to a four-time Olympic gold medalist swimmer. I have experienced and witnessed what it takes to make it to the pinnacle of the sport. Tera had put in the training and climbed the ladder prior to this injury. She experienced excruciating, involuntary backpedaling in her swimming career because no one could figure out what was wrong. She had no idea how long this train wreck of misdiagnoses could last.

We have all been stuck at some point. We've had our hands-in-the-air moments when we plead with God, *What on earth could be beneficial from within this dark cavity of my life?* Janet Erskine Stuart said, "Joy is not the absence of suffering but the presence of God." This life hurts. And our culture tells us it shouldn't. But the Bible never makes such a shaky claim. The greatest human to ever live knew he was not placed on earth to live a life of luxury but to be tortured, mocked, and executed for the sake of those who dragged him through earthly hell.

Our sense of time is minuscule compared to God's. 1 Peter 5:10 says, "After you have suffered for a little while, the God of all grace, who called you to His eternal glory in Christ, will Himself perfect, confirm, strengthen and establish you" (NASB). Our suffering "a little while" can mean a year, a decade, or an entire earthly lifetime. Humans cannot take on a full-time heaven-minded perspective in the deepest ruts of life. Tera didn't. Doctor after doctor failed to restore her and left her with few choices. Either she had to find her hope outside of the operating room or her struggle would become her demise.

Perhaps you're like me and have only recently been thrown for a loop in your otherwise blessed life. Maybe you're like Tera, and you've been struggling for years to understand the "why" behind your pain. We all inevitably experience pain during our short stay on earth, but that doesn't mean we must also experience hopelessness. 2 Corinthians 4:17–18 says, "For momentary, light affliction is producing for us an eternal weight of glory far beyond all comparison. For the things which are seen are temporal, but the things which are not seen are eternal" (NASB). There's so much we cannot see from beneath the dark veil of trying circumstances. But light cannot be shut out by a thin veil.

In *Swimming for Freedom*, you will come to know Tera's tenacious spirit and her road to ultimate freedom, which might not resemble our worldly definition of freedom. Her story will help you see the light of hope through your own weighty circumstances. Whether you're fighting through chronic pain physically, emotionally, or spiritually, Tera's journey will meet you where you are, serving as an empathetic voice of encouragement as to what these trying circumstances could mean for your future. And even if you've reached a point of utter despair, she will remind you that no body, mind, or soul is beyond repair.

Annie Grevers

NCAA Champion and former member of the U.S. National Swimming Team

Prologue

A pensive ten-year-old sat in the back seat of the car as her mom drove her to swim practice. Lost in her thoughts and oblivious to the traffic, she blurted with a confidence bordering on absurdity, "Mom, if I make it to the Olympics, will you buy me a horse?"

Her mom smiled at the faith of her child who was so untainted by the world and its trials that she still believed the impossible to be hers for the taking. And yet, her daughter was the fastest swimmer her age in the country. The casual dream of almost all young athletes could be a reality for her child. She responded with equal confidence, "Sure, sweetie."

"Wait. You mean I don't even have to win? I just have to make the team?" The little swimmer's eyes bulged with incredulity that her mother had agreed so easily to her request.

"Absolutely. You don't even have to get to the podium. If you make it to the Olympics, I'll buy you any horse you want. Deal?"

A grin played at the corners of the girl's mouth as her eyes squinted in unparalleled determination.

"Deal." She paused. "I'm going to name her Freedom."

1

Born to Fight

First they ignore you, then they laugh at you,
then they fight you, then you win.
–Mahatma Ghandi

My body contorted in a twisted fetal position to escape the pain pulsing down my arm. Tears slid gently down my cheeks in silent agony as the words refused to come. I did not have the strength to pray on my knees; that was the position of a warrior. I had only the strength to crumple into the position of a baby. Sobs began to wrack my body. Relentless questions and doubts bombarded my mind, and my receding faith could not muster the strength to fight them.

No logic, wisdom, or truth seemed able to snatch me from the pit of despair that encompassed me on all sides. I sank deeper and deeper. There was no light, no hope, and no answer.

And then, amidst the suffocating anguish, a lone light, barely visible, shone through the darkness. Something from the recesses of my mind fought its way to consciousness: *If you have the faith of a mustard seed, nothing will be impossible for you.* The beacon of hope abated the tears long enough for me to begin to catch my breath.

Words caught in my throat as I uttered a desperately simple prayer. A prayer that I believe changed my destiny: "God, I have fought for years and years and years, and I can't fight anymore. I never thought this world could break me, but it has. And I'm finished. I know I said that your grace was sufficient for me, and I know that I said your strength was made perfect in my weakness, but I can't do this anymore. I can't live this way. Please don't make me live this way. I have been hanging on by a kernel of a mustard seed of faith for years, and I don't have it anymore. I have lost my life because I did what you told me to do. Where are you? Please don't let me live this way."

I paused as one final surge of conviction overtook my mind. I looked up to heaven, tears gathering and threatening to spill over in another torrent. I clenched my jaw with determination, and then I stressed each syllable as I made an audacious demand from an Almighty God: "Heal me or take me home, but don't make me live this way."

Curled up in a ball on my bed, begging for God to take me home, fighting thoughts of suicide, I had finally hit rock bottom. Maybe it took so long for me to get there because I had so far to fall.

I was born to prove people wrong. It was as if I could hear the conversations occurring outside the walls of my mother's uterus, the voices of the doctors telling her I would never make it.

"Do not bond with this fetus," they told her. "This pregnancy isn't going to have a happy ending for you."

Tears rose against her will as my mother fought for the unborn child in her womb. "She's my daughter, not a fetus."

"Well then, do not bond with her. She will never make it. We just don't want to see you get your hopes up only to get hurt again." The doctor tried to curb his blunt bedside manner, but the blow struck deeply.

My bedridden mother had hemorrhaged for the duration of her fourth pregnancy. She had already suffered two miscarriages, and endometriosis had overtaken her body in a vicious attack, painfully relocating and attaching her internal organs to her abdominal wall. Although she did not yet know it, both the endometriosis and tumors inside her uterus complicated this pregnancy.

After a successful pregnancy with my brother, doctors told my mom she should have an immediate hysterectomy. She refused, begging God for one more child. God answered, and I began to paddle around inside her. Now, doctors were telling her that this last hope of a second baby was futile.

Luckily for her and for me, God does not listen to the wisdom of this world. He makes his own rules. It would seem that while God knit me together in my mother's womb, he wove an inextricable patch into the fabric of my being that would never depart: the passion to fight. Before my eyes glimpsed this precious earth and before my lungs filled with oxygen, God knew he would use me to prove the world wrong. He would use me to defy logic, convention, and the standards of others. He would use me to defy the world.

On May 1, 1993, at 12:21 a.m., I won my first battle against the expectations of this world. I was born. Against all odds, I wriggled my little form free and blinked up at the doctors who swore I would never be there. I may have been a month premature, but I made it. I was alive and kicking.

My parents had chosen the name Lindsey for me, but after seeing my frail little form of skin and bones without an ounce of baby fat, they decided I didn't look like a Lindsey. Instead, they named me Tera Elizabeth: *Tera* meaning "tower of strength" and *Elizabeth* meaning "God's promise." Little did they know how those names would come to epitomize my life.

Trials surfaced from the get-go. Within my first few months of life, I looked with disgust on this strange place into which I was so unwillingly thrust. One tear duct would not quit producing a strange goop, and my eye was so full of slimy matter that I spent more time with my eye crusted shut than I spent with it open. Eventually, doctors conducted a tear-duct repair.

Wailing characterized my waking hours more than laughter. With the piece-of-cake infant my firstborn brother had been, my parents could only gawk at their new insomnia-induced lunacy. A few months after my tear-duct repair operation, my mother discovered a prominent lump protruding from my lower abdomen. Doctors took me in to the OR again but this time for a hernia repair. Afterward, I continued to cry in pain and unhappiness until one day, exactly sixteen months after I entered the world, I decided that earth was a habitable place. Much to the relief of my worn-out parents, I stopped crying and never returned to my old antics.

Five months after my birth, surgeons performed my mother's much-needed hysterectomy. The anesthesiologist's eyes bulged above his surgical mask as he observed the damage the disease had wreaked on my mother's body.

"How could this body have borne children?" The attending nurse asked in disbelief.

The surgeon looked up from his scalpel and shook his head. "How could this body have been walking?"

Water has always flowed through my veins. Neither of my parents swam growing up; my mom played tennis, and my dad wrestled. Yet somehow water found its way to my heart, pumping through me with each breath. I would swim in the water forever, and while I may have complained about my prune fingers and toes, I always dove back in.

Even when water didn't surround my sunlit, blonde hair, I pretended it did. In kindergarten, I loved *The Little Mermaid*. In fact, I believed I could be a mermaid. I sang underwater and did my best to open my eyes to see through the pool. I had conversations with King Triton underwater and moved my imaginary tail in smooth undulations to propel myself through the water.

One day, I played on the stairs, entranced in my underwater, make-believe world. Fins were never great for land, and when one of my flippers slipped on the stairs, I heard a crack. Pain seared through my toe, and I deduced I must have broken it.

Mortified that my parents would find out about my amateur mermaid skills, I casually walked downstairs and told my mom, "I think I just broke my toe."

"Sweetie, if you broke your toe, you would be crying hysterically." I wasn't sure what the word *hysterically* meant at that age, but the smirks of my dad from the kitchen confirmed my mom's disbelief.

"I heard it crack!" I retorted with the vehemence of a stubborn five-year-old.

"Well, what were you doing?" she asked.

"Playing on the stairs," I blushed.

My mom looked at me with suspicion and inspected the foot. Nothing looked amiss. "I'm sure you just stubbed your toe," she reassured me.

Ten minutes later, my foot was black from my pinky toe up to my ankle. The doctor confirmed it the next day: I *had* broken my pinky toe.

That day proved two innate characteristics of my heart: First,

I had a pain tolerance that exceeded the heights of Mount Everest. Second, I would gladly face that pain for the sake of water.

My toe healed, and I continued my exploits of algae and mermaid singing. One day at the neighborhood pool, I noticed my mom talking to the lifeguard during one of my breaches for air. The high schooler had been observing my brother and me swimming and asked her if we swam for the local club team, Texas Gold.

"What's Texas Gold?" she replied.

"You mean your kids aren't in USA Swimming?"

"What's USA Swimming?"

"Lady," he said, "you have two breaststrokers. You need to find a coach as soon as you can."

It's amazing how sixty seconds can change someone's life. One word spoken, positive or negative, can change someone's eternity. To this day, I have no idea who that lifeguard was, but he changed the trajectory of my life forever. Because of his comment, I became a competitive swimmer.

Well, technically, my brother, Taylor, became a competitive swimmer. Taylor joined our local summer league swim team, the Georgetown Aquadillos. That year, I went to all his meets, coloring Disney princess pages (probably Ariel) and rummaging through his icebox of snacks. I was bored out of my mind. Sitting for hours watching him seemed like an enormous waste of time, so I decided I should just join him. And the next year, that's exactly what I did. I joined the Aquadillos and asked my coach, Dale Huggins, every two laps what time it was.

"Time for you to get a watch," he would reply.

I hated it. Swimming was cold. You couldn't get out when you wanted. You couldn't sit on the bottom of the pool and sing. You had to jump in freezing water and wallow in the frigid arctic while others finished or while you waited for your coach to give instructions.

I made my parents aware of the torture, showing them my blue lips every chance I got. In the pool, I spent my time saving ladybugs from dying and blowing bubbles while I sat on the wall. Somehow, I kept coming back. My parents never made me swim, and they were the opposite of helicopter parents, but we all realized something—I was good. *Really* good. And I loved winning more than I hated the cold.

With the way the age group system worked in summer league, I had the worst possible birthday. Ages were determined by the age you were on May 1, my birthday. If I had been born a single day later, I would have had another year in each age group. Instead, I was always the youngest a swimmer could possibly be.

Despite this, over the next three years I broke every record the Aquadillos had. My coach would shake his head and say, "She'll be six feet under before those records are broken." Oblivious to his comments, I simply loved the competition. The mother of one of my closest friends promised her a Barbie PT Cruiser if she beat me in the 25-yard Backstroke. My mom told me, and I buried my head in my towel in anger. She often beat me in the backstroke races, but I fumed from the audacity of someone being *rewarded* for *beating me*.

When it was time for the seven and eight-year-old girls' 25-yard Backstroke, I demolished another record, touching the wall in 17.99 seconds. From the beginning, I knew how to channel anger. I subconsciously understood how it worked, and I took advantage of it. I knew I should be a good sport, but secretly, I longed for one of my competitors to talk smack to me. I would smile kindly and then talk my smack in the pool.

This intense competitiveness would bleed over into every aspect of my life. For years, my brother and I had begged our parents for a puppy, and we felt frustrated by their repeated denials. We asked what it would take for them to finally change their minds. Unbeknownst to us, Mom and Dad had carefully calculated how far away each of us was from our respective team records and set what they felt confident was an insurmountable goal because they were intent on maintaining a pet-free home. Pleased with their plan, they promised that if the two of us could combine for a total of six record-breaking swims, then we would get a puppy! Behind our backs, they laughed at the implausibility of such a daunting task.

Four weeks later, Taylor and I cooed as we cuddled Lexi, our new puppy, in the back seat as we drove home from Dallas. Our parents realized they were in over their heads and that my brother and I had more talent than a summer league program could foster. So at age eight, I began to swim year-round, and my world would never be the same.

2

Tera the Terror

It's not the size of the man
but the size of his heart that matters.
—Evander Holyfield

"These girls are going to be shocked when I win their gold medals!"

"Now Tera, it's an honor to even be here. Just do the best you can, okay?" My mom tried to prepare me for the reality I was about to face, but I had always chosen my own reality—and then made it happen.

"You don't think I can beat them, do you?" My eyes squinted in offense.

"Tera, I'm just saying that you are the *only* eight-year-old in the entire state of Texas who qualified under ten-year-old standards. You made six cuts, and you should be proud of that. Some of these girls are almost eleven, and you're eight."

"Yeah, but I have something none of them have."

"Oh yeah, what's that?"

"Mommy, I have kick-butt fire down in my heart!"

Kick-butt fire I had, and I had it in spades. My hatred of

losing propelled me to stardom early on. While I did have talent, my work ethic far exceeded it. I lived to push myself further than I thought possible. I fully believed I could take down Sherrill Thompson, a state champion twice my size, when I was exactly two years younger than she was (it didn't happen, but I never stopped believing I could). By the time I was ten, I could do thirty pull-ups. I lived for the thrill of a close race. No one hated to lose more than I did, and the crowd knew it. Dale, my previous coach, coined the name. I became known as "Tera the Terror."

Timers began to ask me to autograph their napkins or heat sheets. I received standing ovations from crowds of hundreds. Parents of other swimmers told my parents they would pay big money to see me swim because a competitor like me only came around once every few decades. Other swimmers celebrated my birthday because it meant I moved to the next age group, and they wouldn't have to race me again until they, too, aged up. Tera the Terror reigned in Texas.

At nine, I started breaking South Texas records. I won the 50 Breaststroke at every state championship from age nine until I was twelve, garnering eight state titles, including when I was at the bottom of my age group. I broke the team record for Longhorn Aquatics in every event that existed in both Short Course Yards and Long Course Meters, which are the two types of courses in competitive swimming. By the time I was ten, I was the fastest swimmer my age in the country in three events, second fastest in five events, third fastest in three events, and ranked in the top ten in five other events, excluding number-one rankings in three relays.

At the 2004 State Championship, I was ten, and my parents, coaches, and I lined up the game plan to win the High Point Award. This award is given to the swimmer who earns the most points over the course of the meet than any other swimmer. We chose my best events, making sure to leave just enough time between each one so that I wouldn't have to race finals back to back. The meet was stacked, but it looked like I had a shot at winning all seven of my events.

One of the closest of the seven races was my first event, the 200 Freestyle (Free). In swimming, you're never sure how much time a racer can drop at a big meet because we only taper (or gradually reduce) our training until we are supremely rested for two to three meets a year. Because of this, I feared Callie Baker might steal my chance at winning all my events. Callie and I had traded first and second-place rankings in the state for the 200 Free that year, but we hadn't yet raced head-to-head in person. I wasn't about to let her steal one of my gold medals in the first race of the meet.

I dove in for the final and took it out fast, unsure of how Callie paced her races. I didn't know if she finished strong or started strong, so I wanted to set the mood from the beginning. Up in the stands, my mom grabbed my dad's arm without saying a word. I was out too fast. My first 50 was a blistering twenty-eight seconds, and I had never started faster than thirty seconds. The 200 Freestyle is not a sprint, and if you push too hard in the beginning, you won't have enough gas left in the tank to bring it home. My parents knew there was no way I could hang on to that pace, but they were there to stick with me, win or lose.

At the halfway mark, I was a second underneath state record pace; I'd swum it in fifty-eight seconds. *She's going to die. She's going to die,* my parents' thoughts paralleled each other as my mom's hand didn't leave his arm. I extended my lead to a body length. After the third fifty, my parents realized I wasn't dying. The crowd began to realize it too. In the water, my jaw and my third toe started to go numb, a weird phenomenon that only happened to me in the most difficult races of my life. I knew I had a four-body-length lead, but I still had some juice left.

The announcer yelled, "And Tera Bradham is still under the

state record pace! Let's bring her home, folks!" As I took a breath, I saw hundreds people stand to their feet and heard the roar of the crowd. I dug as deeply as I could to will my exhausted body to an even greater feat.

I turned for home and charged for the wall, leaving all my competitors half a pool behind. I gave it all I had, emptying my tank as I touched the wall. Gasping for air, I heard the announcer yell, "And Tera Bradham has demolished the state record by over two seconds! Your new state champion in the 10 and Under 200 Yard Freestyle, with a time of 2:03.56, Teraaaa Bradhaaaaam!"

I looked at the clock to confirm he had read the time correctly. I had broken a twenty-year-old state record by over two seconds, an eternity in a sport where hundredths mean everything. I turned to the right and looked at the crowd still on their feet in a standing ovation. My parents couldn't believe it, but at the same time, they could. They understood the simplicity of the matter to their daughter: I just didn't want to lose to Callie Baker.

The lady next to them turned and said, "That record will *never* be broken." That year, no other girl my age swam a 200 Free that fast in the United States. It was my first number-one ranking in the nation.

Later, during that same meet, my swim cap slipped off my head in the backstroke leg of a 200-yard Individual Medley (IM) during the championship final. At the time, I did not wear hair ties under my cap, and my hair flowed down well past my shoulders. I stifled panic as I pushed off for my breaststroke pull out and resisted reaching out to grab my cap floating to the bottom beneath me—to break stroke would have caused a disqualification. Luckily, I wore my goggles under my cap, so I could still see, but the drag created by my hair cost me seconds of time. I knew I had a few-body-lengths lead on my competitors, but I couldn't let an equipment mishap cost me a victory, so I kept racing, almost choking on the freestyle leg as I tried to breathe with a mouthful of hair. Even with the monumental disadvantage, I won the State Championship by over six seconds.

This was the competitor I chose to become. I loved being the Terror. Nothing could break my intensity. No challenge was too big. Did I believe someone could defeat me? Theoretically, yes. But I knew if she won, I was going to give her the fight of her life, and she would have to earn it. My mental toughness knew no limits. Even when I did lose, it didn't shake my confidence; it only fueled my anger to prove someone wrong the next time.

Once, when I was eleven and a year younger than most of the competitors in my age group, I lost an event at the State Championship. Most age-group swimmers were beside themselves with joy just to make it to finals at the State Championship; I, however, had a meltdown after placing second. That night, I cried myself to sleep because I lost. My mother had tried to comfort me, telling me what an incredible accomplishment it was to be the second-fastest swimmer in the state of Texas, but her message fell on deaf ears. I was inconsolable. My eyes burned with tears of embarrassment that night as I refused to let go of the defeat. The next day, I returned to race my offender. I turned my hurt pride into vengeance that fueled me to not only beat her but to also demolish another state record in the process.

I made sure no one ever questioned who the real champion was. No swimmer ever beat me without due punishment. It was my duty to make sure all swimmers knew where they stood on the totem pole. Other swimmers sometimes said I was the most intimidating person they had ever raced. My confidence flirted with the impossible on a daily basis. To me, impossible was only a challenge to make it possible. I never doubted myself. I knew that when I got up on the blocks, I was going to win. If anyone ever beat me, they would rue that day for the rest of their lives. I would make sure of it.

After the cap mishap in the 200 IM, my parents still believed I could break the state record in that event, but they also knew that required competition. Since my best races were always when someone was pushing me, my parents scoured the nation for someone who would give me that race. They found it in Madeline Dirado, also known as Maya Dirado. Swimming for PASA Aquatic Club, she had a best time that was one second faster than mine in the 200 IM, and she was competing a few weeks after the Texas State Championships at Far Westerns, a championship swim meet in Northern California known for attracting a speedy group of competitiors. My mom and I flew to California, and the talk of the town was the girl who traveled from Texas to California in an effort to steal the High Point Award. Maya Dirado didn't seem too keen on letting that happen.

I started the meet off strong, always one to love the change of environment and the pressure of a travel meet. Maya and I had opposite best strokes, Maya excelling in the butterfly (fly) and the backstroke, while my specialties were the breaststroke and the free-style. She won all the butterfly and backstroke events, and I won all the breaststroke events. We split victories in the different freestyle events, but we had to race head-to-head for the Individual Medley, known as the king-of-the-mountain event in swimming because the event demands you race all four strokes.

In preliminaries, girls lined the sides of the pool to watch me race and then Maya. Maya's technique was flawless; mine looked like a freight train barreling through the water. Maya cut the water like glass, almost no splash apparent in the finesse of her form. Coaches shook their heads when they watched me, unable to believe how good I was with so much room for improvement. I just *wanted* it more than other people did.

That night, Maya and I raced in a showdown final. As expected, she took an early lead over me in the fly and back. But

I loved the chase, and I knew my strengths. When we turned for breaststroke, the hunt commenced. Like a predator, I ate up inches as I made my way to her feet, then her hips, and then her head. We turned for the freestyle homestretch neck and neck and duked it out until the finish. The race came down to the wire, and all eyes shot to the scoreboard to tell who had touched first.

My hand had touched the wall first with a time of 2:19.49, shearing over a second off the Texas State Record. Maya and I high fived in the water, knowing neither of us could have swum our times without the other. Those two times ended up being the number one and number two times in the country for the 10 and Under 200 Yard IM that year. At the end of the meet, Maya and I tied for High Point, and our picture together made it into *Swimming World Magazine*. If the name Maya Dirado sounds familiar, it might be because she won the Olympic gold medal in the 100 Meter Backstroke and the silver medal in the 400 Meter IM in 2016. Her loudest fans cheered for her in Austin, Texas. From an early age, she has been a class act and a fierce competitor, and my family and I wouldn't have wanted anyone else to win.

But back in 2004, we were both on track for Olympic glory. My coach, Randy Reese, told my parents that unless I fell into drugs or became sidetracked by boyfriends, nothing should keep me from making an Olympic team. In fact, he was excited that I would have a chance at three or four Olympics: one at fifteen years old, one at nineteen, one at twenty-three, and possibly one at twenty-seven.

Around this time, parents of other swimmers started interrogating my parents, asking them what my schedule was like, what they fed me, how much I slept, and what I did to prepare for a meet. My parents shrugged their shoulders and confessed, "Well, every morning of the meet, she eats sausage gravy on biscuits." The questioners gawked at the frivolity of parents who didn't understand the champion-in-the-making whom they were obviously neglecting. My parents just laughed. Sausage gravy and biscuits was my tradition, and it worked. They figured I would have more than my fair share of discipline and crazy-athlete habits when I got older. At age ten, they let my competitiveness do the work. You can fix eating habits and sleeping routines; you cannot teach kick-butt fire.

After Far Westerns, I was the target to which all arrows pointed, but I was fine with that because I knew swimmers couldn't hit a target that moved farther and farther away. In fact, I set my own targets. Some of them included the older swimmers on my team. Even though I was the fastest swimmer my age in the country, I certainly wasn't the fastest in the country overall. Luckily for me, I swam under Randy Reese, former Olympic coach and coach of eighteen Olympic gold medalists.

When my parents saw my talent developing, they made the commitment to drive me to the Circle C swimming pool in South Austin, a forty-five-minute commute one way, twice a day. I completed homework in the car as gas guzzled away my parents' bank account. Randy Reese was worth the drive. If I was the epitome of an intimidating swimmer, Randy was the epitome of an intimidating coach. He walked the pool deck and said little, but when he spoke, you knew to pay attention. He may not say anything to you for a few days, and then at the next practice, he would give you a life-altering tip about the angle of your arm and how it affected your stroke. He kept you on your toes while you waited to hear his one-sentence game changer.

Randy was known for no excuses and for training the good ole way: pounding toughness into swimmers through long-yardage sets. My dad heard stories about how he trained his swimmers at the University of Florida who captured two National Championships. Apparently, he had them swim the St. John River . . . upstream. When the current became too much for them, he would yank them into the boat long enough to recover and then toss them back in to develop endurance.

Randy was also an innovator. He invented the pulley system that almost every college swim team uses for strength training. He bought some metal baskets, hung a wire across poles thirty feet in the air, attached the basket to a pulley, and put a belt on the other end of it. That belt wrapped around a swimmer, and then weights were thrown into the basket. It was our job to hoist the weighted basket through the air as we swam to the other side of the pool with resistance. Pulleys were brutal. Sometimes, as we gasped for air on the side of the pool, Randy would decide that we weren't pulling enough weight, and he would toss additional dumbbells into our baskets.

Swimming outside, I braved the sea of black crickets that swarmed the pool in the summer, and Randy told my mom she could bring a net to scoop them out of my lane if I couldn't handle it. There is nothing quite like taking a breath and almost sucking in five crickets or taking off your suit to find insect body parts that worked their way in as you swam. My terror bordered on phobia. Randy's swimmers also procured attractive tan lines thanks to his method of having us wear basketball shorts and old sneakers for resistance. But nothing could keep me away from the challenge. Winning meant more to me than crickets or tan lines.

Randy had more than just potent swimming knowledge; he had superpowers. Storms would come raging in, lightning jagging through the sky off in the distance, yet one patch of bright light shone in a circle above the pool. One day, his superpowers took a day off, and the sky unleashed torrents of rain while we were swimming. We knew rain wasn't enough to get us out of practice. But then, it started hailing. We all looked up to Randy's umbrella, and he could see the hope in our eyes through our goggles. Above the downpour he yelled, "Keep swimming!" We swam another two hundred meters and stopped again at the wall as the hail bounced off our swim caps. "Fine," he said. "Get out." We hooped and hollered as we ran through the ice to the locker rooms. No excuses were allowed in Randy's practices, and we relished that one opportunity from Mother Nature.

Somewhere in the dry-humored, intimidating man was a soft spot for the youngest swimmer by three years in his National Group. I was always a terrible kicker, and one day, we were kicking vertically in the pool. The lightest weight Randy allowed anyone to hold was a twenty-pounder above his or her head. I kept sinking so badly that I would plunge to the bottom of the pool and have to kick off the bottom to surface for air. Randy came by, smiled, and began to laugh, a rarity for the man. Then, he walked away without offering to let me change the weight. Randy understood my personality and how to motivate me. We both knew his laughter would draw out Tera the Terror, and she would meet whatever challenge he presented. I kicked harder and laughed at myself.

Randy also had a habit of throwing the last bit of his coffee into the pool at me while I swam backstroke. I was his favorite target for his lukewarm leftovers, probably because of the reaction he got. Never seeing it coming, I would choke on the sugar and whirl around the pool until I found Randy's smiling face above me. I would immediately start laughing and try to hide my smile, and Randy's lips would form a smirk under his mustache. The coffee routine was our inside joke.

Randy certainly didn't cut me any slack. He saw my potential, but he knew potential without progress was exactly that: potential. Kicking always being my weakness, I couldn't make a 1:30 base interval for 100-yard repetitions of freestyle kick in the National Group. Fed up with people not making the interval, one day, Randy said anyone who couldn't make ten 100s Freestyle kick on 1:30 had to stay after and do ten 100s Butterfly. I had always survived the kicking sets by using breaststroke kick, but he tore that rug right out from under me.

I was the only swimmer in the group who couldn't make the interval, and Randy made me stay after practice to complete ten 100s Butterfly. After about four, he walked out the back doors of the natatorium and left me there to finish the set on my own. Crying from humiliation, I transformed my hurt pride into an anger that fueled me to keep swimming. I finished the set, and I started to make the kicking intervals too.

I had no issue chasing national champions and Olympic medalists at practice; to me, they were just my teammates. Randy saw me train with a fire and a passion known to few in the world; he saw me rise up to compete with his athletes with the confidence of a world-class star. I never realized there was a reason to be intimidated by those studs. Age didn't matter to me, and as far as I was concerned, if I could beat them even on a bad day, then I belonged with them. Randy understood that I refused to accept defeat. He knew I would rather die than lose.

My dad often talked to Randy on the pool deck at Circle C, their conversations usually consisting of University of Florida football rather than swimming. Always unassuming, my dad never brought me up unless Randy offered information. One day, Randy turned to my dad in seriousness. He told my dad how rare it was to find someone who fought like I did. I simply refused to lose. Combine that ethic with his coaching skill, and Randy knew what my caliber of determination could produce.

"Charlie, all we have to do is get her to the meet where she can qualify for the Olympics. If we can just get her to Olympic Trials, she'll fight her way onto the team. It doesn't matter if she's in lane eight. If she makes the meet, she'll make the team. All we have to do is get her to trials."

At twelve years old, I was already one to two seconds away

from qualifying for multiple Olympic Trials events. Randy had been an Olympic coach. He knew what it took to make the team. Compliments from Randy were rare, and when he gave them, the recipient took them with utmost sincerity. If he said you could make the Olympic team, you could. I didn't see any reason why I wouldn't make the team. In my mind, it was my destiny.

3

Swimming through a Wall

Everybody likes to win,
but those who win are those who hate to lose.
–Eddie Reese

Just one more race, Tera. You've got this. I psyched myself up for my third event of the night and my final race of the 2006 State Championship. We could hear the boys finishing their race, and only seconds remained until it was our turn. The coach who barricaded the door then waved his clipboard at us, signaling the eight finalists to begin our march to the starting blocks.

"Please welcome your finalists for the Women's 12 and Under 50 Yard Freestyle!" the announcer's voice boomed into the natatorium. Hands clapped as the walk-out song reverberated, and the crowd cheered. With my CD player tucked inside the pocket of my parka and my hood up Rocky Balboa-style, "Eye of the Tiger" pounded its way through my headphones. Because I was always the only hooded figure, the audience knew who I was, but all they could see was the metallic glint of my goggles underneath my hood. No one could break my concentration or match my intensity. No one hated to lose as much as I did. People would joke that I'd swim through a wall to win, and I knew if it came down to it, I probably would.

I walked with the confidence of a thirty-three-time Texas State Champion. I had been the fastest swimmer in the country my age for three years. I had broken and still held six Texas state records. And to top it off, I had already added two state titles to my belt that night. I owned the Texas Age Group State Championship (TAGS). I was the best, and I knew it. My confidence did not waver, but I also had a profound respect for my competitors. I had won six of my seven events thus far at the meet, and my goal was to sweep the championships with a perfect seven golds. I had accomplished this very feat at ten years old, and a newspaper had called it a "Spitzian performance." Just like Mark Spitz had won an unprecedented seven golds at the Olympics, I had won an unprecedented seven golds at the State Championships that year.

I could reach my goal but not without this final event. Of the seven events I was racing, the 50-yard Freestyle was by far my weakest. The 50 Free is the shortest race in the sport of swimming, consisting of only two laps. Down and back. The whole race takes between twenty and thirty seconds. Hundredths of a second are the difference between first and eighth place. One mistake costs a swimmer everything. A bad start, a bad turn, or a breath too many could sacrifice the entire race.

These thoughts filled my subconscious as our parade ended and each swimmer broke from the line to go to her lane. A man announced our names and teams as we stepped up to our blocks. I took my headphones off, shoved them in the pocket with the CD player, and dropped my parka in the basket behind the timers' chairs.

I could feel my chest pounding with adrenaline. I took my goggles off my face and ran my index fingers in circles along the inside to clear the fog created by my body heat. I pushed them back down over my eyes, making sure the rubber suctioned into a good seal to prevent leaking. The announcer's voice barely registered in my mind as he went down the lineup. Some swimmers liked to smile and wave at the crowd as they heard their name over the speakers, but I never wanted to break my concentration by waving.

As lane one waved at the stands, I walked up to the edge of the pool, splashed water onto my chest three times, and threw it once onto my back. I stood up as the announcer made his way through lanes two and three. The adrenaline worked its way through my body as my arms began to shake with energy. I took practice strokes in the air and shook out my legs.

"Swimming in lane four, your TAGS champion in the 50 and 100 Butterfly, swimming for City of Richardson Aquatics, Meee-gaaaan Connollyyyy!" Megan was the favorite in the event, and the cheer from the crowd confirmed it. She had won some events in these championships and had taken second to me in others. I planned to keep it that way.

I let the cheer from the crowd fuel my motivation to prove them wrong as I shook my arms and legs. "Swimming in lane five, your TAGS champion in the 50 and 100 Breaststroke, the 100 and 200 IM, and the 100 and 200 Freestyle. You've already seen her break a state record this weekend. Swimming for Longhorn Aquatics, Teraaa Bradhaaam!" A faint cheer echoed. I thrived off the fact that more people wanted to see me fail than win. I relished their chagrin each time I won.

Three girls remained to be announced. I knew I did not have a technique as refined as Megan Connolly's. She was a freestyler and a sprinter, and her form put mine to shame. People said my strokes weren't pretty and that I won because of willpower, not technique. But I knew something else: no girl would push as hard as I was going to push. I was willing to hurt more than anyone else. I wasn't willing to let Megan fight as vehemently as I was going to fight.

I continued to pump the adrenaline through my body by swinging my arms back and forth, keeping my muscles loose and ready. Lane seven's name flooded the natatorium as I stared down the length of the pool. *Down and back. Down and back.* I could feel the adrenaline starting to make the tips of my fingers tingle. The feeling enthralled me. The more nervous I was, the more energy I had to channel into my race. The more pressure I felt, the more I liked it. The bigger the audience, the more determination I had. I fed off the energy of the crowd, the closest of races, and the expectation of breaking a record. Now, the pressure was on. This was my prime time.

Eyes briefly rested on the swimmer announced in lane eight. Then they turned to lanes four and five for the showdown. A whistle sounded, signaling the swimmers to step up on the blocks. I took two steps up on the block and crouched in the starting position, every muscle tense with anticipation. The natatorium quieted. I clapped five times, my habit before every race. My heartbeat pounded in my ears. My fingertips wiggled in anticipation. I took two steady breaths.

"Swimmers, take your mark." I wrapped my fingers around the edge of the block; my mind focused, waiting for the first wave of sound to hit my eardrums.

Beep.

In an instant, all my muscles tightened and propelled my body through the air. Water enveloped my body as I dolphin kicked three times and then flutter kicked into the breakout. My arms pulled as quickly as I could make them while my feet motored up white water behind me. I knew I could not afford more than three breaths in the race, but breaths were my only way to see where I was in the pack. Just before the first turn, I took one breath to the right to see Megan Connolly. Neck and neck. I flipped my body upside down, and my feet hit the wall. I pushed with all the force my legs could muster and swam for home. Three more strokes, and I took another breath. Behind.

Fight, Tera, fight. I took a few more strokes. I could feel the lactic acid starting to lock my muscles down. My arms felt heavier. I took my last breath. Still behind. *It's never over until I say it's over,* I thought. I dug deep, mustering every ounce of strength left in my body, lunging into the wall at full speed. Pain ripped through my arm as I heard thousands of voices gasp and begin to scream. Cheers erupted through the crowd as applause began. My heart sank. By then, I was well acquainted with the signals of the crowd.

Massive cheering meant one of two things: I was either about to break a record, or I was about to lose. The audience loved seeing records broken, and they loved seeing an underdog beat the top dog. I knew I wasn't close to a record in the 50 Free, so when I heard the crowd go nuts, I knew I had lost. Disappointment swarmed my mind, and I reeled in disbelief. *I had her. I was closing in. I knew it. I fought so hard. I never lose close races. I always win the final push.* After what felt like a minute (but was probably only three seconds), I pulled myself up to see the scoreboard. I at least wanted to see how close I had come.

Wait. There was a one next to my name. Had I won? I couldn't have won. Wait, Megan had a one next to her name as well. I had *tied* for first place! The scoreboard showed that lanes four and five both swam a time of 24.77. We had tied to the hundredth of a second. A smile of relief and amazement spread across my face.

"Wow! Folks, your winners in the 12 and under 50 Yard Freestyle are Tera Bradham *and* Megan Connolly!" The crowd couldn't get enough. I didn't mind sharing a victory; I just wanted a sweep of the meet.

Still catching my breath, I grabbed the backstroke bars on the block and yanked myself out of the water. Pain seared through my shoulder in protest, but I ignored it as I walked over to Megan.

I gave my cowinner a hug of sportsmanship; it was a great race. To me, the race was a personal best time and the means to an end—a perfect, seven-for-seven State Championship meet.

As I walked from the competition end of the pool down to the side of the pool reserved for warming up and warming down, sharp pain pulsed through my arm. I wondered what had happened, but I didn't stop my march of triumph long enough to process the pain. I jumped in the shallow end of the pool to swim a few laps of cool down, and I took a stroke. I winced as pain flooded my senses. I stopped swimming and stood up. I looked at my arm in confusion. Thinking maybe it was some weird mishap or muscle spasm, I dove back underwater and surfaced for another stroke. Immediately, I curled up in a ball in the middle of the pool and stifled a scream. I stopped swimming and walked a few steps. My mind blurred in bewilderment.

Clenching my jaw in determination, I took a stroke with my left arm and then tried a third time to pull with my right arm. The pain retaliated with as much fury as that with which I had tried to defeat it. I stopped swimming and walked back to the wall, deciding I wouldn't warm down. I knew my body would be hurting from the lactic acid at practice in the morning, but the 50 Free was my last race. I could deal with sore muscles. Besides, I had a High Point trophy to accept.

Using my arms to push myself out of the pool, I winced again as another sharp pain overtook my arm. *Whatever*, I thought as I walked to my chair on deck and grabbed my towel. I went to the locker room, showered, and changed, noticing I couldn't accomplish either task without daggers of pain deep in my shoulder when I lifted my right arm above my head.

After the awards ceremony, I headed to the proud arms of my parents. They were careful not to display their pride in public to be considerate of other families, but as soon as we closed the car doors, they shared in the excitement as we celebrated all the races my brother and I had swum at the meet. When we pulled out of the parking lot and got on the road, the adrenaline started to die down, and I began to relax. The replays of the weekend exhausted themselves, and the car went silent for a while, each left to the solitude of his or her own reveries.

"Hey, my shoulder kind of hurts," I said into the silence. "I think I may have done something to it on the wall when I finished." My parents asked a few questions, and then the conversation returned to the thrill of the night. I didn't bring it up again.

I pushed the pain from my mind and celebrated with my family as we ate hamburgers and fries, the reward my brother and I requested after every championship meet. With a full stomach and a fuller heart, my eyes grew heavy. We had a three-hour drive back from Dallas, and I had to get up at 4:30 to go to practice in the morning. As the youngest swimmer in the group, no one else had come to an age-group State Championship. Randy expected me to be back at practice with the others on Monday.

As I drifted off to sleep, I replayed the victories one more time. After all, once tomorrow hit, the celebration was over. The accomplishments were in the past, and it was time to work toward my next goal. *That was a close one*, I thought, thinking about my last race. My only thought about the 50 Free was that it had sealed my perfect championship. Sure, it was a best time, but the other races that weekend far overshadowed it.

I didn't realize that the 50 Free that weekend was the most important race I had ever swum. I had no idea, falling asleep in the back seat that night, that when I lunged into the wall, stopping the clock at 24.77, the time also marked the exact moment when my life changed forever.

4

Rice Krispies

*The most important thing in the Olympic Games is not to win
but to take part, just as the most important thing in life is not
the triumph but the struggle. The essential thing is not to have
conquered but to have fought well.*

—Pierre de Coubertin

knew I had a good relationship with Randy, but knowing I was
going to have to walk up to the authority figure in my career and
tell him I couldn't lift my arm so much as two inches was not a
conversation I looked forward to. I dreaded it the entire drive to
practice.

After we had driven back from the state championships, I
went to bed, and the pain had woken me up twice during the night.
I didn't think much of it, but when I got up for practice the next
morning, I could hardly move my right arm. The searing pain was
intolerable, even for me.

When I got to practice, I was apprehensive about breaking
the news to Randy, and for some reason my nervous instinct was
to grab my throat with my left arm. I walked up to him, right arm

dangling and left arm looking like I was choking myself—a glorious sight for anyone at five o'clock in the morning. Without meeting his eyes, I muttered, "Something happened to my shoulder last night. I can't move it."

Randy asked a few questions and then told me to get into the pool and see how it felt. I agreed and jumped in, and then I tried to take a stroke. I almost screamed each time, and I could not force myself to swim through the pain. I got out and told Randy the bad news.

"Alright, well, we'll just kick today," he responded. I couldn't tell what he was thinking.

I moved down the pool to a lane away from everyone and began the first practice of hundreds kicking instead of swimming. I started out with my arms on a kickboard, only using my legs to propel myself through the water, as is the natural way to kick at practice. But holding my arm up on the kickboard was every bit as painful as swimming, so I had the humiliation of trudging up to Randy one more time and telling him even the kickboard was too much to handle. I could feel my cheeks burning, and I didn't take my goggles off so that Randy wouldn't be able to see my tears of frustration.

I kicked on my back with my arms at my side for the rest of practice. My mind flew through stages of confusion, grief, frustration, pity, and anger. Every time I got back to anger, I tried to take a stroke. The forceful attempts started off with vehement retaliation as I refused to accept the state of my body. As the pain escalated, the strokes became more and more timid, and eventually, I stopped trying to weasel strokes in altogether. Unable to accept resignation, I walked off the pool deck after practice in humiliation and confusion.

The next day was no better. Neither was the next. Or the next. The injury did not appear to be minor but something that would require time and healing. My parents, Randy, and I decided that I would kick for a while to see if the pain got any better. After kicking the entire summer without my arms, swimming off and on when I could, the pain was barely better, and Randy referred us to a local surgeon to see if he could diagnose the issue.

Sitting in the surgeon's office, I had much to learn about medicine. I assumed that every time you went to the doctor, they would find what was wrong and give you a solution. I had no doubt that I would be over this little injury in no time. I winced as the doctor did strength tests on my arm but, apparently, not convincingly enough for him to ascertain a true problem. He told us I was too young to have a major injury, and the pain must be due to tendinitis or a rotator cuff impingement. Since I trained with such an advanced group, maybe lifting weights so young had been hard on my body as it developed at the same time.

The surgeon decided to inject a cortisone shot into each shoulder to reduce the inflammation. He left the room and returned with a two-inch needle, large enough to make most thirteen-year-olds have a slight anxiety attack, but I trusted the person who went to medical school. He said it would help me return to my sport, so I shrugged off the needle's appearance as it poked the back of my shoulder, between my shoulder blade and spine. I felt the whole two inches of needle sink deep into my shoulder joint. Then, it felt like burning ice was shot through my shoulder, and the pain expanded as the medicine seeped through my ligaments and tendons to invade the entire shoulder capsule. None of this showed on my face as I made a point of not showing pain. The surgeon proceeded to the other shoulder and did the same. He figured he might as well get the inflammation out of both shoulders. We ended our visit, and I headed to afternoon practice.

Immediately, I felt a difference in my arm. The pain was significantly reduced, and I knew we had found the solution to my problem. Overjoyed to be back to normal, I pushed my body like

41

my old self. I chased down my teammates and grappled with the water to achieve victory. Glad to put the shoulder trial behind me, I headed to bed that night feeling better than I had in three months.

The next day was my third day of eighth grade, and it started out like every other school day. I had my outfits laid out for the entire week, and I was excited to show off my new back-to-school wardrobe. I woke up at 4:30 a.m., carefully folded my orange-striped top and jean skirt beneath my towel in my swim bag, ate a small Power Bar, and zombie-walked to the backseat to sleep for the forty-five-minute drive to practice.

"Mom," I mumbled while getting into the car, "something's wrong. I can't breathe."

"What does it feel like? Describe the pain," she inquired.

"I don't know. I've never felt it before, but my chest hurts really badly. It hurts every time I take a breath." Sleep clouded my eyes, but it could not overtake the strange feeling in my chest. I dozed in and out until we arrived at practice.

Getting out of the car, something was amiss. I was in worse pain than the pain I felt with my shoulder, which was substantial. However, this pain was deeper and covered more area. It was more of an ache than a sharp pain, but it was the most excruciating ache you can imagine. It was as if a pair of hands was inside my chest trying to pop my lungs like water balloons.

I began practice, which ironically happened to be geared towards hypoxic work—holding your breath for long periods of time. I started the practice leading the lane and then dropped farther and farther back as I let person after person pass me.

"Go ahead, I can't breathe," I told my teammate. Surprised to see me dropping so far back, she asked, "Are you sure?"

I nodded, and she stayed in front of me as I held my breath for twenty-five meters over and over. Each time I came to the wall, I debated getting out and talking to Randy about the pain. I hoped he might notice me swimming in the back or the grimace on my face and save me the trouble of disappointing him with another injury. However, my teammate noticed and asked me if I should get out. "No, I'm fine. I think I can make it."

As I continued to swim, I started to imagine my funeral. I wondered who would miss me if I were to die. I imagined who would come to my funeral, and I pondered if I had lived life well. Would I regret anything if I died today? Did I do everything I was supposed to do? Would I be in a casket? What would I look like? Who would speak? Would all my teammates go to my funeral?

The pain was to the point where I subconsciously knew it was serious enough to kill me, and yet I kept swimming. An innate desire to overcome fueled me, stroke by stroke. I could not tell people I had *another* excuse to not be able to train as hard as everyone else. The idea was humiliating. I knew this pain was valid, but I also knew other people would not know it. They had started to talk about why I wasn't training the same way I used to. I heard whispers of teammates who didn't think it was fair that I kicked so much; they said I was trying to get out of the hard sets. I wanted to prove them wrong. But more than that, I wanted to prove my body wrong. It was as if my organs were consulting each other without my knowledge and rising up in rebellion. But I could defeat them.

And I did, miraculously finishing the practice. The breaths were causing sharper and sharper pains and made full inhalation impossible. The aching had worsened to an exploding bomb on the exhale and a knife-blade cut on the inhale. The pain didn't get much better when I stopped swimming. On the way to school, I told my dad, "Dad, there's something really wrong in my chest."

"I'm sure it's just a sinus infection," he assured me.

"I don't think so. I need a doctor appointment as soon as possible."

"I don't know if they can see you today, but I'll call."

Never a great advocate for how much pain I was truly in, his response sufficed. Through divine provision, the doctor's office had a cancellation. By the time my dad picked me up from school, my voice had changed. It had heightened to the point where I sounded like I had sucked in helium. I sounded like Alvin from *Alvin and the Chipmunks*.

"You sound funny," my dad said, half joking and half concerned.

We arrived at our family doctor's office, and my doctor began his normal examination procedures. He checked my throat. I held out my tongue and said "ahh." He looked in my ears and took my pulse.

"I don't see anything wrong," he started.

"One more thing," I added, as I realized he might find this detail interesting. "When I was in class today, I started feeling my neck, and I felt all these bubbles." I rubbed my throat to emphasize my point. The doctor's brow furrowed underneath his glasses. He began to feel my throat where I had pointed. The creases in his forehead deepened.

"It feels like . . . Rice Krispies," he muttered. He remained calm but silent, feeling the length of my throat. Bubbles permeated my neck from my collarbone to my chin. He took a step back and leaned on one hip. Returning to his computer, he said, "Well, I'm going to send you over to the ER so that they can run some additional tests. Just take these slips and hand them to the personnel over there, and they'll get you all set up."

He started to hand the slips to us but decided to walk my dad and me over to the ER, which was a few buildings away from his office. My dad, always the calm in the storm, didn't let any worry surface.

"Is something really wrong?" I asked.

My doctor assured me we just needed a few more tests done.

My dad made me feel like we were simply taking a detour around the park on our way back to our car. We walked through the automatic sliding doors, and I took a seat on a blue chair in the waiting room.

As my dad checked me in, I noticed a countdown showing how many people were in line to be seen. Then I noticed the other people in the waiting room. Some had casts, some donned smeared blood, and some closed their eyes as they rested on a shoulder, unable to look up. All the people accompanying them wore haggard or terrified looks. These were some of the sickest people I had ever seen.

I saw a sign that read "EMERGENCY ROOM" and realized that's what ER must stand for. These other people clearly had emergencies, but surely mine was not. That must be why they called everyone else before me; my case was not as urgent. I just needed some tests done with more sophisticated machines than our family doctor had. That's all.

Finally, we went back with a nurse, and a man wearing light-blue scrubs came in to talk to me. We repeated my symptoms, and then they told me to change and put on a gown. In a daze, I followed instructions and headed back to a CT scanner. They walked me over to a huge, white donut that they claimed was a multimillion-dollar machine. I laid down as instructed while they looked at all the screens. I listened to the thumping of the machine and gave thanks that I wasn't claustrophobic inside the center of the donut. Then I went back to my room where my mom had just arrived.

My mom wasn't as good at hiding her emotions as my dad. She tried, but the relief that flooded her face when she saw me said it all. We waited and waited, and I listened to my mom as she called her parents and filled them in. About half an hour later, my grandparents arrived, and a doctor let them listen to the crackling in my chest through the stethoscope.

The head doctor eventually came back in. "Well," he started, "we know what happened, but we're not really sure *how* it happened." My parents and I waited for the verdict. "You have something called a tension pneumomediastinum, which is a hole in your lung."

Our looks confirmed the shock he expected, so he plunged ahead.

"What's fascinating about your case is that you are one of the least likely candidates for this condition. You're young, an elite athlete, and have no abnormalities. This sometimes happens to elderly people when they are exerting themselves at high altitudes. It also happens to tall, lanky teenagers who are growing too fast for their bodies, but you are neither of those. Nonetheless, you have one of the worst cases of this condition we have ever seen. Not only do you have a hole in your lung, but because you swam on it, you also pushed all the air out of your lung, into your chest cavity, and all the way up to your throat. Those are the bubbles you feel."

"So what does this mean?" my mom asked.

He sighed. "Well, it means if she had gone to another practice, it is likely that her lungs would have collapsed, and she could have died before paramedics could get to the pool. She's a very lucky girl."

My mom took a deep breath as she grasped his explanation. I quietly observed the adults talking about my body, but I had only one concern: "When can I swim again?"

"That's up to your body," the doctor replied. "This isn't exactly a common occurrence, so we're just going to have to take it one day at a time. But I'd guess you could start swimming again in maybe two or three months."

My eyes bulged. I had never taken off more than a Sunday, not counting our allotted one week off per year since I started year-round swimming. Coaches' voices replayed in my head, "For every day you take off, it takes three days to get back to where you were."

The short calculations I added up terrified me. A break that long would make me miss a state championship. My team would be talking about my injuries, and the entire state would soon know I couldn't swim.

I barely had time to process my future before doctors began filing in to talk to me and feel the bubbles in my neck. The condition was normally something doctors only learned about in textbooks and rarely witnessed in person. Not only was it uncommon, but I also had an extremely exaggerated case. I was a freak show, even to doctors who spent every day dealing with freak shows. After it seemed like the whole medical staff on duty that night had come in to see me, my dad started making jokes about how he could pay for the entire ER bill if he charged each doctor a few dollars to gawk. I was an anomaly, and medicine had saved the day. The only problem was that doctors had no explanation for how this had happened. I had just mysteriously woken up one day with a hole in my lung.

We left the ER, and I began my new restricted life, following protocol the best I could. Doctors said they couldn't do anything to heal the lung; it just had to heal on its own. My mom warned me not to go up the stairs too quickly at school as the doctors told me to avoid anything that might increase my respiration rate. My parents even offered to talk to the administration to get me a key to the elevator at school, which I contemptuously refused.

For the first time, fear entered my life. I had come within a few hours of death, and I wanted to make sure I knew where I was going after life ended here on earth. Before, I had taken life for granted, but after feeling the breath of death on my neck (and inside it), I embraced a new perspective.

I remembered when I was about five years old I observed my dad as he washed dishes in the kitchen, and I asked him how someone became a Christian. He told me a person prays and asks

God to forgive them, and then that person is a Christian forever. Never needing anyone else's input, I made up my mind that I wanted to be a Christian, so I went over to the couch, buried my head in the cushions, and asked God to forgive me for my sins. Then I marched back over to my dad and said, "Okay, finished! I'm a Christian now!"

My dad laughed and told me it wasn't that easy, but that is the first time I remember truly understanding salvation. I was full of innocence and childlike faith, but I know that my prayer was genuine. Yet, after my near lung collapse, I wondered if maybe it had been too easy. Maybe I wasn't a good enough person. I argued with myself all day contemplating the mysteries most people delve into when they're older than thirteen.

To be honest, I was a good sport most of the time, but I had my fair share of bratty moments. I was the fastest swimmer my age in the country, and although my pride only leaked out a few times, it had hooked little roots of arrogance into the soil of my heart. The hole in my lung and its aftermath started tugging at those roots. After all, I knew how to be stubborn. However, the lung injury made me realize how small I was and how fragile life would always be. These thoughts became a catalyst for my faith.

The hole in my lung also disheartened me because it was yet another injury that was invisible to the naked eye. I didn't go to my club swim practices, and at school I had to sit out on the sidelines in athletics. I felt like everyone thought I wanted attention, and pride pushed me to come back to activity sooner than I should.

Healing from my tension pneumomediastinum was easier than my shoulder because it was diagnosed, and we knew exactly what had happened, even if we didn't know *why* it had happened. Partially due to naivete and partially due to my own stubbornness, I still didn't question whether I would come back to swimming.

I took the setback in stride and made adjustments to get back to work as soon as possible.

Meanwhile, as I continued planning my inevitable return to the sport, my parents called Randy, who showed uncharacteristic concern for me. "Well, I guess her shoulder was finally out of pain, so she pushed so hard she gave herself a hole in her lung. Go figure." He told my parents not to let me come back to the pool until I was ready.

I sneaked into practice one day a couple weeks later and claimed I could start dry land, which is what we swimmers call all other exercise (besides weights) done outside of the water. Randy told me I wasn't supposed to be there and that I needed to heal more. He was right, and I needed people to protect me from myself.

As part of my two-month recovery, I had to see a pulmonologist a few times. I would stare at posters of lung disease—enough to decide to never smoke a cigarette—while I waited to blow into little tubes to test my lung strength. I was an interesting case, even for a lung doctor. He had no idea what had caused the hole either and considered me a one-in-a-million case. I was young and the epitome of health. No compelling reason existed for me to have been in his office. He also couldn't believe I had intensified the injury by pushing so much air out of the hole to other parts of my body.

The pulmonologist talked to my dad as if I wasn't in the room, a practice with which I was becoming familiar. The doctor shook his head and said, "I've seen a grown man curl up into fetal position on the floor of this room, unable to cope with the pain of breathing with a tension pneumomediastinum. But your thirteen-year-old daughter swam an entire practice with it."

I started physical therapy for my lungs at home, blowing up balloons and then trying to suck in all the carbon dioxide back in to fill my lungs to their capacity. After breathing as shallowly as possible for weeks, it felt as if my lungs had shrunk. Frustrated, I did everything I could to get back into the pool. On the bright side, we all figured this forced break from swimming was divine intervention; my shoulder was finally going to get the rest it needed to heal too. I didn't believe God created my lung collapse any more than he caused me to run into a wall at the end of a race and damage my shoulder, but I did believe he used circumstances to work everything together for the good of those who believed in him.

Sometimes, I wondered if God would give me an injury to force me to slow down, but most of the time, I knew better. Still, my story had started to sound a little bit like the beginning of an athlete-Job narrative. God may not *cause* bad things to happen to people, but that book of the Bible certainly made it clear that he *allows* bad things to happen to people sometimes.

I was determined to learn my lesson so that I wouldn't have everything taken away from me, like Job. I would be good, rest, and heal up; that way, I would finally be my old self when I got back into the pool again.

5

The Enemy Within

Do not measure yourself by what you have accomplished
but by what you should have accomplished with your ability.
—John Wooden

As my lung began to heal, the pain in my chest slowly dissipated, and the number of bubbles in my throat decreased. I remained faithful to my physical therapy exercises, but I became restless. I had always wondered what it would be like to have a life like my classmates: wake up around seven o'clock in the morning, go to school, maybe do an hour of practice for band or athletics, and then go home. I could spend the night at people's houses on Fridays without Saturday morning practice, and I wouldn't have to do all my homework in the car.

Thanks to my lung injury, my dream finally came true. I came home from school, finished my homework, and watched TV, which was something I never did. Then I read for fun, sketched drawings, and played fetch with my dog. By the time I did all that, it was about 6:30 at night. Finally, I wrote a report on a Zoo Book for fun until my parents got home from work and from bringing my brother to practice.

After a week and a half of my glorious freedom—doing all the things I believed swimming had deprived me of—I felt bored out of my mind. That's the funny thing about freedom: it's never quite what we think it is. We believe freedom is a lack of commitments and an ability to do whatever we want, but it's within the confines of structure that our innermost gifts are freed to reach their utmost capacity. Many times, what we see as walls of confinement are only guidelines directing our power in a fixed direction so we can fly higher and higher.

To stay busy, I started taking my wiener dog on walks, which turned into jogs, which turned into runs. I was careful—nearly dying had certainly freaked me out—but my body craved exercise, and my heart craved a challenge. I needed to push the boundaries of everything in my life. And this compulsion, combined with a weird need to follow rules, created a rebellious yet simultaneously obedient teenager. My thirst for the incredible fueled me to shatter whatever boxes the world tried to trap me in. It wasn't that I didn't trust doctors; I just didn't like being controlled. Doctors thought they understood how I worked, when I knew they didn't. The very confines they placed on me for recovery became deadlines I needed to surpass for no other reason than to have the sheer fulfillment of beating the status quo. If most people should have taken three months off for this lung injury, then I would only need one.

Because of this boundary pushing, I ran a cross-country race four weeks after I almost died from a hole in my lung. I finished in the middle of the pack, irate that I did not win like I used to before the injury. I mean, of course, I had just suffered a gargantuan trauma to a major organ, but in my mind, that was just an excuse. It should have only been a minor setback. The running loss further cemented that it was imperative to get back to the pool as soon as possible.

About two weeks after the cross-country race, I returned to the pool. Swimming had such a different breathing pattern than running, and the pain in my chest shocked me as I struggled through each stroke. In fact, breathing while running and breathing while swimming are opposite. While running, you breathe in through the nose and out through the mouth; while swimming, you breathe in through the mouth and out through the nose. The pain I felt in my lungs was much deeper while swimming than running. It permeated my chest, and a skill I used to take for granted became a mind-consuming task.

The words of my parents and doctors telling me not to exert myself too much came back to me, and I felt scared of the water. Since no one knew why I developed a hole in my lung, we all assumed I had "pushed too hard," which was a surprise to no one. Now, I feared that if I trained too hard, I might create another hole in my lung. If it happened once, who was to say it wouldn't happen again? For the first time in my life, I held back. I didn't push as hard as I knew I could, and a spirit of timidity that I had never known suddenly gripped my psyche.

Three years later, my parents figured out the cause of my near lung collapse. They were talking to my teammate's dad, who was an orthopedic surgeon. When they described my lung injury to him, he immediately said the cortisone shot I received the day before my lung pain began was exactly what had caused the hole. The lungs have many vessels in the back, and lots of doctors choose not to place cortisone shots through the back of the shoulder because of this, opting instead to insert the shot through the front of the shoulder. My doctor had accidentally nicked a pulmonary artery when he injected the cortisone shot, causing a hole in one of my lungs. Because I swam an entire practice with it, I caused the hole to enlarge and become potentially fatal. But I had only recently returned to the sport and wouldn't know any of that for three years. For all I knew, I had either created the lung collapse, or it had been a random, freak occurrence. Both options birthed a new fear in me that subdued my all-or-nothing spirit.

Worse yet, my shoulder pain had not subsided with time off. In fact, it had hardly improved at all. Although the pain wasn't as bad as those first few initial practices where I couldn't lift my arm, it still hurt enough to cause me to change my strokes in order to lessen the pain. My head started to tilt sideways during breaststroke, and I began to recover with my arm straight during freestyle rather than bent at the elbow. I looked like a boxer, trying to sling my arm around the side of my body instead of pulling it through the water gracefully. And let's not even think about butterfly. It was my worst stroke before the shoulder injury, and it became an absolute torment after it. By far the most strenuous stroke on your shoulder, butterfly became the bane of my existence as an IMer.

As hard as I fought the setbacks, the new mixture of fear and injury prevented me from training like I used to. I gained almost twenty pounds because I continued eating the way I had before the injury, but I wasn't burning as many calories. After Randy talked to me about it, I worked to lose the weight. Somehow, God protected me from the body image issues that are so prevalent in a sport whose outfit leaves nothing to the imagination. Plus, I think God knew I would have more than enough to deal with coming up, so I simply buckled down and lost the weight. However, I lost a few more months of improvement in the process. The incident created another dip in my career, which had changed from a perfect upward slope to a roller coaster of the unexpected.

Although I conquered the weight gain, my original problem remained, the problem I could never overcome: intense shoulder pain. Eventually, I couldn't hide the results of different training at meets. I stopped improving, and people's malicious prophecies came true. I became the twelve-year-old wonder they claimed I would become. I lost my edge. And I started to lose. A lot. Instead of bouncing back like I used to, the injuries and the voices took up residence in my head. An old African proverb says, "If there is no enemy within, the enemy without can do you no harm." My enemies had always been external and thus easily defeated. But now, I faced myself. I faced a challenge I could not overcome, and it originated in my body and in my mind.

In late fall of 2006, my physical therapist (PT) took my dad aside, slightly outside the half-closed door, leaving me to do my exercises alone.

"I think you need to take her to a sports psychologist," he told my dad. "We see this a lot in athletes who are too good at too young an age. They get older, their bodies change, and they can't perform the same way they did before puberty. Your daughter experienced such success that she now can't handle her fall from fame. In my professional opinion, this issue has to do with her head, not her shoulder."

My dad calmly listened to the PT suggest that my injury might be a figment of my imagination that I was milking for all it was worth to justify my downfall.

"Well, we will consider that, but Tera has never been one to make things up. She also has a super-high pain tolerance, like grotesquely, unhealthily high. I don't think she would create this injury for attention."

The PT pretended to listen, even though he had already made up his mind about my psychological diagnosis. He nodded, and then the two of them returned to the room.

I found out later what the PT had told my dad, although my dad softened the blow. I fumed that people seemed to love to say things about me behind my back but didn't have the guts to tell me to my face. I vowed I would do my PT's exercises so well that my shoulder would get better, and I would return to my former prime, and he would shake his head at how mistaken he'd been.

The PT was not the first medical professional to suggest I needed to see a psychologist. I had always been exceedingly honest, almost to a fault. I was open with strangers, and I had no issue sharing my story with doctors. I thought if they knew the prowess from which I had fallen, they would be more willing to help me get back to that level of competitiveness. It turns out that my transparency had only fostered their doubt about the validity of my injury. Fixing what they could, they all eventually concluded that my true injury was in my head. My parents constantly took work off to bring me to a new doctor, who would begin bright-eyed but inevitably give up, stumped after a few weeks.

Another avenue we ventured down was deep-tissue massage and Kinesio tape, or K-tape. I saw multiple AIRROSTI (Applied Integrated Rapid Recovery of Soft Tissue Injuries) doctors. They would use the Rolfing technique, which was a deep-tissue massage that helps chronic pain and soft-tissue injuries. Although much more painful than your average massage, I saw the pain as beneficial, and I could feel my muscles release as the AIRROSTI doctors worked their hands more and more deeply into my tissue. After each treatment, the doctors applied K-tape to my shoulder in different ways to support the work they had just completed on my arm. The tape was a strong adhesive bandage designed to help an athlete's body in the natural healing process. Since I saw the AIRROSTI docs once or twice a week, the tape wound around my shoulder became a new accessory.

Nowadays, many overhead athletes wear the colored tape for support of joints and muscles. But back then, the cutting-edge invention garnered questions and stares. I proudly wore my pink and blue tape and rolled up my sleeves during outdoor workouts to show it off. A part of me felt justified, like there was finally something visible to show for all the internal pain that no one could diagnose. When it turned out that my skin had an allergic reaction to the adhesive and caused welts, I still asked the doctors for more. Probably part mental and part legitimate, the tape did alleviate a little of my shoulder pain. I felt like my shoulder was more stable and supported with the tape while I swam, and my muscles seemed to recover a little better.

In the meantime, my parents researched every doctor they could think of, and we knocked down doors that led to experimental treatments, muscle massage therapy, physical therapy, chiropractic work, orthopedic diagnoses, and oodles of other treatments. I did hours of therapy at home. I tied resistance bands to my four-poster bed, and I froze ice in Dixie cups to soothe my shoulder after each practice. If you can think of it, we probably tried it. But after almost three years, nothing worked. I began to manage the pain, and I started to wonder if I would ever know what life felt like without it. I didn't give up, but everything was like a Band-Aid, a temporary treatment that would help for anywhere from a couple of hours to a couple of days, and then we would be back at square one. Nothing ever resolved the pain; it only masked it.

Slowly but surely, I watched an entire country of swimmers pass me. Swimmers I used to demolish now passed my times and continued on to incredible careers. I heard people talk about the indomitable champion I used to be. I fought to prove them wrong, but I couldn't break through. I did not get a single personal best time for three years. The best swimmer in the country at twelve became a slightly above-average swimmer at fifteen. Even though some would say I posted respectable times for my age group, competitors like Maya Dirado now left me in the dust.

6

Sacrificing Freedom

If our identity is in our work, rather than Christ,
success will go to our heads,
and failure will go to our hearts.
−Tim Keller

In the fall of 2007, during my freshman year of high school, my family started considering moving to South Austin to get closer to my team's practice. My brother and I would have to change schools and start over making friends, but it was a small price to pay. Most of our friends were our teammates anyway.

My mom showed me some houses online, and I started to daydream about a new room and a shorter drive to practice. Things started rolling along until a train crashed into our plans: Randy Reese moved back to Florida. After coaching me for nearly seven years, the man for whom we were about to uproot our family was moving halfway across the country.

We looked at our options of teams across Austin, but we were at a loss as to where we should go without Randy. Should we stay at Longhorn Aquatics and see who his replacement would be, or should we try something different? In the end, we decided it would be smart to try a new up-and-coming team called Nitro Swimming. They had just built a pool seven minutes away from our house.

I walked onto the pool deck for the first time and sensed it could be a good place. The atmosphere was different. Even though I weathered a fair share of whispers about Tera Bradham being at Nitro and withstood the "What's up with her now?" and "Oh, she's still swimming?" comments, I liked the training at Nitro overall. I stayed and bought into the program. I didn't know much about training other than Randy's, so I feared the results of changing the philosophy that I knew had produced some of the best athletes in the world.

The switch ended up being exactly what I needed at the time. My new head coach, Terry Olson, still gave us long yardage sets, but the change of scenery and tempo did me good. I started improving under Terry's training. In December, having only trained with him for four months, I dropped eight seconds in my 400 IM at our first shave meet, and I ended up getting best times in all the other events I swam—a miracle for my mindset after not improving for three long, discouraging years. Although I was improving, my shoulder pain was no better. It would give out far before my aerobic capacity or my muscles did. Still, the success from that meet kept me in the sport. I hadn't improved enough to regain the status I used to enjoy in the swimming world, but I started competing at the national level again. I wouldn't have my pick of universities like I did before, but if I kept improving, I could earn a scholarship to plenty of Division I programs.

After my freshman year of high school, I went on a mission trip for two weeks to Guatemala. While there, I escaped the expectations of the swimming world. I served people who barely had enough to eat or wear, and I realized how insignificant my problems were. God revealed to me that I put swimming before every-thing, including him, and I felt mortified by how important I had thought my shoulder issues were—especially when compared to the problems of people living in true poverty.

By the time I returned to the US, I could not come to terms with the fact that I swam in a 660,430-gallon swimming pool every day while, in developing countries, nearly 80 percent of illnesses were related to a lack of clean drinking water. I couldn't under-stand how some people begged for food while I ate between three and five thousand calories a day just to fuel my body. I didn't want to think about the fact that I raced in a $500 swimsuit while other people would not earn that amount of money in an entire year.

I finally faced the effects that my stubbornness had taken on my spiritual life. While my resolve had propelled me to radi-cal heights of perseverance, the same resilience had kept me from fully surrendering to God. I trusted in God for my salvation, but I trusted in my own ability for my performance. While I believed in Christ, I had never given him full authority over my heart. Thank-fully, nothing is too big for God to handle, and nothing is too small for him either. He cares deeply about the most minute details of our lives. God knew swimming was a huge part of my life, and my dreams mattered to him, but he was much more concerned with the state of my heart than he was with the state of my shoul-der. Physical injuries he could heal in an instant, but matters of the heart he had to dig up millimeter by millimeter.

The human heart is given to idolatry. We were made to wor-ship, and worship we shall, whether it is a person, an object, an image, a paycheck, a job, a relationship, or ourselves. We all wor-ship something. We can identify what we worship by analyzing what gives us our ultimate highs and our ultimate lows. What you think about when you have nothing to think about is what you worship. For as long as I could remember, swimming had always given me the best moments of my life as well as my worst agonies. Breaking a state record left me fueled to carry on for months, and losing left me in utter despair, wondering if life had value if I wasn't the best.

My sport now came head to head with my God. Which did I value more? The spiritual battle ate me alive, and I showed up to practice in tears, unable to even get into the water. I've never been adept at hiding my emotions, and seeing the crazy in my eyes, my coach intervened. Pulling me to a bench outside while the other swimmers started their warm-up, he asked me what was going on.

"Terry, I can't do this anymore. I've made swimming an idol in my life. I've put it before God, and I need to go home. I need to quit swimming."

My declaration hung in the air. Certain this was some passing, teenage phase, Terry tried to talk me down from the ledge. He told me to remember all I had overcome, to remember who I was, and to realize I had unlimited potential. But that was the problem. This wasn't about who *I* was but who God was. After three years of barely improving in the sport and losing my dream of making the Olympic team, God finally broke me. I was willing to give it up.

I told Terry that I would pray about it, and I did exactly that. I discovered that the personal values I had cherished and fought for collided with the new values I found in Guatemala: helping people, realizing that the world was bigger than a swimming pool, and sacrificing myself for the benefit of others.

The demons I faced from within were confronted by what I thought was another demon at the time: the voice of God giving me a solution to it all. All of my struggles stemmed from an injury and a sport that I idolized. After all I had endured, I still hadn't quit the sport because I couldn't live with myself if I gave up. But I realized that I wasn't giving up; God was giving me instructions to give *it* up. That would have been lovely, but who in the world was going to believe that God had told me to quit swimming? The swimming world would believe I quit because I couldn't handle my downfall anymore.

I shouldn't have cared, but I did. Resentment and anger fueled me, and not only was God telling me to give up the idol my sport had become, but he was also asking me to let go of my pride and my need to prove others wrong. My sport was my identity, and only one thing could sit on the throne of my heart. Which did I value more: swimming or God?

I chose to value God more than my sport and more than myself. I chose to give him reign over my life. I was prepared for the swimming world to laugh at me for having become a washed-up has-been after all. But I did it: I quit the sport of swimming for a week . . . and it killed me.

Then, the Holy Spirit whispered, *Go back.*

Um, excuse me, I responded. *This is not a game. This is my life. You told me to quit, and now you're telling me to go back?*

I felt like God had spoken straight to my heart: *I see that you are willing, but I put this passion in you for a reason. I gave you this talent for a reason. Go back and swim for my glory instead of your own. Go back and I will give you a greater platform than you ever could have had without the sport.*

I returned to swimming, resigning myself to the fact that my shoulder pain would never go away. Since God revealed arrogance and idolatry controlled my heart, I figured God would use my shoulder pain as the thorn in my side to keep me humble. My motivation for swimming completely changed, as did my goals. I gave up Freedom. I would no longer swim for my horse or for the Olympics as that seemed impossible with my incessant shoulder pain. I would love my teammates and do my best to show them Christ as they may never have seen his genuine love from someone else. I would try to qualify for the 2008 Olympic Trials. Many times,

US Olympic Trials were faster than the Olympics themselves, so I would at least be happy for the rest of my life knowing that I qualified for one of the fastest meets in the world.

I managed to convince myself that I was only aiming for the Olympic Trials cuts, that is, until the 2008 Olympics came around. Before my injury, my coach had said that 2008 would have been the year I would have had a shot at the team, but instead, I had an inexplicable shoulder injury and an ego that I was in the process of surrendering. Idols don't stay defeated once you choose God. They try to resurrect themselves and dethrone the rightful king any time you are the least bit lacksadaisical. And the 2008 Olympics was my first real test since having made the decision to surrender my sport to God for his purposes rather than my own.

"Hey, Tera," my dad called from the living room. "Michael Phelps is racing. Don't you want to see if he wins his seventh Olympic gold?" I shrugged and walked upstairs. I turned on the TV to watch the race alone because I didn't know how to process my emotions by myself, let alone in the presence of others.

Somewhere deep down, I knew how hurt I was by the way my life actually looked compared to how I thought my life would look at fifteen years old. Since Guatemala, God had changed my heart towards swimming, but the Olympics brought back feelings in me that I couldn't deny. A part of me still longed for greatness and wondered if I could make the Olympic team if I could become healthy. But I wasn't healthy. With a derailed career and my shoulder pain as unrelenting as ever, I struggled to come to terms with the swimmer I knew I could be and the swimmer I thought God wanted me to be. It seemed like a huge sacrifice to swim solely for the sake of showing Christ's love to my teammates, who might possibly come to know God, while I lived in pain every day. But it also seemed clear that God did not intend to heal my shoulder, so what was he asking of me when he told me to return to the sport?

I submitted to what God asked me to do and continued training, but I felt a strange sense of betrayal. I knew in my head that God's plan for my life was better than my own, but I didn't yet fully believe that truth in my heart. He could change my life's circumstances if he *wanted* to. But God was not intervening in my life; he was intervening in my heart.

God had my attention, and my eyes looked to him, but they couldn't resist looking back now and then at what could have been. A little part of me still knew what could have been if only I hadn't raced the 50 Free at the State Championships at twelve, and those thoughts lingered in the back of my mind. I never verbalized it, but what I wanted desperately was the healing of my shoulder. It turns out that sometimes God is not saying no; he's saying *not yet*. When God doesn't change our circumstances, his goal is often to change us. He had too much to accomplish in me to leave my heart engulfed in its own egocentrism.

7

Numb

What does this world need:
gifted men and women outwardly empowered?
Or individuals who are broken, inwardly transformed?
—Gene Edwards, A Tale of Three Kings

Resigning myself to not being the best in the country, I no longer used swimming as a reason for living. The drive to make it back to the top never left my heart but instead lay dormant. In addition to my fall in the sport of swimming, my family started to collapse. Parellelling my sport, the issues began while I was in middle school, and by the end of high school, my family had all but disintegrated. I was losing everything. I didn't know how to cope with the overwhelming emotions I was feeling, so I suppressed them. I felt so intensely about everything that subconsciously I knew it would be better not to feel anything at all.

When someone loses everything, she will most likely try to find value in something else. Amidst their life struggles, many girls found their worth through a relationship or through fitting in. I wasn't tempted by the in-crowd, drugs, or guys, namely because it took quite a bit for me to care about someone, and I wasn't going to sabotage my swimming with drugs. Peer pressure had never had much effect on me either because I derived most of my identity from going against the norms of society. Not only did I not care about fitting in, but I also never *wanted* to.

Instead of falling prey to those temptations, Satan found the one that fit my fancy: perfectionism. I had always been an extreme perfectionist. I liked competition and winning, but my dedication came from wanting to see how far I could push myself in every endeavor. Thus, with my family falling apart, my swimming career at a standstill, and an untested faith to stand on, I turned to the one thing left I could control: my grades. I poured everything I had into school, beating myself up internally if I made anything less than a ninety-eight in advanced placement (AP) classes. I went to morning practice, then school, then afternoon practice, and then I went home, enclosed myself in my room, and lost myself in a textbook to ignore the tension in the house.

Studying became my escape, and I knew that an education would open doors for me in the future. I became mechanical rather than passionate; survival drove me. I pushed through my days suppressing my emotions until, once every couple of months, I couldn't take it anymore. I would cry myself to sleep, making sure no one saw or heard, and then I would wake up the next morning and start the grind all over again.

Words have always sunk deep with me, whether positive or negative, and with the constant voices telling me I couldn't compete anymore, the stressors at home, and my constant inner critic, I decided I didn't like those voices anymore. In turn, I vowed to never let anyone make me feel anything I did not want to feel again. Instead of surrendering to God and allowing him to heal me, I fended for myself and solved my pain the one way I knew how. No one would control me, and I would be my own master.

The only emotion I would allow myself to feel was anger. Anger was useful. I could channel anger into good practices and good grades. Pain, hurt, betrayal, frustration, sadness, and disappointment had no room in my heart; none were productive emotions, and I was only going to allow myself to feel a way that could help me accomplish my goals.

Throughout high school, I consciously and subconsciously lost the ability to feel. I didn't want to feel. I could fake it at church and at school, and most people thought I was a happy person, but there wasn't a single person who knew what I was really going through. I became the most isolated person imaginable, and in a sick way, part of me loved it. People would get to know one aspect of what I had been through, and they would tell me I was the toughest person they knew. They told me my life was perfect. This was easy to deny because I had so many flaws that I could point out, but as my mouth denied my friends' assertions, my inner ego fed on them.

My friends thought I was perfect and strong, and that was how I wanted people to think of me. If I couldn't have an Olympic medal or be known on a global scale, at least the people around me would know me as unconquerable. But you can only fool yourself for so long. Other people didn't know what was going on or how badly I hurt, but honestly, neither did I. Most of the time, I didn't even admit to myself that I had emotions because I would have had to admit a weakness in myself, a chip in my armor that had allowed my calloused heart to feel.

From late middle school to early college, I refused to cry. It may have happened in anger or at times when my heart overran my façade, but I did the best I could to never let someone see a tear leak out. Pride developed around my being different from the other "pansy" girls to whom I compared myself. Whereas those girls cried at sappy movies and any time they were upset, I would never stoop to such a grotesquely vulnerable mode of expression.

After three years of this numb existence, I went to Junior Nationals in the spring of 2011. I roomed with a girl who was both my teammate on my club team and my teammate on my high school swim team. We had a class together at school as well, so she saw me daily in every avenue of life except at home. After finals at Junior Nationals, our conversation turned deep in the way those travel-meet roommate conversations always do if you allow them. I started telling her about my family. The words poured out and so did the tears. Suddenly, I was having one of my crying episodes that I usually had in my room alone, except I had unintentionally let one unfold in front of another human being.

She stared at me as if I were an alien that had just told her she belonged to another planet. She didn't smile, she didn't pat my hand or try to comfort me, and she didn't even respond to what I was saying. Finally, growing insecure about her statuesque demeanor, I asked, "What? Why are you looking at me like that?"

Still unmoving, she whispered, "I thought you were a robot."

"What?" I laughed. But she wasn't laughing.

"No, Tera. I'm serious. I told my parents I didn't think you were human. You go to school, make perfect grades; you show up to high school practice and kick everyone's butt. Then, you go to club practice and train your tail off there too. You never falter, and you do it day in and day out without ever showing emotion. I didn't think anyone could work that hard, show that little emotion, and be human. I thought you were a machine."

"And now, because I'm crying, you realize I'm not?"

She nodded silently.

That conversation marked a turning point in my life. I had become the numbest person fathomable, to the point that others thought me inhuman. Perfectionism was one thing; being described as a machine was another. Even though I didn't admit it to myself, I deeply yearned for human connection; I just didn't trust people enough to have those connections. However, I realized that if most people viewed me the same way my teammate did, then I would never have any relationships. I wouldn't inspire people if they didn't even realize I was a human.

I questioned my logic for the first time: was not feeling a good thing? It certainly was productive, but I knew I would never enjoy life if I didn't let myself feel anything. I came to the stark realization that I not only needed a healer physically, but I also needed a Savior emotionally and spiritually. I'm grateful to share that God would eventually completely restore my parents' marriage, but the struggles within my family wouldn't begin to heal until after I left for college. In in the meantime, I had to endure a journey that would last longer than I had bargained for.

8

Career-Ending

For those who believe, no explanation is necessary.
For those who do not believe, no explanation is possible.
—by Franz Werfel

I t's not every day that the team meeting between warm-up and the rest of the practice lasts thirty minutes. My teammates and I were eating it up, hoping the pump-up speech might last long enough to get us out of at least one set. But within a few minutes, our attention piqued not from a possible lessened workload but from the rapture of a speaker who engulfed us in his story.

Coach Doug Russell came to Nitro my junior year of high school and began to help Terry coach the National Group. We were used to other coaches flitting in and out, but this was different. Coach Doug and I were kindred spirits; he possessed a spark in his eye, a perseverance in his gut, and a confidence in his step that helped me through a time when I didn't know how to believe in myself again. It takes most people two to three years to understand how I work, and some people much longer, but not Coach Doug. He was one of the rare people in my life who understood me after watching me swim just one practice. He always knew what to say to me even when I didn't know what I needed to hear.

Coach Doug stood in front of the National Group, telling us how he fought for years to beat Mark Spitz in the 100 Meter Butterfly. Mark Spitz was the Michael Phelps of my parents' generation. He was the first athlete to win seven gold medals at the Olympics, surpassed only by Phelps' eight medals in 2008. Over the course of his career, he broke thirty-five world records. In everyone's minds, he was invincible—except to Doug Russell. Doug had never beaten Mark Spitz head-to-head, but he never stopped believing that he could. And one day in 1968, Doug beat Mark when it mattered the most: the Summer Olympics in Mexico City. He fought tooth and nail to pull off the victory, sealing not only the Olympic gold but also the world record. Coach Doug beating Mark Spitz was like someone beating Michael Phelps at the Olympics today; he beat the sport's idol. To have that person as your coach was a swimmer's dream, but now he was about to take it one step further.

Coach Doug took out a small glass that was sealed with wax to prevent evaporation of the water inside. On the last night of the 1968 Olympics, young Doug had knelt in the gutter, scooped up water from the Olympic pool, and stuck it in his bag. He had kept it as a treasured possession in his home for nearly forty years. But he didn't bring it to practice that day for show and tell. He took a small knife out of his pocket.

"I want you to know how much I believe in this program," he said. He sawed at the wax until the lid popped free and forty-year-old air leaked out in a mist. Twenty sets of teenagers' eyes remained glued to Doug's hands, wondering if he was really about to do what he appeared to be doing.

"I want you to know how much I believe in this group," he continued. "I want you to know how much I believe in *you*." He looked each of us in the eye and then unceremoniously dumped his

71

Olympic water into the Nitro pool. He had created all the build-up with his words; no pomp was necessary to create slack-jawed gawkers in the bleachers. I almost wiped my eyes to make sure I had seen it accurately. Coach Doug had just poured his Olympic gold, world-record-setting water into *our* pool.

Then, it was finished. There was nothing else to say—only work to do. We all jumped in the pool, barely comprehending what had just happened. I gave everything I had that night. How could you *not* have a good practice after the coach whom you respect and admire dumped his heart and soul into the very water in which you were swimming?

A few months earlier in late 2010, we had started the process of finding a muscle massage therapist since, in addition to everything else, I had started to pull my groin repeatedly. If I made it two weeks without straining the muscle, it was a good streak. I had pulled the muscle so often that the scar tissue from repetitive injury was creating a weakness that made me predisposed to pulling it again and thus began a new cycle of injury.

Frustration didn't begin to describe the injury's effect on me. The pain itself was tolerable; it certainly wasn't anything compared to my shoulder. But why was it always *something*? Why did my body hate me so much? Why was *I* always getting injured? Did God just want to curse my body for the sake of my heart? I believed God was more concerned with who I was than what I did, but I thought he should at least have somewhat of a vested interest in the sport that he told me to return to. Why make me go back just to experience more injuries than I did before? I thought I could serve others far better if I wasn't forced to overcome a new health hurdle every other month.

It was humiliating to have to modify my training for yet *another* injury in practice. Instead of having to not wear paddles or to lessen the butterfly yardage for my shoulder, now half the time,

I couldn't even train my strongest stroke, breaststroke, because the kick is one of the most groin-intensive motions of any sport. Plus, with an injured leg, I tried to pull harder with my arms, which made my shoulder flare up, and then I couldn't kick because of the leg injury. I floundered like a fish out of water, except I was a fish in water that couldn't use its fins. It was a nightmare.

After months of torment, we found a muscle massage therapist named Susan Muska. The first time I walked into her office, I noticed the many jerseys that decorated her office. Athletes she had helped recover and return to competition had signed each one. But one caught my attention: it was not a jersey but a pillowcase, and a grateful note with a Sharpie arrow pointed to a smudge of mascara. Even though Susan's treatments were painful enough to elicit tears from the toughest of athletes, all of the best had thought her methods were worth the pain. I hoped she could heal me too. I started seeing Susan multiple times a week for both my groin and my shoulder. She would work deep into the muscles, and I would grit my teeth to bear the pain. I was above mascara stains on pillows, but Susan could always tell how much pain I was in by the squint of my eyes.

Over the next two months, Susan observed that I didn't have muscles in any of the right places for a swimmer. My lat muscles, the ones on the side of the shoulders, were too small for an athlete of a lat-dominated sport, and some of my other muscles, like my traps, were over-developed. At this point, I had been compensating for my shoulder injury for five years. Not only had my strokes drastically changed, but my entire body structure was also transforming as well. For this reason, Susan referred me to a fitness trainer named Carlos Vega. I worked with Carlos on getting my muscles strengthened in the right places, but he noticed muscle dysfunction even beyond what Susan had observed.

"Your left leg looks way smaller than your right one," he said, tilting his head one day and squinting his eyes for accuracy. "Wait one second." He ran behind his desk and rummaged around until he found a tape measure. He proceeded to measure the greatest circumference of each of my legs, around the quad and hamstring muscles.

He raised his eyebrows. "No way. Let me do it again, just to make sure."

The circumference of my left leg was more than an inch smaller than that of my right leg, a huge disproportion for an athlete in a completely bilateral sport. Normally, if someone has a weak arm, it correlates to the opposite hip. Since my right arm had been injured for so long, my right leg had to kick harder in swimming to make up for the lack of strength in my right arm. This made it stronger than my left leg, which didn't have to compensate for a weak arm. All of this explained the groin pulls and the leg dysfunction. My chiropractor always found my hips displaced and my left leg an inch shorter than my right; suddenly, those issues made sense too.

It seemed as if the string of my physical problems was slowly unraveling. All except for one problem: my shoulder. The thorn that refused to exit my side. Carlos fixed my severe muscle imbalances by targeting muscles in our workouts, but he was still baffled that I had as much shoulder pain after the progression as I did when we started.

"It just doesn't make sense," he said, rubbing his goatee. He reached out and felt my shoulder, placing pressure with his thumb on my biceps. I immediately jerked my arm away from him and teared up uncontrollably from pain.

"I'm sorry, Tera. I didn't mean to do that." He sat in puzzled silence, staring at my arm. He looked back up at me. "That's just not right. I saw tears spring into your eyes involuntarily. We've fixed all the muscles, which means the injury has to be internal.

People don't tear up from pain when someone touches their arm unless something is seriously wrong."

Carlos had a torn labrum a few years prior where the cartilage in his shoulder was ripped off the bone. He suspected the same thing might have happened to me and that it had gone undiagnosed for five years.

"I'll tell you what," he said. "I'm going to refer you to the same surgeon who diagnosed my labral tear. He'll order an MRI, and maybe we can figure this out."

I had never heard of a torn labrum, but I immediately went home and googled it. Every symptom perfectly matched mine: sharp pain with overhead motion, deep achy pain, shoulder weakness, clicking or popping. It was an injury caused by impact. In one moment, it all came together: I had torn my labrum hitting the wall at the end of the 50 Free at the 2006 State Championship when I was twelve. I knew it. It all made sense.

The next day, I ran up to Coach Doug at practice, my body wiggling like an excited dog whose beloved master just got home. I couldn't wait to tell him what I had discovered.

"Doug!" I almost screamed. "I know what's wrong with my shoulder!"

"Okay, okay, just breathe and let it out," he tried to calm me down.

"I have a torn labrum! Do you know what that is?"

My eyes were saucers, awaiting the awed reaction I expected from the man who invested so much time and energy into me. His eyes narrowed, and my hopes shattered.

"Yes, I know what it is," he started. "I've been at baseball games my son's whole life, and many throwers have it. Tera," he said in caring disbelief, "there's no way you have that. I see how you train day in and day out, and that is an excruciating injury. There is sharp pain, and sometimes pitchers can't even lift their arms. You train like an animal. There's just no way. There has to be some other explanation."

I wilted internally at Doug's incredulity. He believed in me so much, and even *he* didn't believe I could have a torn labrum. Afterward, my talk with Terry didn't go much better.

"I figured it out!" I told Terry. "My trainer told me about it, and I looked up all the symptoms, and they match like nothing has ever matched before. I *know* this is what I have!"

"Now, Tera, you can't just diagnose yourself on the internet. Max Kerwick had a torn labrum because he dislocated his shoulder out of the socket. That's serious stuff from impact and from a specific injury."

"I know! It happened when I hit the wall at the end of the 50 Free when I was twelve, but no one has found it for five years!" Terry respected me, but he also knew when logic didn't quite add up. He didn't want to kill my joy, but he also didn't believe me for a second.

"Come on, Tera. Just the other week you came in excited that you did twenty-two pull-ups in a row. I don't think you could do twenty-two pull-ups with a torn labrum."

"Just because I did them doesn't mean I did them without pain," I mumbled.

"Well, we have three weeks until Junior Nationals. Don't start swimming differently because you think you have a torn labrum. You'll destroy yourself if you believe that."

Completely deflated by the two men who I thought would be as excited as I was, I put my goggles on to hide the tears and jumped into the pool. I didn't question if they were right; I knew in my gut that I had a torn labrum. For once, everything made sense. It just stabbed my heart that neither of my coaches took me seriously.

Later that week, I strutted into the office of the surgeon Carlos had referred me to, full of confidence that he would confirm what I now knew: I had a torn labrum. Instead, he told me I was much too strong to have a torn labrum, and he prescribed sleeper stretches, which involves lying on your side to stretch the shoulder. The stretches made my pain worse rather than alleviating it, so after a couple weeks of persistent complaints, he agreed to order an MRI. The MRI results came back as a "probable labral tear."

"See, it's just as I suspected. There's nothing there," the surgeon explained to my dad and me.

"Excuse me?" I asked. "It says *probable* labrum tear. Probable means *probably*, right?"

"Eh, not really. These tests are really finicky, and tests come back like this all the time without there being a real tear in the shoulder." I thought the MRI had finally vindicated me, and now I had a doctor contradicting the results he held in his hand.

"You're welcome to get a second opinion, if you want," he added as an aside.

"I think we will," my dad said.

We went to a renowned surgeon in Austin who operated on elite athletes and who had an incredible reputation. He said the exact same thing that the first surgeon had said.

"Well, if you go to Junior Nationals and don't improve your times, then we will consider a scope of the shoulder to go in and check things out," he finally conceded. "But we don't want to do an invasive surgery unless we have to. You're still competing at the national level in your sport, and even a scope can be potentially dangerous."

"I want you to go in. I know I have a torn labrum. Just because I'm still competing at the national level doesn't mean I'm competing at *my* best." My chest swelled as I pridefully defended myself, "I used to be *the* best, not one of the best."

He nodded his head, acknowledging my inability to cope with my childhood wonder days slipping away from me.

Well, fine. Be that way, I thought. Junior Nationals was only a few weeks away, and then he would scope my shoulder after the meet. He would see. I wouldn't sabotage the meet on purpose; that just wasn't who I was. But it turned out that I didn't need to. I didn't hit a single best time, and my pain was as bad as it ever had been.

After the meet, I returned to Austin and saw my surgeon one day before my scheduled scope surgery, when he would observe my shoulder from the inside out. They would send cameras in through small punctures in the shoulder, and if they found any damage, then they would perform a surgery to fix the problem.

"What do you expect to find?" I asked directly, tired of him moseying around the bush of what I wanted to know.

"Well, I think we're going to find some granulation and inflammation," he said.

"So, basically nothing," I deduced.

"No, just some minor causes of chronic pain." He tried to justify it, but I knew it translated to, "You're a baby who can't handle not being the best anymore, but we will pacify you and your crazy parents by going in." He didn't express a shred of faith that I might know my body.

That night, childlike faith rose up in my heart for the first time. No one believed I could have a torn labrum. Not my coaches, not multiple surgeons, nor any of my teammates. My parents might believe me, but I knew theirs was a hope for an explanation, not an assurance of a major injury. Knowing no one believed me, I knelt beside my bed with absolute assurance that the surgeon would find my shoulder torn the next day. I thanked God, as if the miracle had already taken place because, in my mind, it had.

"Thank you, God, for finding it." My head touched the ground. "Thank you for healing me after all these years. Thank you for finally showing them what is wrong. Thank you for the miracle." A couple tears of joy slid silently down my cheeks. "Thank you," I whispered.

The next morning, March 23, 2011, I went in for surgery. The surgeon didn't expect to find anything; I expected him to find everything. For the first time since the removal of my wisdom teeth, I was anesthetized, and I woke up with my arm in a sling. A nurse realized I was coherent, and she came over to adjust my sling and to give me some apple juice.

"How big was it?" I mumbled through the grogginess. I had barely regained consciousness, and those were the first four words out of my mouth. I never asked her if my shoulder was torn or what they had found. I asked her in full assurance of my God. I believed the miracle fully in my heart before I ever heard it with my ears.

"How big was the tear?" I asked, thinking the nurse didn't understand my question.

"I don't know, sweetie," she said. "I wasn't in the operating room. I'm just here to help you wake up." She brushed my question off, albeit with kindness.

Faith is being sure of what we hope for and certain of what we do not see. I had full assurance of the truth the night before my surgery, and it did not disappoint. Not only was my labrum torn, but it was also completely detached from the bone. When I hit the wall fighting to win my seventh gold at the State Championships, my biceps tendon had torn the cartilage in my shoulder from the bone. The tear wasn't the biggest the surgeon had seen, but he said it definitely wasn't the smallest one either. The tear was about ninety degrees, or a fourth of the full circle that creates your labrum. The surgeon placed multiple anchors in the cartilage to reattach it to the bone.

It turns out the first surgeon was right: The pool of dye that had indicated a probable labrum tear on the MRI had turned out to be nothing, but my labrum was completely torn in a different spot, which didn't show up on the MRI at all. Modern medicine only goes so far, and then comes faith in a God who will reveal what tests cannot.

While I was waking up from the anesthesia in the holding room, Terry sat in the waiting room with my parents, eager to hear the verdict from the surgeon. I had swum for Terry for three years, and he had become a second dad to me. After all, the swimmers in National Group spent more time with each other and with our coaches each day than we did with our own families. Nothing could contradict someone cutting my arm open and seeing what was inside. Whether good or bad, we were all about to receive an answer. His being there was a huge show of support, and it meant the world to us.

Finally, the nurse called my parents back to speak with the surgeon. They returned to Terry in the waiting room—my dad calm and my mom crying.

"It was torn," my mom told Terry. "She's been living with a torn shoulder this whole time."

Terry didn't say a word. His eyes widened, and then he immediately dropped them, counting on his fingers. Finishing his arithmetic, he looked up.

"She has time for two more," he said, excitement laced with incredulity filling his voice.

"Two more what?" my parents asked.

"She has enough years left in her career to try for two more Olympics." He shook his head. "If she can swim the way she has with a torn labrum, nothing will be impossible for her now that it's fixed!"

My parents accepted the compliment, but doubt lingered in the air.

"There's something else," my dad said.

"What?"

"I read the surgeon's notes on his clipboard as he was talking to us. He wrote 'career-ending' about her surgery."

Terry shook his head. "Nah," he said. "Don't even tell Tera that. She doesn't need that kind of negativity in her life. Two more Olympics! Two more!" he shouted as he whisked out the door to buy a copy of Josh Hamilton's new comeback book for me.

Terry had gone from not believing I could have a torn labrum to counting the years until the Olympics in a matter of ten seconds. He knew that if I really had a torn shoulder, then I had swum through an injury he never dreamed possible. If I could train like I had with an injury as significant as a torn labrum, then he knew I would return to the top in the country. His belief in me gave me confidence, and that moment forever changed our relationship. In that moment, Terry understood me and everything I was capable of.

Within the next week, I went to practice in a sling and saw Coach Doug for the first time. He gave me half of a giant bear hug, gently avoiding the arm on which they had operated.

"I want to talk to you." He pulled me aside from my teammates. "Tera, I have to be honest with you. When you told me that you had a torn labrum, I thought you were crazy. I've seen pitchers with torn labrums come off the field every day in tears, and yet you . . ." He stopped and teared up. I had never seen this kind of emotion from him.

He continued, "You trained harder than any of those grown men. You fought people with a fervor rare to humankind. You defined a competitor, and not only did you never shed a tear, but you also didn't even talk about it. I don't apologize too often, but I have to apologize to you, Tera. I was wrong, and I owe you a huge apology. I will never be able to tell you how much I think of you as a person and as an athlete. I can hardly believe you swam the way you did through that injury. It's unbelievable. I'm sorry, Tera."

I was almost in tears at this point, which wasn't too common for me either.

"You have my utmost respect." He placed his hand on his heart in sincerity.

Doug's apology meant the world to me, but even with two of the best coaches in the country in my corner, I still had to contend with reality. The same surgeon who had operated on world-class athletes had declared my injury "career-ending."

9

First Comeback

*We rejoice in our sufferings, knowing that suffering
produces endurance, and endurance produces character,
and character produces hope, and hope does not put us to shame,
because God's love has been poured into our hearts
through the Holy Spirit who has been given to us.*
—Romans 5:2–5(ESV)

After all my pain, I finally had an answer. My labrum had been ripped from the bone, and all my struggles made sense. After five years of tolerating naysayers and doubters, the mystery had been solved. In one operation, I went from trying to qualify for Olympic Trials to believing I could make the Olympic team again. After all, I had been the fastest swimmer my age in the country until I tore my shoulder. If my torn shoulder was the reason for my downfall, why couldn't I make it back to where I had been before the injury?

All of my trials made sense. God had used my injury to humble me, and now he was going to bring me back in one of the most awe-inspiring comebacks the sport had seen. He had transformed my heart so that all I accomplished would be for his glory, and I would be able to pour into athletes across the world through my Olympic platform. My dream came back to life in vivid color, and I couldn't wait to make it a reality.

The previous fall, I had gone through the NCAA recruitment process with my parents and Terry. In the college search for recruited athletes, universities pay your expenses to take up to five forty-eight-hour trips to visit their campuses in order to learn the traditions of their schools, their academics, their coaches, and especially their athletic teams. After those five trips, you verbally commit to compete for one of the universities, and then you sign with the university in the spring for a scholarship.

I took recruiting trips to the University of Louisville, Ohio State University, Harvard University, and the University of Arkansas. I intended to take a trip to Texas A&M University, but in the end, I decided against it. Although Texas A&M had an incredible program, it was unlikely that I would receive much of a scholarship, and I had other great offers on the table.

As for Harvard, the fact that I could have attended an Ivy League school spoke to my obsessive perfectionism, but I just didn't feel at home when I visited the campus. I never wanted to wonder, *What if I had gone to Harvard?* And after my recruiting trip, I didn't have to. Harvard obviously gives its students a world-renowned education, but some of the school's characteristics didn't mesh well with who I was. I knew I could have handled the academics, but it just didn't feel right. Although my decision to cross Harvard off the list left many perplexed—and understandably so—I didn't need a brand-name education to open doors for me. I believed God would open all the doors he wanted for me.

My decision between universities ultimately came down to Louisville and Arkansas, and I chose the beautiful campus nestled in the Ozarks.

"Well, I want you to sit on the decision for forty-eight hours," Terry said. "Then, if you come to practice in the morning and 'Call the Hogs' in front of all your teammates, I'll let you commit to Arkansas," he told me.

Sure enough, my decisiveness rang true, and two days later I yelled "Pig Sooie" through the Nitro natatorium. I committed to swim for Jeff Poppell and the Razorbacks, a rising team in the Southeastern Conference. Then I applied for other scholarships at the university, and I was invited to compete for the Arkansas Honors College Fellowship, a full academic scholarship given to seventy-five students a year. In February of 2011, I walked with pride onto my future campus, and I pitted my best essays and my interviews with faculty against those of the other candidates.

When Chancellor Gearheart invited us into his office for a roundtable interview, the other applicants sat straight as corn stalks, hands folded primly in their laps, and asked about research grants, whether they could begin their theses as sophomores, and what kind of academic prestige the university merited. My pectoral muscles always tight from so much forward motion in practice, I tried to mimic their pristine etiquette but settled for my best, slightly slumped swimmer posture. The dryness ate away at my attention span. Finally, I piped up.

"Where does Tusk live?" I asked Chancellor Gearheart.

Snickers resounded around the table at the highly undignified question I'd posed to the head of school. Then, the tickled chancellor enthusiastically told us all about how Tusk, the real wild hog who was the mascot of the University of Arkansas, lived on a farm about forty minutes from campus. I got an answer to my question, and a few years later, Chancellor Gearheart still remembered me.

I was awarded the fellowship, which meant that although I was offered a full swimming scholarship, the athletic department would only need to cover differences in cost between my athletic and academic scholarships, such as the difference in housing costs between my athlete dorm and the dorm I would have lived in if I only had an academic scholarship. With gratitude, I accepted both opportunities to represent the U of A, and I could barely wait for my final three months of high school to pass so I could move to Fayetteville.

In the summer of 2011, I moved to Fayetteville, Arkansas, less than a week after graduating from high school. I was excited to start my first college classes during the summer, begin my shoulder rehab early with their athletic trainer, and get a head start on the upcoming season. My new coaches and I hadn't decided yet if I was going to take a medical redshirt, which allows an athlete to sit out for a season due to injury without losing a year of eligibility. I wanted to do everything in my power to avoid a redshirt season, and I wanted to take advantage of all of the resources that a top twenty program offered in order to make a fast comeback.

It's not ideal to hear your recruit is having a massive surgery right before she comes to swim for you, but my new head coach, Jeff, took everything in stride. Jeff was nothing but supportive, and it had been his idea for me to come to Arkansas early in order to get a head start on my rehab. From my first day on campus, he let me kick with the team, even though I couldn't swim with my arms yet. To be so injured but so included was a testament to the character of my new coach as well as to his belief in my ability to recover.

When I arrived on campus, I moved into the Quads, which were brand-new dorms. My assistant coach, Todd Mann, took me down to the equipment room the next day.

"Here's some shorts and a few shirts," he said as he tossed Nike apparel over his shoulder at me. "You'll get a whole suitcase full of gear in August, but this should be enough to get you through until then."

Trying not to trip over the dangling goodies overflowing my arms, I skipped all the way back to my dorm room, as giddy as a kid on Christmas morning. Training two to four hours a day while being a student athlete certainly wouldn't be cushy, but I planned on enjoying all my free gear and complimentary chocolate milk.

By the time I had arrived in Arkansas earlier that summer, I already had three months of recovery under my belt. I was out of my sling and had started shoulder-strengthening exercises. I had stopped taking my pain meds two days after my surgery because the pain was already less than the amount of pain to which I had been accustomed. Now I had to acquaint myself with a new type of pain: the dull, permeating ache of "surgery pain" caused from the repairs. I faced a formidable road full of this new pain in order to regain the range of motion I had lost due to my immobility after surgery.

Even though I spent two to three hours in the athletic training room completing my exercises each day, we still decided it would be best for me to take a medical redshirt my freshman year. We planned on my shoulder making a full recovery, so it seemed smarter to wait until I could compete well for four years rather than waste a year of eligibility on a mediocre season as I continued to recover from my operation.

As the leaves started to change colors in the Ozarks, I watched the bus drive away for each swim meet as I stayed at home on the sidelines. At first, I could only kick during practice, and I mainly did leg weights, so I didn't mind not being able to travel to meets because I couldn't have swum well anyway. But as I recovered and began to compete more and more in practice, it became more and more difficult to watch the bus pull out to each swim meet without me.

It was like I was a walk-on my first year, rather than the scholarship athlete I was. At first, I received no respect. I was the wiggling worm hugging the wall of the end lane as I kicked my own practices with a snorkel and my arms at my side. Then I began to swim again, starting with the sprint group before moving up to the middle-distance training group.

I improved day by day, and some of my teammates started making snide comments about whether I would replace them on the travel team or take their spots for relay races if I chose to compete rather than redshirting. They were becoming resentful that I only did one practice a day, viewing my recovery from a major surgery as an excuse that gave me the power to beat them rather than the limitation it truly was. It had never been a problem before, but now that I could keep up with them, competitive spirits threw logic out the window.

Their comments became my ammunition, which I stored away in my mind for future motivation when I could truly compete again. And if I could surprise a teammate enough to merit her viewing me as competition, then her insult was my compliment. I kept quiet and bided my time, knowing those girls wouldn't know what hit them once they saw who I was when I had fully recovered.

At college, God was still at work in my heart. I knew a gargantuan number of Christians who fell away from their faith when they went to college, and I didn't want to be one of them. A tennis player, who wound up being a lifetime friend, invited me to church the first week I was on campus. I went to feel it out and never left. From the moment I walked into the Link's college ministry, I knew it was where I belonged. There was only one problem: I didn't know anyone. My pastor later called me gutsy, but I didn't know how else to make friends, so I signed up to go on a whitewater rafting trip to Colorado.

Not knowing anyone on the trip, I met and bonded with the lead pastor and his wife, Josh and Casandra Foliart, as well as many other college students at the church. When we went whitewater rafting, I shoved my arm into my life jacket to avoid using my shoulder and prayed I wouldn't fall out of the raft. I shouldn't have been whitewater rafting after an operation anyway, but all went well, and I laughed through the waves. The bonding on the Colorado trip made my new church a second home, and its people became a second family.

As I hung around my church family more, my values continued to change. I used to cry myself to sleep from losing a race or missing a record, but now I cried because my heart broke for my teammates who didn't know Christ. Since I had to heat my shoulder before practice, I always got to the pool before my teammates, and I would pray over their lockers. I would ask God to start a revival on my swim team. I decided to serve on the leadership team for the youth ministry at church, and I started volunteering at Horses for Healing, a program designed to help children with disabilities ride horses. I started sacrificing my time and my emotions for the kingdom rather than just for myself.

What I didn't see coming with my spiritual growth was how God would reawaken my passions and my vigor for life. After becoming numb to every emotion, he used my new friendships to chip away at the walls I had built around myself. No one knocked the wall down, but it was as if each of them had a little pickax, and as they chipped away, the walls started to crack and crumble. While God was the consuming fire melting the block of ice that held my heart captive, my friends faithfully chipped at the cracks to expedite the process. Through it all, God taught me how to feel again.

All the emotions I thought I had numbed had really only let nasty seeds of bitterness take root, and the glimpses I saw of those issues didn't make me want to pull out a shovel; I thought they should stay buried right where they were. Part of my hesitance to confront my hurts came from naivete; I had never understood forgiveness. I thought I would wake up one day and suddenly no longer harbor resentment or that one day I would have the courage to make the decision to forgive, and then the battle would be over. But God wants to uproot the sins and hurt we've buried so that he can bring them to the surface and heal them.

God taught me that forgiveness was a choice far before it was ever an emotion. I learned that some days I chose forgiveness and laid my bitterness at the foot of the cross, while other days I chose anger, and my own sin ravaged my heart as I lashed out. Forgiveness was not a one-time deal; I had to choose it over and over again—sometimes multiple times a day.

I also had to learn that forgiveness didn't mean I had to be okay with a person's actions; it meant that I was no longer willing to live with the repercussions of his or her sin in my life. When you don't forgive someone, it's almost as if you carry them on your back. They never hop off, and you end up giving them a free ride while you collapse from exhaustion. It's a heavy burden to bear, and it became exhausting. To live with a constant chip on my shoulder didn't hurt my offenders; the only person it hurt was me. Finally, I decided to cut the straps off the people I carried on my back and let my hurt fall to the ground.

The battle didn't end in that moment, but I began to choose victory. I chose to feel, and I chose to believe in the goodness of humanity again. Or rather, I chose to believe in the power of Christ's redemption in humanity to turn our sinful nature to good. The only problem with letting my intense passions return is that it left me wide open to getting hurt both by people and the disappointment that would inevitably come my way.

After my surgeon wrote "career-ending" on my chart, he told me if I ever got a lifetime best time again, it would take at least two years. He warned me that most athletes who underwent that surgery never came back to compete at the same level of competition they had attained before. Almost exactly one year after my surgery, I competed in my first race since the operation. Since I was redshirting, I couldn't compete in a college meet, but my coaches let me swim a 100 Breast during one of the diving breaks as an exhibition. I wouldn't swim in a heat with other people, but I could use the clock and see my time.

Todd had been training me in the sprint group, so it was he who asked me what time I thought I would hit in the race.

"Probably about a 1:07," I responded. "I haven't trained that much, but I think that's respectable. What do you think I'll go?"

"Probably a 1:07, maybe a 1:08," he said.

I dove in for my first race, trying to practice my new form. I loved that the Arkansas fans and teammates were in the stands, even if my race didn't count for anything. My new church family also showed up in the front row, with flowers to boot.

I stopped the clock at 1:05, two seconds better than my coach or I had predicted. The time was still a few seconds away from my lifetime best, but for the first race back from a major operation, it was surprising. Todd furrowed his eyebrows in contemplation as he and Jeff gave me hugs after the race. We all knew what it meant: if I could hit a 1:05 as my first race after surgery, and in a practice suit without resting, what could I do with real training under my belt and other advantages? The sky was the limit. We predicted I could break a 1:00 in a year or two, placing me in the top eight at NCAAs. And the 100 Breast wasn't even my best event.

The race may not have counted for anyone else or for the scoreboard, but for me, that race counted more than any time that had ever gone down in the history books. For as long as I could remember, I had swum through excruciating pain. Now, I was swimming in less pain and was on my way back to the top. I had paid my dues, and it was my time again.

After my first race, I started training with Jeff in the middle-distance group, and I increased my yardage. I still couldn't train as much as everyone else, but I was building up. I trained as much as my shoulder would allow, and in June, after three more months, it was time to give Olympic Trials one more shot.

I hadn't raced the 400 IM since my surgery, but it was my strongest event and my best shot at qualifying for Olympic Trials. I was pumped, and I knew my shoulder would probably only last long enough to give the endurance race one chance, so it was then or never. Because I hadn't swum the race in so long, I didn't pace it correctly, using my legs too much on the backstroke. I came home a little more slowly because of the flawed strategy, and I ended up missing the Olympic Trials cut for the event by a little over a second. For the first time racing the event in over a year, the time was incredible, but I had still missed the cut.

Not giving up that easily, I decided to go for the qualification standard in another event. Two weeks later, I drove to Omaha to compete in a last-chance meet for Olympic Trials qualifications. We decided I would go for the 200 IM, half the distance of my best event, since my shoulder couldn't handle swimming the 400 IM repeatedly just yet. My prelim time qualified to swim in the finals. I placed top three at the meet but missed Olympic Trials by less than half of a second. When I saw the time, I wanted to crumple into a ball of tears. All of my rehab had been for nothing. Four years earlier, I had missed five Olympic Trials cuts by two seconds or less. Now, I missed them again but by a smaller margin, and it was even more painful because of how much I had overcome to compete again.

Since the cuts for Olympic Trials usually get faster every four years, my times in Omaha would have qualified four years earlier. I had returned to the sport after a major operation, and I had swum lifetime best times in less than a year, but I had still missed the cuts. I knew Jeff and Todd would be proud of me. To swim those times foreshadowed nothing but incredible things to come in my future. I had come back, I had beaten the odds, and I was on the rise. I still had four years of eligibility left.

The timing would be perfect: I would end my college career at the same time I aimed for the Olympics one more time. Only, I still faced two problems: First, I had so much pain in my shoulder that I couldn't lift my arm . . . again. Second, the coach whom I loved and respected, who recruited me and helped me through a trying year of rehab while believing in me all the way, had resigned. Jeff Poppell was moving back to Florida, and I was headed back to the operating table.

10

Bubbles

Assurance after all is no more than a full-grown faith;
a masculine faith that grasps Christ's promise with both hands—
a faith that argues like the good centurion,
if the Lord 'speak the word only' I am healed.
Wherefore then should I doubt?

—J.C. Ryle

After my meet in Omaha, I still had to finish summer school classes. One day during my Spanish class, pain shot involuntarily through my arm, surging so suddenly and so excruciatingly that I jumped out of my seat with a gasp. The class was small, so the outburst was obvious. Everyone turned to look at me.

"¿Estás bien?" my professor asked me.

"Sí," I responded quickly, wanting eyes off me so I could process what had just happened. I tuned out the Spanish literature and lost myself in thought. While the past few months and weeks had been filled with confusion, it was as if that one jolt of pain awakened me to a sobering reality: I needed a second surgery.

I didn't know what was wrong, but I knew that God created

pain as a signal for us to realize that something isn't right in our bodies. I had numb patches on my arm as I continued to lose sensation, I woke up from pain regularly, and now I couldn't even sit in class and take notes without surges of pain diverting the attention of both my classmates and me.

Before my first surgery, everyone told me I was crazy, and then doctors found a torn labrum inside my shoulder. Because of that, I had confidence in my ability to know what pain I should push through and what pain I shouldn't. As educated as doctors were, they could never feel the pain I felt, and I knew my body better than anyone. Logic told me something was still very wrong inside my shoulder.

Although I had been careful, I figured I must have pushed too hard, or I must have come back too quickly after surgery. I had to have torn the repair to the labrum; there was no other explanation that made sense. But another surgery? I loved God humbling me and bringing me back for his glory, but one surgery was enough to accomplish that. God had already written an incredible comeback narrative. I was supposed to be on the rise, not back under the scalpel.

I had prayed for God to give me a word for the year, a word that represented a theme he wanted to teach me about. The word I felt the Lord impressed on my heart was *fearless*. As I argued with him about another surgery, I felt him tell me he was going to bring me back again and that I shouldn't fear a worse outcome.

You have to be fearless, dear one, he whispered, as I pictured Aslan the lion talking to me as if I were Lucy.

But I was afraid. Being fearless does not mean that you don't experience fear as much as it signifies your refusal to accept fear as something to define your actions. If I had another surgery, and they fixed a tear once again, what was the point in swimming afterwards? Wouldn't I just tear the repair all over again like I had done this time? I could understand having another surgery, but how did swimming again fit into the equation?

I apparently didn't know how to train properly enough to prevent reinjuring myself, but without training with Olympic-level intensity, how did God ever expect me to be able to make the Olympic team? And if I didn't make the Olympic team, then I had no idea how he was supposed to give me a platform through my sport, as I felt he had told me in high school. Try as I might to remain fearless, all the consequences of a second surgery sent shivers down my spine.

I continued to turn to my Bible, and I ended up reading it in its entirety over the span of my freshman year of college. While I was reading through the book of Jeremiah, the Holy Spirit quickened a word to me and gave me what I came to call my life promise. The verse is about Jerusalem, but I felt like God told me this was the promise he wanted me to claim for my life.

Written as if God were speaking it over me, Jeremiah 33:6–9 says, "I will bring health and healing to you. I will rebuild you as you were before, and you will enjoy abundant peace and prosperity. I will forgive all your sins of rebellion against me, and then you will bring me renown, glory, praise, and honor, before all the nations on earth that hear of what I do for you, and they will tremble and fear and be in awe of the abundant peace and prosperity I provide for you."

When God works something in my heart, I grab on with both hands. I've always been an all-or-nothing person. So when God told me this was his promise for my life, I latched on and believed him with all my heart, mind, and soul. I trusted that God's promise meant that he would heal me, it would be for his glory, and he would take me to the Olympics so that every nation would hear of his testimony in my life.

But we were suddenly taking yet another detour. And God

was asking me to have faith that even with another surgery, he could accomplish what I believed he was telling me. Plus, I did the math in my head, and by the time I recovered from another surgery, I would only have three years to come back for the Olympics, rather than four. Was he serious? After not one but *two* surgeries? Indeed, he was immovably serious. I couldn't shake the feeling in my gut that God was calling me to remain in the sport of swimming.

Well-meaning Christians had taken me aside for years and asked if I thought my shoulder pain was a sign from God to quit swimming. I emphatically said no, even more so after I received my life promise from God. Those little voices now resurfaced in my mind; how sure was I that they *weren't* right?

Other Christians calmly accepted my pain and explained it away with the "thorn in your side" theory. Maybe my experience was much like the experience of the apostle Paul, who wrote that God let him have a constant thorn in his side to humble him. At times, I believed this theory too. God knew my heart better than I did, and he must have known I would have been too arrogant if I didn't have an injury that constantly limited my capabilities.

Still, other Christians told me that God's healing should always come and that if I wasn't being healed, then I had to have some sin in my life that I hadn't dealt with yet. Maybe God was punishing me for my lack of repentance. I honestly searched my heart and found many imperfections, but nothing surfaced for which I had not asked God's forgiveness. I begged God to show me what I was hiding if I had deceived myself. He didn't reveal a buried sin, and he didn't heal me.

I always came back to my promise. It's all I could cling to because it was the one thing that I felt sure of. He had said he would heal me, so he must be waiting for the opportune moment. But even if healing was coming someday, God certainly hadn't felt like healing me yet. It wasn't happening through people's distant prayers, the laying on of hands at church, or the anointing of oil by the elders. My church family and I exhausted all the methods of healing that are present in the Scriptures—all to no avail.

Since God was not intervening on my behalf, one option remained: another surgery. Doctors at the University of Arkansas agreed to scope my shoulder again and possibly cut off the biceps tendon, which connects the biceps muscle to bones in the shoulder. A new cutting-edge surgery had suggested that cutting off the biceps tendon reduced pain tremendously for labrum repairs, but it was still experimental. Was I willing to risk my dream on an unproven operation?

Shortly after my surgery revelation in Spanish class, I showed up for practice with a war raging inside me about whether I should opt for a second surgery. At the time, the Arkansas swim team had a volunteer assistant coach on staff, Chris George, and I always felt a strong connection to him because he, too, had undergone multiple shoulder surgeries. This coach had watched my journey for the past year, including how I had been kicking with a snorkel with my arms at my side ever since the meet in Omaha.

Chris approached me as thoughts raced through my mind. "Tera," he said, "I've been thinking about whether I should say this to you or not, but I don't think it's right if I don't. I want you to think long and hard about what you're doing. Look at me."

He lifted his arm, showing a severe lack of motion; he couldn't raise his arm completely above his head. "This is what happened to me because I kept swimming after my second surgery. I don't want you to end up like this. There is so much life left after swimming ends. Think about picking up your kids one day. Don't you want to be able to do that? I don't know if I'm ever going to be able to do that," his voice drifted off.

I knew how much it must have hurt him to relive his own pain in order to prevent mine. I sat in silence. It wasn't the first time someone had told me these things, but hearing it from someone I respected made the nail sink deeper.

"You have your whole life ahead of you," he continued. "Just have the surgery, and then let that be it. Swimming after two surgeries could ruin your quality of life. Just think about it, okay?"

I nodded and jumped in the pool, fighting the tears rising inside my goggles. I kicked lap after lap with nothing but the sound of passing water for company. My coach's words undulated in my mind like the waves I created with each dolphin kick.

Kicking was much slower than swimming, even with fins on, and once my teammates started the main set, I had to stop on the wall to let them lap me. As I waited for all of them to come by, my teammates upturned tons of bubbles as they came into the wall. Welcoming the distraction from my chaotic thoughts, I swatted at the bubbles. My lips turned up playfully around my snorkel as I marveled at the physics of a bubble. No matter how many tiny bubbles spawned from my breaking the big bubbles, they still rose in unison to join the air outside the water. They were so resilient, so persistent, and so undeterred by the giant snorkeled fish trying to destroy them.

Then, unbidden, God whispered to me, *You're a bubble, Tera.*

I would like to say I gasped with realization and praised God for his mightiness. Instead, I sneered with sarcasm into my snorkel, *Well that's real nice, God. What on earth is that supposed to mean?*

I had heard God's small whispers before, which usually only lasted a sentence, so I was shocked when I felt his response in my spirit: *You're a bubble, Tera, because you will always rise. Not because you're trying to, and not because you want to, but because like a bubble, it is your very nature to rise. You can do nothing else. And it is not truly your nature but my nature. I have risen from everything. I have risen from the grave, and I have risen from everything you will face in your entire life. Because I am in you, the more you grow with me, the more my nature becomes your nature. Thus, you will always rise.*

My giddy bubble traipsing nose-dived into choking conviction. I saw the war on the horizon, but hope shone a glimmer of sunrise on the battlefield. God's love rose like a bubble inside of me, squelching all fear. He was good regardless of my circumstance. If I never swam again, he was still faithful. But I *would* swim again, and I would rise from the ashes. How could I not? I was a bubble.

On July 18, 2012, two surgeons operated on my shoulder for the second time, and although they found gargantuan amounts of scar tissue and other symptoms, they said the repair of my labrum looked perfect. My first surgeon's work was impeccable, and my shoulder looked so good that these doctors decided not to cut off my biceps as planned, opting not to end my career with such an invasive surgery. They concluded my "discomfort" must be due to residual operational pain and bursitis, and they cleaned out the scar tissue. I could barely wrap my head around this much pain being simply "surgical pain," but that's what the second surgery had confirmed. If surgeons said my shoulder looked perfect, I had nothing to dispute.

Spiritually, it seemed a bit extravagant to go through an entire operation—again—just to assure me that nothing was wrong in my shoulder. But God's ways are higher than ours, so I accepted the mystery. If that's what it took for me to believe I didn't have a torn labrum, then so be it. God had thrown the ball back into my court and assured me it was safe to swim on my shoulder.

I returned to the pool within two weeks. Now I had the full assurance I needed to believe my pain was tolerable. Many athletes came back from shoulder surgeries, so if they could face surgical pain, I sure could. My comeback depended on it, and I was confident that I would come back stronger than ever. After all, I had more memories swimming with pain than I did without it. Pain and I had taken our relationship past the friend zone back in high school. We knew each other intimately, even though the toxicity of the relationship threatened my sanity. But, like all dysfunctional relationships, I was relieved to know that I could return to pushing the boundaries of logic. I believed that God had given me the reins to gallop headlong into what would become my worst nightmare: having no limits to how hard I could push myself.

If I could just overcome the pain, then I would rise to victory. It would be excruciatingly difficult, but it was nothing I couldn't handle. If the end result was the Olympics, I could push through just about anything. I had already swum with a torn shoulder for five years; what was swimming through surgical pain now that I knew everything was fixed? I could be truly fearless now because I had proof that I had no reason *not* to be.

11

Paving the Way for a Miracle

Even if the healing doesn't come,
And life falls apart
And dreams are still undone
You are God, You are good
Forever faithful One
Even if the healing doesn't come.
—"Even If" by Kutless

Do I live in the past? I asked myself this question, which had just been posed to me by Blake Johnson, the head coach who had taken over the swim program after Jeff left. I sat in his office shortly after my second surgery, having come to participate in what I thought would be a productive conversation with my coach. But somehow the tables had been turned on me.

"I mean, I don't think so," I told him. I paused to genuinely consider the question again. "I think I almost struggle with living too much in the future. But I know what I can be in the future because I know who I was in the past, before my injury."

After returning to training at lightning speed, I was back to training full practices and swimming respectable times, but my shoulder still put me in as much agony as it did before the second operation. I would try to start practice fearlessly, and when the pain inevitably came, I tried to pretend it didn't exist. I ignored it and told myself my shoulder was fixed but to no avail. The pain was preventing me from training to my potential.

I thought Blake would help me work through what was going on and give his best advice about the root of the problem. Instead, he pressed his theory that the true root of my problem was that I was struggling to move on from past success and accept reality. Nothing was wrong with Blake's perspective. I understood all too well how the state of things looked on paper; Blake thought I needed a reality check. He didn't have a reason to believe in my God or in me, but I did. I knew who my God was, and God was not confined to the reality of his own making any more than I was expected to succumb to its confines. I believed he had given me a promise that he would complete, not because of the reality of my situation but *in spite of it*. And whether or not Blake believed in me, I believed in my God's ability to resurrect who I used to be. I did not live in the past; I simply used it to frame the possibilities of my future.

"I really don't think I live in the past," I continued. "I want to understand why my arm still hurts so much. I have a grotesquely high tolerance for pain. Just yesterday Kara got a cortisone shot in her hand and complained about it all day. A cortisone shot to me feels like a mosquito bite. When I am in pain, I know it's something serious because I know how much I can handle."

Suddenly, Blake accused me of believing myself to be better than all of my teammates. He twisted my words in a way that left me speechless. I couldn't comprehend how he could misconstrue my intention so much. I was simply trying to use a recent comparison to describe my pain tolerance, not put someone down. I didn't think Blake would appreciate the analogy of swimming through a near lung collapse since, to him, that might indicate I was living in the past. I meant no disrespect toward my teammate; I only wanted to clarify my own grievances by using a present illustration. But the pains of misunderstanding had only just begun.

Todd knew me a little better than Blake as he had been with me throughout my entire recovery from the first two surgeries. He had trained me under Jeff before I could swim in the distance group, and now he was my coach under Blake since he trained the distance group while Blake coached the sprint group. Todd knew my heart, and I knew he cared about me like a father cared for his daughter. I knew he had my back. One day, we talked in his office, trying to put words to the confusion.

"Tera, why do you always want everything to make sense? Sometimes, you just have to let things go."

"But Todd, it just doesn't make sense." I knew I was repeating what I had already said, but I couldn't think of a better way to describe it. "I don't think my body would still be in this much pain if something wasn't wrong with it."

"You've had two surgeries, Tera. You're going to be in pain as long as you keep swimming. That's just how it goes after you've had two surgeries."

"I know that, but I really think this is different. I don't think this is just surgery pain. I know my body."

He sighed. He wanted me to be okay, but he didn't have answers for me. No one did. And who could blame him for trying to help the best way he knew how? Outside of God, nothing made sense. Surgeons had found no reasonable cause for my pain to be as obscene as it was. The results were in, and you couldn't argue with what doctors had witnessed inside my arm . . . unless you had faith. Faith is seeing what is unseen and hoping for the impossible.

It is taking God and his Word at face value and not adding or subtracting anything.

Tears rose up out of anger and frustration. It didn't make sense, and I desperately wanted it to. Todd was right; things in life didn't always make sense, but I believed God had given me a promise that he would heal me in this life, not in the one to come.

"Why do you need it to all make sense?" Todd asked me again, his voice laced with compassion.

With a faith I can only ascribe to the Holy Spirit, I looked at him and declared with passion, "Because when my God heals me, your only explanation will be that it was he who did it."

As I fought each day to convince myself that all I had to do was push through surgical pain, I was bombarded on all sides. Neither of my coaches believed my pain could be the result of a genuine physiological issue other than the obvious two surgeries I had endured, and the athletic trainer I worked with every day had no more faith than they did: "Tera, if anyone trained as hard as you did, she would be having the same pain you are."

I tried to wrap my head around my athletic trainer's logic. What part of already having had two shoulder surgeries would make my pain anything like that of what my teammates experienced? Conversely, she had just paid me a huge, backhanded compliment. She essentially told me I trained harder than anyone else did without meaning to make such an implication. She was right; I *did* train harder than most swimmers. It's just that I seldom had the opportunity to prove my abilities because of the debilitating pain that never ceased to radiate through my arm.

I couldn't think of a single practice where I felt I could push my heart to its aerobic capacity or my muscles to exhaustion; my shoulder always gave out due to excruciating pain before I could push the rest of my body to its limits. I was always fighting to try to push myself to the point of which I knew I was capable.

Another pointless meeting with Blake that day already had me sparking angry fireworks when I walked into the makeshift training room at the natatorium. After dealing with Blake's disbelief for an entire meeting and then hearing my athletic trainer parroting his doubts, I couldn't hold my anger in any longer. I turned on her in unrestrained frustration.

"No, that's actually not true. I was always capable of training this hard and pushing myself this hard before I tore my labrum. I understand that most people can't push themselves to the limits that I can. Even if they did, they would not feel the same pain that I do because they haven't had a torn shoulder for five years and two surgeries on it! I know I am capable of pushing myself more than other people can, and I did until I tore my labrum. My work ethic never irritated my shoulder before I tore it, and that training intensity is why I was the fastest swimmer in the country!"

I was yelling by the end of my outburst, which was a first throughout all my years of trial. I had never screamed at anyone in a position of authority in my life, although I had come close. But that day, I lost it. I was sick of people acting like they understood me and putting me in a box that they could comprehend instead of trying to find the real answer to my pain. I was sick of people's sheer disbelief in my intellectual capability to determine when something was still very wrong with my body.

Of course, Blake happened to arrive at the pool in time to catch only the last of my outburst. Perfect timing. The incident added one more feather to his cap of understanding the lunatic athlete who couldn't get over her fall from fame. He pulled me into his office later and told me he'd never seen a swimmer talk to an athletic trainer like I had. He deemed it totally unacceptable, and he was right.

"I know." I stared at my feet, trying not to cry from shame and anger. I knew losing my temper was wrong, but I still felt completely misunderstood and misrepresented. "I'm sorry. It was unacceptable, and it won't happen again."

Later at afternoon practice, I apologized to my athletic trainer and told her I knew she was doing her best to help me. Swallowing my pride was the right thing to do, and I needed to take responsibility for my words, but internally, I couldn't help but also wonder why neither my athletic trainer nor my coach ever apologized to me.

Then, a week before the Southeastern Conference Championship (SEC), I was physically incapable of swimming a full practice. My pain was so intense that I had to quit after warm-up and kick the rest of each practice. I kept pushing past what I should because I was terrified my coach would make the decision to not take me on the travel team. Not only would it seem ludicrous to take an athlete to SECs who couldn't complete a practice, but I also swam one of the biggest endurance races in the sport: the 400 IM. If I couldn't train properly before the meet, it also meant I wouldn't have the endurance to perform well in my race.

Todd, who had since been promoted to associate head coach of the Razorbacks, saw me trying to swim through excruciating pain. He squatted down in the gutter. "Tera, what are you doing?" I heard the care in his voice, and concern wrinkled his forehead.

"I can finally compete this year," I said. "I didn't come all this way and go through two surgeries to back out of SECs a week before the meet. I can do it, Todd. Even if I can't train at all, I'll show up and compete. I've done it my whole life. Trust me. I can fake through the pain."

He sighed. "I know," he said. "You don't need to convince me. No one is taking your spot, Tera. If you're able to swim on Tuesday when we leave, I'm taking you." Relief poured over me, but doubt tugged the back of my mind, *Would I be able to swim on Tuesday?*

I pushed through and found myself on a plane flying back

to one of my favorite pools: the Texas A&M Natatorium. Growing up, I had won many state championship races there. Texas A&M had just joined the SEC, and they had one of the nicest pools in the conference, so this year, they had the pleasure of hosting.

We arrived, and I jumped into the pool. The water felt fast. Once you get to a certain level of swimming, you can tell if a pool is fast or slow based on a myriad of factors like temperature, depth, gutter type, and the number of people creating waves from sharing your lane. To a normal person, the pool would have felt cold and wet. To me, I could tell it was faster than the pool I trained in. It felt like game time.

My first race was the 200 IM, in which I swam a 2:01:64. I missed qualifying for the C final, which includes competitors who placed between the sixteenth and twenty-fourth places in prelims, by 0.45 of a second. I competed in a couple of relays, and a few days into the meet, my main race was up. My shoulder was barely hanging on at this point, but I had made it. It was time to convince myself that I no longer hurt. I faked myself out, raced the prelim, and miraculously qualified for the C final.

That night, I could barely force myself to lift my arm to take each stroke to warm up for my race. Usually, I felt confident that adrenaline would carry me through the race no matter how bad my shoulder felt, but this time I wasn't so sure. I told one of my teammates I might need to scratch the race. I feared I was going to have to stop in the middle of it and get out of the pool, and no one does that unless it's a medical emergency. I would rather scratch than face that kind of humiliation.

I didn't do my normal warm-up. The change in routine would be enough to throw many athletes off, but I was trying to cut as much yardage as I could in order to make it through my race. I did about half of a normal warm-up and then did pace 50s, which are 50-yard repetitions at my target speed, with my coach. I walked over to my blocks, and my shoulder seeped with pain as I swung my arms in circles.

When I got up on the blocks, carnal Tera took over. I took the race out strong, especially considering fly was my worst stroke and the most painful for me. I was in lane one, one of my favorite places to race since my open turns faced the whole pack of swimmers to the left. My backstroke leg was weaker than normal, and when I turned for the breaststroke part of the medley, I was in last place. I could see all of the other swimmers on the first turn, and I began the hunt. One by one, I picked some of them off, knowing that I could anchor the freestyle leg with sheer guts. The announcer commented on my surge, and I heard my name over the speakers. That had to be good.

I turned for freestyle and churned through the water, fighting with all I had left. I finally flipped for the last fifty yards and brought the race home like there was no tomorrow. Somewhere in the back of my mind, I knew that it might be my last race, and I wanted to leave it all in the pool. I loved to finish strong, and I ended up negative splitting my last 100, meaning I split my last 50 faster than the first 50, with a split of twenty-eight seconds—quite a feat for someone as undertrained as I was. I hit the wall at 4:17.09 and placed fourth in my heat. It was a personal best time and an NCAA B Cut, which is a time standard that allows you to qualify for the national championship through rounds of selection, but it was not fast enough for me to be called to the championship.

I had done it. I made it through the race without having to climb out of the pool, and I had somehow pulled off a miraculous swim by faking myself out. I even earned points for my team. I didn't have to fool myself with mental tricks anymore. The race was over, and I didn't have to fight the pain. I took some high fives from the coaches and tried to enjoy it. I barely warmed down and only swam a few laps.

Finally, I swam the 200 Backstroke, an interesting choice made by my coaches since my best stroke was breaststroke. I had been training well enough in backstroke that they wanted to see what I could do. Since the 400 IM was over, my only goal for this race was to finish well for my team. I swam a 2:01, which wasn't an incredible race but also not bad for essentially only swimming warm-up for the past month.

I didn't even warm down. I had no reason to. I missed qualifying for the finals, which was a relief because it meant my meet was finally over. Deep down, I felt certain that was the last time I was going to get into a pool. This was different than all the other times I had come back. This time, I knew my career was over. If something didn't change, I knew that was the last race I was ever going to swim.

As I walked towards my backpack, one of my previous strength and conditioning coaches hugged me on the sidelines and said, "That's a long way from the operating table." It was indeed a long way from my first and second surgeries, but neither of us knew it wasn't far from the third operating table either.

A couple of months before SECs, the doctors working with the University of Arkansas had tried more cortisone shots in my shoulder, which I asked them to insert from the front for fear of nicking another artery. I had overcome the fear of pushing my breathing too hard, but the last thing I needed was another hole in my lung.

Then my shoulder started going numb and itching like crazy around my biceps. I told my athletic trainer I had lost sensation of my arm around the tendon. She blamed the cortisone shot, but the last time I checked, no cortisone shot had ever made an arm lose feeling. On a good day, I could feel most of my arm. On a bad day, I lost sensation in about a three-inch square on my shoulder. Sometimes, my entire arm would start itching so badly that I would scratch as if I had chicken pox.

No one realized how damaged my nerves were becoming because they thought my symptoms were a result of the cortisone shots. After I came back from SECs unable to swim, the last idea the doctors at Arkansas had was to do a CT scan of my neck to make sure I didn't have a pinched nerve. As I sat in the giant white cheerio of a machine with its sounds pounding through my earplugs, I fell asleep. I was so accustomed to CT scans, which made some people feel claustrophobic, that I could fall asleep during one.

All of the tests came back negative, and even though I had lost the function and the feeling in my arm, no one had any more ideas. Although I couldn't swim after SECs, I was kicking at practice because Blake thought I should. I couldn't lift weights, and running on the treadmill, which was supposed to be a leg substitute for arm work, hurt my arm. One of my best friends on the team had a great relationship with Blake, and she came to my defense by explaining to him how much pain I was truly in.

After their conversation, he approached me later to verify I was in pain while kicking. Befuddled as to why he suddenly understood now that it came from someone else's mouth—but simultaneously grateful he was attempting to understand—I tried explaining it once more.

"Yes. I'm always in pain. I'm in pain walking around. I'm in pain in class. I'm in pain at home. I'm in pain trying to go to sleep. Yes, I'm in pain with any kind of exercise, even if I'm not using my arms."

Blake suggested that maybe I shouldn't be swimming at all.

"Yeah, no kidding," I responded.

With that, I decided to quit the sport of swimming. For good. Even though I still felt like God had told me I was supposed to swim, I no longer considered it an option. After persevering through horrendous pain for seven years, my body flat out refused. I couldn't have swum even if I wanted to.

12

Giving Up and Taking Charge

Don't believe in miracles—
depend on them.
—Laurence J. Peter

My dad has always been low-key and one of the most laidback people you'll ever meet. He could make friends with just about anyone, and it takes a lot for him to confront someone. He gives people chance after chance to prove themselves, and he has an ability rarely seen on earth to forgive and see the best in others.

Up to this point, my dad had given Blake many chances to help me. My dad didn't want to butt in, and he tried to let me handle everything since I was an adult in college. But after all of Blake's failed attempts to help me, my dad decided it was time to have a conversation with him, man-to-man. After the SECs, my dad called Blake to hear his opinion about my whole situation.

"Now that my daughter is in so much pain that she can no longer swim, what's the game plan?" he asked.

Blake shared that he'd had doctors perform MRIs and CT scans and that I was still doing physical therapy.

"You mean the same therapy that hasn't worked for the past two years? I haven't intervened because I wanted your doctors do their thing, but I'm not convinced that you all are fighting for Tera anymore. My daughter now has no quality of life because she continued swimming for your institution. Do you have a plan to help her?"

Blake stressed that they were doing all that they could.

"It sounds to me like you don't really have a plan at all. Have you given up on my daughter?"

Blake repeated the same strategies that hadn't been working for the past seven years.

Unconvinced, my dad said, "Blake, I'm going to ask you that question again." Stressing each word, he asked, "Have you given up on my daughter?"

Blake sighed on the other end of the line and paused. Then he said yes.

My dad paused as he heard Blake admit to what he had suspected all along then charged forward. "Okay. Well, I'm not going to let my daughter live this way, so I'm going to take her to doctors who can figure out what's wrong. I would appreciate it if you all released her from your doctors and let me take it from here."

Blake relinquished—probably glad to finally be rid of the situation.

I tried an acupuncturist for the first few months after quitting swimming. In addition to the traditional needles, she used a laser on my shoulder, which somehow shot pain through my hand. She said the damage in my shoulder was unlike anything she'd ever seen, and even she could not determine the root of the problem. Her needles ended up pricking my emotions rather than healing my shoulder, but I wasn't ready to accept constant pain.

With one more type of treatment added to the list of trial and error, I returned home for spring break with a referral to see a person whom some deemed the "witch doctor." Other people called him Jesus. He was neither, but his nicknames came from his ability to heal people in unconventional ways. I had heard of Dr. Noah Moos from my teammate's mom, who swore he could figure out the answer to any physical problem, no matter how severe.

Dr. Moos was a holistic doctor who considered the body, mind, spirit, and emotions in his treatment. He held a chiropractic degree and had unique experiences studying with some of the great minds of alternative medicine and acupuncture in China. He combined all of his knowledge in his quest to solve people's issues and let their bodies function the way they were meant to function. He was the doctor people went to when all other doctors had failed.

An extreme skeptic by now, I was not convinced Dr. Moos could solve my mystery, but I was desperate enough to give it a try. I was home in Austin and ready to visit him. I expected his office to feature a bamboo curtain from which he would emerge with long hair and walk through mist before ushering me into some sort of strange practice. Much to my surprise, his office was practical and traditional. Perfectly normal.

"Do you want me to tell you what's wrong?" I asked when I finally met the surprisingly kempt man.

"Nope," he said as he began an examination unlike anything I had ever experienced before. Parts of the exam resembled a typical orthopedic exam: he asked me to resist different movements. Other parts of the exam used instruments that measured the energy output of the body and helped detect areas of stressed tissues. I had never seen anyone do what he was doing. He moved his fingers in some kind of sign language over my face, shoulders, stomach, and legs. I should have been freaked out, but these things had long since lost their shock factor on me. In fact, they piqued my curiosity.

"What on earth did you do to your right shoulder?" he calmly asked.

He'd never seen me before, and I hadn't breathed a word of my medical history to him. Dr. Moos earned himself some credibility with me with that comment. I chuckled, and then we launched into a discussion about my injury and medical history.

"Well, among many things, you have what's called double crush syndrome, except yours is triple. A number of muscles are not working correctly in your shoulder, neck, elbow, and wrist. Since these muscles aren't working correctly, your body is trying to splint those areas so that you don't move into a motion it cannot support."

Dr. Moos continued, "When muscles become too tight, not only can they cause pain at the attachment site, but they can also affect the nerve. Dysfunctional muscles also have trouble supporting the bones, which can affect the nerve; this is happening at your first rib, your elbow, and with a bone in your wrist. The pain you feel is likely the result of the nerve being crushed by the muscle and bone in these areas."

Considering the hand pain I had felt for the past few years and the fact that he explained perfectly in ten minutes what no doctor in seven years could explain so succinctly, I was swiftly becoming a believer in Dr. Moos.

"Furthermore," he went on, "your body is very low in some key nutrients. Your body will have a hard time healing itself, even if it wants to. This has been going on a long time, and your body has tried so hard to fight it that it has depleted all its resources. Since you're only in Austin for the break, I'm going to order blood work to confirm the nutrients I believe you are missing."

Dr. Moos shifted all the bones back into place and worked

on the muscles, and I left feeling more encouraged than I had in years. Bloodwork later confirmed Dr. Moos' suspicion about my nutrient deficiencies. The body is supposed to make sense, and all of Dr. Moos' explanations gave words to my pain. That's all I needed. I just wanted an explanation, no matter how dreadful the diagnosis. That way, we could move forward.

Dr. Moos also recommended hyperbaric oxygen therapy. Before I headed back to Arkansas, my parents and I walked into a room where an unimpressive white tube large enough for a person to be zipped inside waited. Doctors created this machine to heal injuries that wouldn't heal. It works by increasing the amount of oxygen your blood can carry, thus allowing more oxygen to reach injured tissues. This temporarily restores the level of blood gases in your body, so it can fight off infections and promote healing.

Why not, right? I thought as I entered the room. I didn't really understand the science, but I was so accustomed to putting my health in other people's hands that I blindly followed instructions by hopping into the mysterious chamber. I felt like I was entering some sort of sci-fi alien tank inside of which my body was about to be cryogenically frozen for the next hundred years, or I would be put to sleep until I awakened on a distant planet twenty years later.

Instead, the experience was anticlimactic. A doctor zipped me up as I laid down inside the little tunnel. I looked through a small window and imagined my view must be similar to that of an astronaut looking out of his or her helmet. My therapy session lasted two hours, and all I had with me in the tank was my phone. After taking some amusing selfies with my oxygen mask on, my attention span dwindled. I prayed, I tried to take a nap, and I let my mind wander to hope.

My newfound hope was expeditiously squashed when I returned to Arkansas after the break. I saw slight improvement for a couple weeks, but then I was back to square one. I stayed in communication with Dr. Moos, and my sudden downturn after everything he had fixed left him concerned. He knew there must be more to the puzzle.

In the meantime, even though I could no longer swim, I was still a scholarship athlete, and I wanted to keep my coaches posted on my progress. When I thought Dr. Moos had found the long lost problem, I had excitedly told Blake and Todd about what he'd found. Now that things appeared to be taking another downturn, Blake scoffed at the possibility that a random chiropractor had supposedly figured out the shoulder issue that top surgeons couldn't diagnose. He did his own research and said double crush syndrome was debated, and many doctors claimed it didn't exist. In his mind, I had fabricated yet another excuse for my shoulder pain.

But back in Texas, Dr. Moos wasn't giving up just yet. He asked for copies of my MRIs and sent them to his friend, who specialized in reading these complex tests. His friend called him and said my MRIs definitely were not normal. He saw a number of things wrong, including something highly concerning: a bubble-like formation on my biceps, a possible sign of my body fighting internal infection.

Dr. Moos reached out to my parents: "Tera needs to see an orthopedic surgeon. She likely needs to have a third surgery to address the spot on her bicep."

I tried to keep on keeping on, but my pain remained undeterred, and my mind remained in turmoil. The path was getting darker and darker, and I was running out of options. But many miracles are complete and utter tragedies before they are miracles. In fact, what most people see as a door closing is really a miracle waiting to happen. We read stories of people healing from cancer, being instantly cured from drug addiction, and having paralyzed limbs restored, and we see the glory. But we don't think about the pain these people first endured before experiencing the miracle.

Without the tragedy, the issue, the brokenness, the lack, or the failure which necessitate the divine, miracles would cease to exist. Before Jesus healed a woman, she bled for eight years, was ostracized from her community, and considered unclean for a condition she could not control. If the flood never came, people would have seen Noah as a crazy lunatic who built a boat large enough to house the world's animals. Abraham had to lift the knife to kill his son before God provided the ram. Jesus changed the world when God raised him from the grave, but before that, he let others slaughter him in the most gruesome death Roman torturers could conjure.

Not all tragedies become miracles, but it is through the opportunity of adversity that the path clears for a miracle to take place. I thought I was nearing my end, but I was actually only getting to the end of *myself* and my resources so that God could do what only he could do. Behind the scenes, he was paving the way for a miracle.

13

The Fog

chucked my Bible across the room and screamed, "You are not a good Father! No parent could watch his daughter suffer like this for so long and do nothing, all while being fully capable of healing her!"

I crumpled on the ground in tears. Canker sores laced my throat as I tried to swallow. I couldn't even be angry without physical agony. Over the past few months, these sores had become a constant companion. Before my outburst, I had used a mirror to count ten of them covering my mouth and throat. Afterward, I had been dutifully trying to complete my quiet time when I read, "Now to him who is able to do immeasurably more than all we can ask or imagine, according to his power that is at work within us, to him be the glory . . . for ever and ever" (Ephesians 3:20–21).

I had spent years claiming promises and believing God would honor my faith through this crazy trial. If God really could heal me, then he certainly couldn't be a good Father because he hadn't healed me. The picture Ephesians portrayed was so different from the Father I saw in my life that I couldn't react in faith anymore. Anger was all I had left.

Pain coursed down my arm from throwing my Bible, and it further justified my anger. But my feelings were so complex that I wasn't sure how to sort them. I crawled over to the Bible on the floor, its pages bent out of shape in the same way I felt God's words had bent out of shape in my life over the years. I picked up the Bible carefully, like a baby, and started to fix the pages. My anger ebbed; my tears escalated.

"I'm so sorry," I whispered. Part of me felt conviction, and part of me felt anxious for having thrown an omnipotent God's holy book across the room. He might smite me into a pile of ash. Smoothing the pages, I closed the Bible and crawled to sit with my back against the bed. I held the book across my chest in crossed arms, dropped my head against my legs, and talked into my knees.

"God, I can't believe you. Belief is too painful. It's easier to succumb to a life of pain. What am I holding onto? If this verse is true, why haven't you healed me? You say you can do immeasurably more than we can ask or imagine. I can imagine healing, which means you must be able to do more than that. But so far, you haven't even done what I can imagine, much less more than I've asked."

I sat in the silence, waiting to feel God's arms wrap around me. I felt nothing. My anger transformed to self-pity. *Why me? How much longer?* I ran out of questions, so I tried to clear my mind with steady breathing. I had already asked everything I could ask.

As I sat in the silence, I felt God console my heart, *Hang on, baby, hang on. Answers are coming.*

Chronic pain is like fog. It's a difficult concept to describe if you've never experienced it, almost like trying to explain snow to someone who has lived her entire life in the Bahamas. Chronic pain does not assault or attack the senses like a physical injury, nor does it invade the heart and penetrate the mind like heartbreak or emotional pain. It is a creeping pain. Slow and sure, like a fog gently spreading across a field. As you're walking around, you might notice a little mist in your vision, but you figure it's nothing to worry about. After all, you can still see where you're going. But after a while, your vision blurs. You know you're walking in a field, and the landscape is predicatable, so you figure it shouldn't cause you too much harm to continue.

Before you know it, you're surrounded. The fog is so thick that you could cut it with a knife. It closes in around you, suffocating all your senses. Your vision is destroyed, and your perspective becomes disoriented. Panic begins to set in. You claw at the air, trying to clear a way to a visible path. You spin in circles, frantically searching for any sign of light penetrating the darkness, only to find more gray fog. It is unchanging and imperceptibly growing denser. No matter where you run or turn, the fog is there. It is immovable, unrelenting, and unforgiving.

The panic fades, and apathy replaces it. You accept the fog and succumb to your new reality. You learn to live within its confines. Sometimes you curl up into a ball of hopelessness, tears streaming down your cheeks in a slight mental breakdown, as something in the recesses of your mind recalls what a sunny day looked like. You know nothing will truly change, so you eventually get up and start walking again, but this time you're resigned to your blindness. You may throw a small pity party for yourself every now and then, but to be honest, you've become comfortable in the fog. You've found safety in the obscurity. To the rest of the world, you have become invisible.

But that comfort only lasts so long. You were created for the day, not the night. You wake to the reality that you have no idea where you are. The people you leaned on have all disappeared, and the truths you built your life upon have faded into oblivion. You are utterly lost and alone, and it's too late to find your way out. These lies begin to suffocate you until you believe the fog has become impossible to escape. The suffocation turns to desperation.

As pain began to fully consume my body and my mind, strange thoughts began to surface. Ideas that had disconcerted me before now twistedly made sense. The fog had been creeping in for years, but I didn't know it. I had slowly faded into darkness. The fog deteriorated my mind to the point where all I could see were the people in the fog with me, not those who walked in the sunlight.

Something in me knew that I wasn't thinking clearly when I had thoughts about amputating my arm. BIID, or body integrity identity disorder, is when a person believes one or more of his or her limbs are not supposed to be a part of their body, and often-times, they have a strong desire to amputate the limb. I had heard of people with BIID trying various "home procedures" to damage the limb to the point that necessitated amputation. Some tied a tourniquet around their limb and attempted to cut off all circulation from the appendage until it was so damaged it had to be removed. Others froze the unwanted body part with dry ice until doctors amputated the limb in order to save the person's life.

These methods seemed valid enough, except I realized in order to amputate my arm high enough to cut off the pain at its source, doctors would have to cut off my entire shoulder, and that would be too close to major arteries. Too risky. I didn't want to die; I just wanted to get rid of the pain.

Then I pondered Bethany Hamilton, who lives an incredible, fulfilled life and testifies to God's grace every day with one arm. I thought, *Okay, God, if I go to shark-infested waters in Australia, go surfing, and dangle my right arm over the surfboard, would you send a shark to come bite off my arm exactly where it would need to be cut off? Then I could bring glory to you and be out of pain too!*

My mind churned ahead and envisioned an incredible story. Not only would I be out of pain, but I could also go to the Paralympics! Yes! Surely, this is what God had planned all along; this must be why he placed the desire to go to the Olympics in my heart. It was just a different Olympics than I thought! Everything made so much sense. I paused with satisfaction at having reached a conclusion for my future.

But then that still, small voice gently whispered, *I already have a Bethany Hamilton. I need a Tera Bradham.*

But why can't you have two? I pleaded. True to my nature, I wasn't backing down without a fight.

True to his nature, God didn't feel the need to explain his reasoning. He just repeated, *I need a Tera Bradham.*

One would think that his words would inspire me, and my faith would arise. After all, I had received a promise that God was going to fulfill. Surely, I would get up and patiently await my miracle with renewed fervor. I sorrowfully admit that I did none of those things. I had reached a point where I thought living with one arm would be better than living with searing pain. I thought about how I would have to learn to write with my left hand. I thought about my previous surgeries, after which I couldn't use my right arm. Without it, I couldn't do the simplest of tasks, such as put up my hair or eat without spilling food all over my lap. Still, even this life seemed like a preferable alternative to the one I currently lived.

Pain was my life. My shoulder had been injured for so long that I couldn't remember what life was like without pain. How many memories do you have from before you were twelve years old? The degree of pain varied, but it had the perseverance of a two-year-old begging for candy. Annoying at its best and debilitating at its worst, the pain was relentless. After seven years of praying for healing, seven years of seeing every doctor imaginable, and seven years of trying to cope, my willpower waned. I was now willing to sacrifice the ease of two-armed life for the less painful but still challenging one-armed existence.

As a former fog-dweller, let me tell you something: There is danger in the fog. It is not normal. You are not made to stay there, nor do you have to. If you do not find a lifeline, you will continue to wander helplessly in any given direction. Eventually, that easy, predictably flat field on which you were wandering will turn into a slippery slope. If you don't grab onto something for support, you will plummet down that slope. And sometimes, you won't even get the grace of bumping into a hill first. Sometimes, you'll walk straight off a cliff.

That's what happened to me. I didn't even realize how the fog came in or how long it had been there until it was too late. It closed in around me, all at once, and before I knew it, I was suffocating, running, and utterly desperate. I walked right up to that cliff. At the time, I didn't even know I was standing on the edge of it, but looking back, it's scary to see how close I was to the point of no return.

I never could have imagined the deepest, darkest, blackest pit of hell in which I found myself. The fog wasn't a dull, downcast gray; it was pitch black. It was hopeless. My story had ended in tragedy. But even all the darkness in the world cannot overcome the light shed by a single flame.

Sometimes, that flame is a person who assures you that no matter how dark it gets, you're not alone. Morgan was one of my best friends since the summer before our freshman year of college. After meeting at church and hanging out all summer, we helped each other move into our new rooms for the fall semester. To our surprise, not only did we live in the same dorm, but we also ended up as next-door neighbors! I practically lived in Morgan's room during my freshman year.

We moved into the same complex for our sophomore year and complained how the now thirty-second walk to each other's apartments was too far compared to the two-second walk of freshman year. Morgan was my staunchest supporter, and she stood by me through trial and victory. She saw all my ups and downs, and her compassion and support buoyed me through my toughest tribulations. She also had an uncanny way of knowing exactly what I felt—even when *I* didn't even know what I felt.

When I told Morgan I was finished fighting, she stared at me with a look of horror. Beneath my words, she could tell I had begun to truly give up on life.

"Oh, Tera," she stumbled. She looked in my eyes and realized the light in them had vanished. Morgan knew this wasn't simply a trial as others assumed. This was my life-and-death battle. She started to cry.

"Tera," she said through the tears, "I have no words." She held my hand, and we cried together. After a few minutes, her hand tightened around mine, and I looked up. The sadness in her eyes had changed to a fierce strength I had never seen before. Her voice was unwavering and her conviction steadfast.

"Too many people's eternities depend on your story for you to give up now. You've come too far. Don't you dare give up now." She held my bloodshot eyes with resolution. "Tera, you can't let Satan win."

Everyone likes a comeback story. I had been the fastest swimmer my age in the country, then tore my shoulder, and then appeared to be on the rise once again. Everyone was in my corner when it looked like I would triumph against all odds. But when you have another surgery, and doctors find nothing, and the pain worsens until you have no quality of life, and you're hanging onto something God told you that seemed absolutely absurd, people stop wanting to hear that story. I had countless supporters my freshman year, but few people wanted to hang out with the once-bubbly person who now soured in her struggle to survive.

No one wants to persevere with someone at rock bottom. No one likes a story of defeat, sorrow, and confusion. But one person found me in the fog. Morgan mourned with me when nearly everyone else walked away. She understood how lost I was, and she brought a flashlight into the darkness. Although I didn't know it at the time, her light was a lifeline amidst the fog, and it would prove to be just enough to help me hold on.

Hang on, baby, hang on. Answers are coming, God whispered.

14

Sufficient Grace

If you can't fly then run,
if you can't run then walk,
if you can't walk then crawl,
but whatever you do,
you have to keep moving forward.
—Martin Luther King, Jr.

t is one thing to experience pain that is understood. It is another
to experience pain without explanation. Normally, when someone has an injury, they go to a doctor, take time off, rest or take
medicine, and then the injury gets better. But for me, I went to
doctor after doctor, and no one could even begin to tell me what
was wrong, much less make it better. For five years, I went without
so much as a diagnosis. After two more years, surgeons had been
inside my shoulder twice, and my pain was worse than ever. Were
they missing something? Not likely. The problem was clearly with
me. It seemed as if the only plausible explanation was that I needed
to fix something inside of my own head.

But deep down, I believed the universe happened with causality because it was created with intentionality. Pain indicated something was wrong because that is how human bodies were designed. I believed there had to be a legitimate reason for my pain. I read books about regrowing nerves, convincing myself I had been in pain for so long that my nerves had created "bad habits," and even though the problem was now fixed, they hadn't received the message that they no longer needed to emit pain signals. Nerves heal millimeters at a time, so I figured it would take a long time for my brain to stop sending danger signals to my body. Like everything else, nerve science was a part of the puzzle, but it proved to be only one small piece.

In mid-spring of 2013, I saw another muscle massage therapist to try to speed up the healing process, and we started to see improvement. My pain decreased a little, probably from the placebo effect. Thankfully, this doctor sincerely cared about helping me manage my pain and discovering its cause, and over the course of a few months, my pain seemed to lessen. During one session, he took a scraper to some of my rotator cuff muscles—all of the tiny muscles in your shoulder that hold it in place. Scraping comes from the traditional Chinese medicine of Gua Sha, and it is believed that by scraping the surface of the muscles and creating bruises, bad toxins release, and blood flow increases to the injured area. By releasing the lactic acid build-up, an injury is then able to heal. The treatment is not supposed to be overly painful, although a Google image search suggests otherwise.

Like most treatments, my body did not react normally to scraping. During the scraping process itself, the pain was so intense that I wanted to bite down on a rag. But I was gladly willing to endure any kind of temporary pain that might alleviate the permanent pain to which I was so accustomed. That night, I tossed and turned and woke up so many times that I began to count the interruptions in my sleep. By morning, I had woken up at least four times, and I was unable to lift my arm. Yet another treatment that was supposedly great for others was literally a nightmare for me. I did my best to get through the day and attended church that night. Worship began, and I cringed. Normally, I loved to lift my arms while singing, but now it was impossible. It didn't matter; I didn't want to worship God at all that night anyway. Why did he promise healing when all I seemed to experience was increasingly intensifying pain?

Then, the band started to play one of my favorite songs. My faith began to fight my doubt. I may not have been able to use my competitive streak in the water anymore, but I could use that fire to fight in the spiritual realm. *I will worship, even when I have no reason to. I will see my miracle come to pass,* I thought. I reached my arm above my head, almost screaming from the pain. I dropped my arm but tried again. Try as I might, I could not straighten my elbow. I forced my arm as straight as I could and held it still as an act of defiance toward my circumstance and in the belief that my God was not yet finished in my life.

It is easy to worship God when our lives go as planned, but when life isn't going our way, or we don't like the song, or we don't feel like worshiping, we tend not to worship—at least not as passionately. But worship doesn't have much to do with us; it has everything to do with the One we worship. Regardless of our circumstance, and regardless of our emotion, God is still worthy of our worship. We move the heart of God when we praise him—especially when we feel as though we have no reason to praise him at all. Admittedly, these thoughts were not on my mind as I held up my arm that night. I only knew that something in me had to worship God because, deep down, I knew he was worthy. Tears ebbed at the corners of my eyes, and I held them shut throughout the chorus. Only when the song mellowed did I return my arm to its limp dangle at my side.

A season of profound dependence on God that I had never known before began that night. God wanted my complete dependence on him, and he got it. I had no other option. My heart was peeled back, raw and beating in his hands, and I had to let his grace sustain me—moment by moment. The pain was so relentless and my heart so frail that I had to turn to God to sustain me. At first, this degree of dependence humbled me, but it also made me feel like the last part of my strength had deteriorated. I had turned to God before, but I had never reached the point where I couldn't make it through the day on my own. The last ounce of my false sense of independence evaporated.

Multiple times a day, I needed to ask God to fill me and help me carry on. I would see people in wheelchairs or glorifying God through cancer or horrendous infirmities and realized that maybe God wanted to use me in this way to inspire others. Finally, I surrendered.

God, I prayed, *if I have to tell myself that your grace is sufficient for me one hundred times a day, then it is worth it if this is how you want to be glorified in my life. Help me live for your glory, because I cannot do it on my own.*

I woke up each morning to pain and repeated, *Your grace is sufficient for me.* Pain pulsed in my hand as I tried to write in my journal. *Your grace is sufficient for me.* I tried to cook breakfast but couldn't lift the pan. *Your grace is sufficient for me.* I had pain brushing my teeth. *Your grace is sufficient for me.* I used my left hand to open the door. *Your grace is sufficient for me.* The pain forced me to move my hands to the bottom of the steering wheel to drive. *Your grace is sufficient for me.* Sometimes, I had repeated that verse over twenty times by the time I got to campus. Faking it to make it had failed, and I desperately hoped that depending on God until I made it would succeed.

One day, I was sitting in the car with four people and my

pastor, Matt Huie. We were driving home from a retreat w
college group.

"As I was preparing the sermon this week," he began, "I f
like God wants someone to share on stage about God's grace in
their life."

He paused. I felt a little nudge in my spirit, which I promptly
laughed at internally. *I am the last person in the world who could
speak about grace right now,* I thought. *I am in the fight of my life, I
have absolutely nothing figured out, and I'm desperately struggling to
believe God's grace is enough for me each day.*

I was in the car with three other people on the leadership
team at church—one of them would surely volunteer.

Silence.

"If one of you feels led or if you know of someone who might
be good, let me know," Matt said. Some said okay. Others said
they'd pray about it.

I stared out the window, pushing the Holy Spirit down in
my gut without a hint of emotion on my face. *No,* I said to God.
No way. I continued to stare out the window until I successfully
ignored the Spirit within me . . . until later that night. I could not
fall asleep, which was an oddity for someone who usually gave way
to the REM cycle within sixty seconds of her head hitting the pillow. Whenever I couldn't sleep, it was often because God was trying to tell me something.

Fine! I thought, slamming my fists on the mattress. I looked
up at the ceiling. *I'll do it tomorrow. I'll tell Matt I'm the one who
is supposed to speak. Just let me sleep!* A hint of anxiety pulled at
my mind since public speaking had always terrified me, but peace
filled my heart. I fell asleep thirty seconds later.

The next morning, I dragged my feet through the church
lobby up to Matt. Without so much as a hello, I started, "I think I'm
the one who is supposed to share about grace tonight."

pulled at his cheeks. "I know."

one God wants to share. He told me it was
...et him speak to you too."
...confirmation. That night, I spoke in front of more
...e hundred peers about what God was doing in my life. I
shared my testimony, about how I had no idea what was going on,
and about how I got up each morning and begged God for his grace
to get me through the day. Tears rimmed my eyes as I declared
God's promise to me to my peers: "I will bring health and healing
to you. I will rebuild you as before, and you will enjoy abundant
peace and security. I will forgive all your rebellion against me, and
you will bring me renown, glory, praise, and honor before all the
nations on earth that hear of what I do for you, and they will tremble and fear and be in awe of the abundant peace and prosperity I
provide in your life" (Jeremiah 33:6–9).

I paused and looked out across the audience. My voice
shook: "I will *die* before I give up on that promise."

There is power in declaring God's goodness to a group of
people amidst your pain and uncertainty. Declaration moves the
heavens to action, for it justifies your faith through action. You
must be willing to take God at his Word and claim it, even when
you can't see it. It was a bold statement. It was also a challenge that
the enemy was more than willing to take me up on.

The enemy's first method of attack was isolation. Within the
same church where I spoke that night, I enjoyed a group of people
whom I considered family. But since my lack of improvement after
my second surgery, one by one, people started slipping out of my
life. No dramatic falling outs took place; I just wasn't the pursuer of
people I used to be. I used to initiate conversations and hangouts
and coffee dates. Now, few returned the favor. Although most people were still in my life, they withdrew to a safe distance in fear of

getting too dirty. They would ask about my shoulder, and I would shrug or tear up, so they would leave it alone, not knowing what to tell me when my healing never came.

The same team who had cheered for me on the big screen at church during my Olympic Trial qualifier now left me alone; it was easier for them to do than I ever expected. I didn't think I could slip out of their vision so easily, but I did. It wasn't that they didn't care; they each had their own lives, and after a while, when a story doesn't improve, people don't want to be a part of it anymore.

No one knew what to do with the girl who never had her comeback. No one knew what to do with the girl who never got any better. No one knew what to do with the girl who had lost the fire that used to light up her eyes. I would have given anything for someone to wrap me in a hug and not let go, to tell me that it was going to be okay and God had a plan, but I didn't know I needed that. I certainly never portrayed that I wanted it either. Instead, I sank further and further into the darkness of isolation.

"Stop dangling your arm at your side. If you don't move it, it's never going to get any better. You're making it worse." In May, I had come to the pool to see my athletic trainer, even though I wasn't swimming anymore. I was still diligently doing my rehab exercises, hoping that the exercises that hadn't worked for seven years would somehow yield a different result. Some might call that the definition of insanity.

"I can't use it without pain!" I almost shouted back. "I have pain when I write, I have pain when I walk, and I have pain when I put on my backpack. For crying out loud, I have pain just sitting here! I can't use my arm anymore!"

"Well then, you shouldn't be exercising, should you?" The condescending tone insulted whatever shred of ego I had left.

"You're right. I shouldn't have been exercising or swimming for a long time. But I did." My stubbornness retaliated with equal bite.

"Well, now you don't have an option. If you're really in that much pain, then you don't need to be doing any kind of exercise or movement."

"I agree." I conceded.

"Well then," she replied, "until you can put on a backpack without pain, you're not allowed to exercise anymore."

"Fine." I threw my hands up in resignation. In my anger, I decided it was a motion worthy of the pain, and I stormed out of the natatorium.

I did my shoulder exercises and went to class, but I quit any form of exercise I had been attempting outside swimming. Not only had I lost my dream, my sport, and my promise, but I also lost all the endorphins that exercising normally produced. If I lived in frustration before, now I started to tread the paper-thin line between dejection and depression.

I found solace in walking. It was a fundamental necessity for life, and they couldn't ban me from that form of exercise. If you follow Dickson Street up into the hills, you will find a campsite bundled into the side of a miniature mountain. The sign introduces you to Mount Sequoyah, a cluster of buildings used for camps, retreats, conferences, and weddings. The road there creates about a mile loop. On one side of the street, there is an overlook of the entire city of Fayetteville. From there, you can see Old Main, the University of Arkansas campus, the Square, and the mountains on the other side of I-540. At this lookout is also a cross that stands at the height of two people, and it lights up at night for the world to see.

Often, I would climb up to the cross to spend time with God. One night I went to Mount Sequoyah with friends as we sang "God of This City" over Fayetteville. I would sit in the cross's shadow to muse with friends for hours about the complexities of life. Sometimes, my mentor and I would stare out across the city as we listened to worship music in the car when it was too cold to sit outside.

But after I was confined to no exercise, Mount Sequoyah took on another identity: it became my refuge. I would park at my friend's house and walk the rest of the way to the cross, relishing the only chance I had to slightly raise my heart rate. I walked prayer circles around the loop at Mount Sequoyah. Sometimes I would only walk one loop, and other times I walked for hours. Without practice consuming five hours of my day, I had nowhere to be. Sometimes, I walked aimlessly, having nothing left to say to God and not hearing anything in return. Other times, I walked with purpose, claiming my promise and circling that mountain like the Israelites circled Jericho.

Inevitably, I ended my time sitting at the foot of the cross, looking out at the city that had become my home. Sometimes, a change of scenery is the best way to change your perspective, and I have always connected more to God in nature. Sitting up by that cross, looking out across the city as far as the mountains on the other side, my head would feel as clear as the view.

The days I knelt in the grass under the foot of that cross, I would ask God hard questions. I often received hard answers to those questions or no answers at all, but sometimes I received the sweet seed of partial revelation that gave me just enough hope to carry on.

One day, I felt God whisper to my spirit once again, *Answers are coming. Hang on, baby, answers are coming.* God almost never tells us things in full, for then we would have no need to depend on him. I desperately needed an answer that no doctor or person on earth could provide, and now, God told me answers were coming. All I could respond with was, *Your grace is sufficient for me. Let your grace be sufficient for me until the answers come.*

15

A Kernel of a Mustard Seed

Truly I tell you, if you have faith as small as a mustard seed,
you can say to this mountain, 'Move from here to there,'
and it will move. Nothing will be impossible for you.
–Matthew 17:20

My mother died before I was born. At nineteen years old, her heart stopped beating, and a Code Blue was announced over a hospital PA system. A team rushed to her room to begin resuscitative efforts. Doctors performed CPR and used a defibrillator to force electrical currents into her body and jolt it back to life. After four minutes and twenty seconds, her heart began to beat again.

My grandmother had been bringing my mom to various doctors around the country for the past seven years, including the Mayo Clinic in Rochester, Minnesota, in vain attempts to ascertain the reason why her daughter experienced seizures and fainting spells. My mom would frequently pass out during tennis tournaments, and my grandmother would either rush to find a hospital in an unfamiliar city or summon an ambulance. Between middle school and college, doctors treated my mom for hypoglycemia and then epilepsy, but her prescribed medications were treating non-existent conditions.

"Her lips and fingernails turn completely blue," my grandmother would tell the doctors. "It has to be something in her heart." But doctors didn't listen to her. In seven years, not one doctor ordered an echocardiogram. That is, until my mother died and cardiologists finally confirmed what my grandmother had known all along: a problem with her heart. Doctors finally diagnosed my mom with a mitral valve prolapse, a condition in which the mitral valve does not close properly, allowing blood to regurgitate back into the left atrium when the left ventricle contracts, instead of pumping blood out through the aortic valve (like it should) and eventually delivering it to her veins and arteries. A correct diagnosis finally put a name on the insanity their family had faced for years, and an effective treatment was implemented.

Now, a generation later, my shoulder crisis forced my mother to relive her multiple misdiagnoses. She never would have wished her years of pain and confusion on her worst enemy, much less on her own flesh and blood. And yet, my mother found herself in her own mother's shoes, dealing with seven years of misdiagnoses and a daughter who could not handle the pain anymore.

In fact, the pain had become so severe that I found myself back in the doctor's office and speaking to one of the two presiding surgeons who had operated on me in Arkansas. He essentially told me that my injury and pain were in my head, that I couldn't handle losing my sport, and that there was more to life than swimming.

"Just go to Spain," he said. "Get your mind off of everything that revolves around swimming and see how big the world is. I'm sure with a change of surroundings, your pain will go away. I think you'll be just fine when you come back, and I see no repercussions of this injury for your future."

Ten minutes earlier, he had walked into the room and performed the shoulder strength tests that had become second nature to me. "Push here. Resist here. Good. Okay, turn your hand thumb down, and try not to let me push your arm down." Doctors never saw any flaw in those strength tests because I had always been able to execute them with adequate resistance.

This time, though, the pain that I usually gritted through was almost unbearable. The surgeon placed his fingers on my shoulder and pushed down with his thumb, feeling the biceps tendon. Stunned by the immediate pain, tears sprang up involuntarily. It was like his finger was a knife he had shoved into my arm, even though he had barely touched me. Frustrated at failing to hide the weakness, even more tears threatened to spill out from anger.

My surgeon looked at me and quipped words I've never forgotten: "I don't take your tears seriously anymore. You're just really emotional about this." He walked out of the room and returned to tell me he thought studying abroad was the best option. Even though barely touching my arm caused me to cry involuntarily from pain, to him the solution was mental, not physical.

I wanted to burn with anger and let it fuel me on to greater things, but that stage of my life had passed. I could no longer make myself angry. I resigned myself to the mediocrity my life had become—a life of no solution and no resolution, a life of endless limbo, endless circles of faith and doubt, and endless debates without winners. I couldn't fight for myself anymore. I had exhausted all my options, and I didn't know what else I could do. The prayers of others had failed. My own prayers had failed. Doctors had failed. Science had failed. And by my estimation, God had failed.

I remembered Matthew 17:20 where Jesus says, "Truly I tell you, if you have faith as small as a mustard seed, you can say to this mountain, 'Move from here to there,' and it will move. Nothing will be impossible for you." I loved that verse. The mustard seed was the smallest seed with which farmers in Jesus's time would have been familiar. His parable means that if you have the tiniest bit of faith—even if it's as tiny as a seed that can easily disappear into the crevice of your hand—you can move a mountain.

Except sometimes, the mountains didn't move. I felt like there were moments where I had more faith than plenty of people who had been healed, both in biblical times and in present day, and yet I remained in pain. Where was the justice in that? I mean, I must have had a mustard seed of faith, right? But according to the Bible, which was supposed to be my ultimate source of truth, if I had the faith the size of a miniscule seed, God would move my mountain. And he hadn't. That reality left me with two options: either my faith was not as grounded as I believed it was or God was not who he said he was.

Naturally, I chose to believe the latter. My body had been deteriorating for seven years, and my faith had begun to deteriorate with it. One by one, it seemed everyone in my life had eventually given up on me, including God. Before, I could always banish the naysayers from my mind because I believed in myself even if they didn't, and I believed God was fighting for me when others weren't. But when I felt God's loss of belief in me, I finally gave up on myself. If he wasn't rising to my defense, why should I defend myself? I had held firm to the idea that if we were the authors of our lives, God wouldn't defend our stories, but if *he* was the author, he would come out in power to defend the story he had written.

Now, I couldn't help but wonder if maybe my imagination *had* created it all: the promise, the healing, all of it. Maybe God was a figment of my imagination, wishful thinking for a hurting heart. After all, we all need a hope to cling to. Maybe God was what I fell back on simply because my upbringing had taught me to. Maybe I was wrong about everything all along, including the reality of a loving God. I was alone, and the weight of the world had crushed the unconquerable spirit people had once so sought to emulate. I was no longer capable of fighting for myself, and no one was stepping up to fill the vacancy that the abandonment of my promise left. No one, that is, except my parents.

I don't want to live anymore, I texted my mom from Spain. She asked me how I was handling my pain overseas, and I responded in honesty. Even pursuing the treasures of the Louvre, exploring my childhood fascination of the Coliseum, and booking my days with tours and my nights with blogs, I couldn't block out the pain. I even had to stop mid-conversation while eating a croissant in Paris, unable to finish a thought as pain surged through my arm. I fumbled for words in Spanish to describe my story to my host mom, but how could I explain it to her in another language when I couldn't describe in English? So, I didn't. I did my best to learn the architecture of Spain's cathedrals and sucked it up.

Studying abroad and the busyness that accompanied it kept me sane in the midst of insanity. While there, my parents followed Dr. Moos's advice and began researching the best shoulder surgeons in the country. They texted me off and on, updating me on their findings. They narrowed their list to two of the best shoulder surgeons in the country: one in New York and the other in Denver.

Then, my dad was listening to a talk show on the radio one day when the hosts announced a surprising guest: Amy Van Dyken, former swimmer, Olympic champion, and world record holder. She talked about her shoulder surgery and her return to the sport and to the Olympics—again. My dad couldn't help but think her experience with undiagnosed shoulder pain sounded similar to mine. Perhaps her surgeon could fix my shoulder too.

"But how would we ever get ahold of her?" my dad asked my mom. Desperate for an answer to my pain, my mom took matters into her own hands. She made a Twitter account so that she could tweet at Amy Van Dyken and ask her for the name of the surgeon who reconstructed her shoulder. Within a few hours, Amy tweeted back: "Dr. Schlegel with the Steadman Hawkins Clinic in Denver. He's amazing!!"

Thus, I found myself meeting my parents outside the Dallas airport during my layover on my trip home from Spain. Instead of continuing to fly on to Arkansas as planned, I walked out of the airport, hopped in my parents' car, and headed to Denver. On our way, we met with a pastor who my parents knew. He prayed over me and for my healing. I appreciated the gesture, but I was so used to people praying for my shoulder that it was hard to believe this prayer would produce a different result.

I climbed back into the car and zoned out for most of the ride, not even thinking about what could happen in Denver. I subconsciously numbed my mind. Deep down, I knew this surgeon was a last-ditch effort, and if he failed like everyone else had, then I had no idea how I could cope with my pain. Since I had lost control a long time ago, I simply awaited my verdict in passive resignation.

My parents and I arrived in Denver, checked in to a hotel, and walked into the Steadman Hawkins Clinic. We divvyed up the paperwork, watched young athletes come in with casts and braces, and then filed into the renowned surgeon's office.

From the moment he walked in, I could tell Dr. Schlegel was different than most of the surgeons I had encountered. There was no golden cloud of god-complex surrounding his head, and he kept his medical jargon to a minimum. He was personable, a rarity in the bedside manner of top surgeons, and he seemed like he genuinely cared about finding the solution to my pain.

After talking to us and taking his time, Dr. Schlegel ordered more MRIs and tests. At this point, waiting didn't surprise me. I sighed as I went in for another round of machines to confirm what humans wanted them to say: the pain was all in my head. We were only delaying the inevitable outcome, when a top surgeon in the country would join ranks with the other surgeons to tell me I was crazy. I would have much rather ripped the Band-Aid off immediately and gotten it over with, but timing isn't up to any of us, and answers almost never come when we expect.

My parents extended the stay at our hotel, and we busied ourselves venturing to Pike's Peak and climbing the 2,744 steps of the Manitou Incline in Colorado Springs. A few days later, Dr. Schlegel relayed the predictable news: the MRI was not normal, but they thought they had discerned most of my pain stemmed from the biceps tendon. Go figure. Exactly what my second surgeons had said, and they had decided *not* to cut off my tendon once they were inside my arm because they didn't want to "end my career."

My parents and the team of doctors all decided we would try four weeks of physical therapy with a certified physical therapist and see if it helped. They said we could schedule a third surgery, hoping we wouldn't have to follow through with it, but by booking it in advance, we would at least be able to squeeze into the packed schedule of a thriving orthopedist.

Dr. Schlegel looked at me and asked me what my goal was for this surgery, if it were to happen. He wanted to know if I wanted to try to swim again.

"If it's a possibility, then of course I want to swim again. But I don't know if that's ever going to happen, so just do whatever you can to take away the pain." Tears welled up in my eyes. "Just give me my arm back."

The previous Christmas, I had met one of my pastor's friends who was a PT visiting from out of town. She really wanted to figure out the root of my shoulder pain and texted me exercises and advice in the following months. Right at the time I was getting back from seeing Dr. Schlegel in Colorado, her friend, Dalton Smith, a trusted physical therapist, moved to Rogers, Arkansas, just twenty minutes north of Fayetteville.

When Dr. Schlegel assigned my treatment to a PT, I chose

to see Dalton Smith. He watched me as I trudged through the doors wearing all black, a symptom his psychology courses told him denoted depression. I slumped in the corner of the waiting room, curled over in terrible posture, filling out paperwork for the millionth time. I circled the part of the body on the chart that hurt, I put down my past medical history, and I wrote that I had no allergies to any medications. I could have filled out the chart in my sleep.

Before he began to work with me, Dalton took me into a side office to talk. After introducing himself, he asked me one question: "Do you believe you can get better?"

No one had ever asked me that before, especially someone in the medical world. His bluntness exposed the sensitive part of my heart that I hid from doctors for years. Unbidden tears arose.

"Yes. I mean, I don't know, maybe . . ." I stammered. "I don't really believe doctors can do anything, no. I believe God can heal me, but I don't know if he *wants* to heal me." I stared at my feet.

"The reason I'm asking," Dalton explained, "is because if a patient does not believe she will get better, she won't. I've seen people come in with a knee scope, the least invasive and the easiest of surgeries, and not recover because they don't believe they can. I've also seen people come in with major surgeries and return to high levels of sports competition because the opposite is true: they believe they can. This all depends on you."

Great, I thought. *Exactly what I don't have left to give. Me.*

"Okay," I responded. "I'll give it one more shot. Maybe I've just never received the proper physical therapy before." I wanted to pacify him more than I believed therapy would help, but I desperately wanted to believe it would. With that, we started on some exercises and some manual work. Dalton combined massage with strengthening exercises, and we set up a physical therapy plan for the next four weeks.

I dutifully finished my exercises at home, and I started seeing baby steps of improvement. Whether it was the power of suggestion, my buying into Dalton's mindset of believing I could get better, or something actually physically happening, it didn't matter. I didn't care. Tiny steps of improvement gave me hope, and a person can live off a mustard seed of hope. A mustard seed of hope can birth a mustard seed of faith. I lived on this seed of hope for three weeks. Then, the day came that crushed my seed.

I knew to avoid things like grabbing a gallon of milk with my right hand or shampooing my hair with my right hand, but I still tried to maintain some function of my arm to convince myself my arm could recover. So, without thinking, I reached to turn off the kitchen light in my apartment.

Stunned by the overwhelming pain that shot through my arm, I sucked in air and doubled over, clutching my arm to my stomach and clenching my eyes shut. The pain moved through the top of my arm like someone running a knife drenched in poison along my biceps tendon. I held my breath.

Slowly, the pain subsided, and I let the air out of my lungs. I remained keeled over, inhaling air, my mouth forming a grimace, and my eyes closed, terrified if I let go of my arm the pain would return. After about a minute, I stood up and let my arm dangle. The pang of realization sent a sobering shiver through my spine.

I can't even turn off a light switch, I thought. *I'm twenty years old, and I can't turn off a light switch.*

Everyone was right. All the people who had told me I was crazy for years were right—all of them. I was never going to pick up my kids. I was never going to throw a ball to my dog or put my hair in a ponytail. I couldn't even turn off a light switch. Like the switch I had just turned off, something in my mind flipped irrevocably: I would have the third surgery. I had to. It was my last chance.

That night in bed, my body contorted itself into a twisted

fetal position to escape the pain pulsing down my arm. Hot tears slid gently down my cheeks in silent agony as the words refused to come. I did not have the strength to pray on my knees; that was the position of a warrior. I had only the strength to crumple up like a baby. Tears began to cascade, which slowly turned into sobs that wracked my body.

Relentless questions and doubts bombarded my mind, and my retreating faith could not muster the strength to fight them. No logic, wisdom, or truth could snatch me from the pit of despair that enveloped me on all sides. I sank deeper and deeper. There was no light, no hope, and no answer.

And then, amidst the suffocating anguish, a lone light, barely visible, shone through the darkness. Something from the recesses of my mind fought its way to consciousness: "If you have the faith as small as a mustard seed, nothing will be impossible for you" (Matthew 17:20). The beacon of hope abated the tears long enough for me to begin to catch my breath.

Words caught in my throat as I uttered a desperately simple prayer. A prayer, I believe, that changed my destiny: "God, I have fought for years and years and years, and I can't fight anymore. I never thought this world could break me, but it has. I'm finished. I know I said that your grace was sufficient for me, and I know that I said your strength was made perfect in my weakness, but I can't do this anymore. I can't live this way. Please don't make me live this way. I have been hanging on by a kernel of a mustard seed of faith for years, and I don't have it anymore. I have lost my life because I did what you told me to do. Where are you? Please don't let me live this way."

I paused as one final surge of conviction overtook my mind. I looked up to heaven, tears gathering and threatening to spill over in another torrent. I clenched my jaw with determination, and then I stressed each syllable as I made an audacious demand from an Almighty God: "Heal me or take me home, but don't make me live this way."

16

Covenant Scar

I'm a surgeon at heart.
A chance to cut is a chance to heal.
—Kevin Beam

By the time we returned to Colorado, I had no hope left. My parents took me to P.F. Chang's for my last meal before I had to stop eating for the operation. I sat in the booth outside, trying to focus on the taste of the food instead of the headache that felt like hammers were pounding my head. Whether from stress or other physical factors, horrible headaches had become my companion recently. My mind just couldn't handle my body constantly being in so much pain anymore.

The next afternoon, August 6, 2013, I went in for my third surgery on the same shoulder. I had no expectations and no grand revelation of faith like I did before my first surgery. I had prayed all I could, and I resigned myself to whatever happened. To me, this surgery was just a final shot in the dark.

My parents prayed for me, and nurses had me initial my right arm in Sharpie, affirming it was the correct shoulder on which to operate. Then the anesthesiologist came in. He started pumping drugs into my IV, and I immediately became dizzy. They wheeled me back to the operating room, and as the three nurses in blue scrubs met me, they could tell I hadn't lost consciousness yet.

"Could you help us, dear? Move your body onto this table for us." I helped them transfer my body from the gurney onto the operating table.

"Thank you so much for helping me," I said. They smiled. I barely had time to take in all the bright lights and metal contraptions before darkness encapusulated me.

Meanwhile, Dr. Schlegel had just finished his fourth surgery for the day. His final patient was a twenty-year-old female swimmer from the University of Arkansas. He perused her charts one last time:

Name: Tera Elizabeth Bradham
Allergies: None
Medications: None
Previous Operations:
Date: 3/23/11
– SLAP lesion, labral repair
– Career-ending
Date: 7/18/12
    – Bursitis
    – Capsule debridement
    – Inflammation
    – Labral repair appears perfect
    – No invasive repair

More notes from my second surgery followed, and then Dr. Schlegel's own pen dotted the page:

> – Patient appears healthy and of good mind
> – Two previous, unsuccessful surgeries
> – Severe pain in the biceps tendon
> – Pain on some days a 10 of 10
> – Patient will do four weeks of physical therapy
> with a trained specialist
> – Patient will return if no improvement is seen

Dr. Schlegel put on a new pair of gloves, and his nurses placed a mask over his face.

"Let's get started," he said.

First, he tested my shoulder for mobility. Since I was under anesthesia, I couldn't resist him moving my arm, so these tests were more accurate than anything done in previous evaluations.

"Well, there's one of the problems," Dr. Schlegel spoke softly under his surgical mask. When he moved my shoulder back and forth, it gave way far too easily. Dr. Schlegel discovered my capsule had severe multidirectional instability, meaning my shoulder capsule was too loose and moved too freely, causing excruciating amounts of pain.

Because I had swum for seven years with a damaged shoulder, all of my muscles had incurred side effects. No doctor had been able to diagnose those because, paradoxically, since I had kept swimming, the muscles guarding the capsule remained stronger than they otherwise would have. Even when I thought I did strength tests correctly with doctors, my muscles subconsciously guarded the injury, rendering the tests almost useless compared to what my lack of control displayed under anesthesia.

To fix this problem, Dr. Schlegel was going to tighten my shoulder capsule, almost like folding the bottom of a t-shirt up and tucking it in. But before they could start that repair, they had to cut me open. Purple Xs were drawn on my shoulder where they were going to cut with the scalpel. Then Dr. Schlegel opened the two-inch incision along the front of my shoulder and cut two smaller holes to insert arthroscopes, which are long tools used to help operations in joints. The nurses helped him stretch my skin and pin it back, revealing the interior anatomy of my entire shoulder. Normally, as the biceps muscle turns into tendon, it becomes smaller, wraps around the humerus, and attaches to the top of the labrum—the cartilage in the shoulder. My first surgeon had repaired the torn labrum, but no doctor had yet investigated the biceps.

Dr. Schlegel avoided all the intricate muscles of the shoulder, the most complex joint in the human body, and found the biceps tendon. Next, he began a tenodesis procedure, which meant he cut off my biceps tendon. Severing the tendon, he flipped it up to reveal the bicipital groove, where the tendon lies inside the groove of the humerus bone. Underneath, he could see what was not visible to any of my previous surgeons. "Well, well, well. Look what we have here," he muttered.

Gratitude filled Dr. Schlegel's heart. When an elite athlete who has already had two previous unsuccessful surgeries lies on your operating table, a surgeon can't help but wonder what more he can do to help. But Dr. Schlegel had agreed to try to help me, hoping he could find something to fix. Fortunately, he had already discovered severe instability in my arm, but now he found something else: the tissue of my biceps tendon was bright red instead of the normal white. Immediately, Dr. Schlegel knew he could fix a second source of my pain. The bright red tissue signified synovitis, or inflammation, around a damaged tendon. My biceps had begun to degenerate.

Dr. Schlegel cut off my biceps tendon from the top of the shoulder near the labrum to the head of the humerus bone, removing about two inches of tendon. Because my tendon had started degenerating, it could no longer heal on its own, and it needed to be removed. Dr. Schlegel reattached my biceps to the bone, began the intensive process of repairing my shoulder capsule, and placed sutures in my arm.

My parents waited in the lobby, trying to distract themselves from the worry nagging their hearts. The surgery was supposed to take forty-five minutes, and it had already lasted more than two hours. Did they find something? Did something go wrong? The minutes ticked away in agony until a nurse finally appeared in the doorway.

"Dr. Schlegel wanted me to come out and tell you that everything is fine and not to worry. He found a lot more than expected, so it's going to take a little while, but everything is going well."

My parents breathed a sigh of relief, and my mom grabbed my dad's arm. After seven years, could this be the miraculous surgery for which they had prayed?

Finally, Dr. Schlegel walked into the lobby to visit with my parents and shook my dad's hand. "We found two major problems that were causing your daughter a severe amount of pain," he started. Then he explained both the degenerative tendon and the multidirectional instability. Dr. Schlegel wasn't surprised by what he had found as much as he was shocked by the fact that I had swum through it. "Either issue would have given her severe pain," he said, "but the two together would have been unfathomable."

My parents closed their eyes and held back tears of gratitude.

Back in the recovery room, my eyes blinked open. I could barely glimpse a nurse handing another patient a juice box around the curtain. Then I looked at my body. My right arm was still completely numb from the block shot, so I couldn't move it even if I tried. But my stomach looked large, like there was something under my gown. I used my left hand to touch it and then to tap its hard surface.

In my grogginess, I thought my six-pack had either suddenly turned to steel, or the doctors had put me in some bionic contraption. I looked at my right arm, which was suspended on a pole out to the side in a sling I had never seen before. It appeared the pole attached to a brace on my side, which connected to my newfound abs of steel.

I looked up at the clock. It was almost five o'clock. The surgery was supposed to finish at three. I read the clock multiple times, trying to figure out if I was hallucinating due to the anesthesia or if the surgery had really taken three times as long as they told me it would.

Then, I put two and two together: with the body brace and the time lapse, I had one coherent thought: *They found it*, I marveled. *I don't know what it was, but they found it.*

My parents drove me back to the hotel, where the staff was enthusiastically and compassionately supportive. Knowing that we had driven all the way from Texas for a surgery and that having to recover in a hotel wasn't ideal, the staff had assembled a tray with ice cream and every kind of treat the hotel had to offer and sent it with my parents up to our room. They also sent a card that was showered with encouraging notes, like "Tera, you are a trooper—this one will do it!" and "We wish you a speedy recovery!" The card was replete with a signature paw stamp from Smokey, the hotel cat, and they even included a printed Florida Gator logo with an arrow pointing towards a handwritten "Tell Dad, go LSU!" Someone must have had some rivalry chats at the front desk.

I stayed in bed watching Shark Week and sleeping, propped up by multiple pillows. My parents gave me straws for Gatorade and heated up chicken noodle soup, which was just about the only thing I could eat on pain meds. I sat there staring at the bowl, unable to force myself to eat its contents. I knew I had to eat to make the nausea go away, as I was familiar with the potent painkillers' effect on me, but I couldn't bring myself to eat it. I stared at my mom and then back at the bowl. Then, I started crying.

That bowl of soup seemed like Mount Everest. I had competed at the highest levels of swimming as an elite athlete, but in that moment, trying to eat a bowl of soup seemed like the biggest hurdle anyone had ever asked me to jump.

Two days later, we went back to the Steadman Hawkins Clinic to have my stitches removed, see Dr. Schlegel, and start physical therapy. I couldn't do much in physical therapy since I was in a body brace and completely immobile for three weeks, but a physical therapist on staff at the clinic, Mike Allen, showed me exercises to help my blood flow for the time being.

Afterward, we headed to the office, where Dr. Schlegel explained the procedures to me, and then the nurse came in. Up until that point, I hadn't seen my stitches, and I assumed I would have a bunch of small incisions like I had from other surgeries. She carefully removed the bandage and revealed my shoulder underneath.

I saw my mom's eyes turn to saucers before I looked down myself. An uncontrollable grin spread across my entire face.

Yes! I thought. *I finally have something external to show for all of my internal pain!*

Due to the elasticity of our skin, the size of a surgery scar shows that the skin was actually opened twice that size and in each direction. That meant that my two-inch incision had revealed my entire shoulder and biceps tendon during surgery. The scar covered the whole front of my shoulder, and I could not have been any happier.

I love scars. Most girls hear the classic scar conversation come up among a group of guys and head in the opposite direction, noses crinkling in disgust at the gruesome brazenness of the opposite gender. When I hear men start to describe a scar, I get so excited I almost run to get a chair. The stories simply enthrall me. The reason? Because scars tell stories. My scar is my favorite thing about my body. I purposely wear one-shouldered tops and dresses that show my scar, and I love that a red circle still appears around my scar when I vanquish a challenging cardio workout. Some days, I almost wish my scar showed more prominently than it does because, to me, it is the symbol of all of God's faithfulness in my life.

A few months after the removal of my bandages, I noticed something about my scar. I looked in the mirror to see how the incision was healing, and I began to count. I knew the big scar had seven stitches, but what I found next floored me. I counted over and over to make sure I had counted correctly. Not only did the biggest scar have seven stitches, but when I counted all of the little arthroscopic scars (through which surgeons had stuck their utensils), there were also seven scars in total, including the largest one. I understood their significance immediately. God had given me a covenant scar.

Some people say seven is God's perfect number, but it is so much more than that. If you consider biblical commentaries and what scholars have said about the number's appearances in Scripture, the number seven is a sign of perfection and completion. Whenever you see a seven in the Word of God, it is something that God is completing and perfecting, or it is a sign that something is already completed and perfected.

My scar was God's final seal upon his covenant. A covenant is a promise or an agreement between two people, and God's covenant to me had been Jeremiah 33: God would heal me, and the nations would tremble and fear at what he had done in my life. Like the Holy Spirit seals us until the coming of our Savior, God designed this perfect mark of seven stitches—seven scars upon my arm—as a symbol of the sealing of his promise to me. And for the record, he placed it there after seven years of trial.

After the third surgery, my seven-year nightmare ended. The fight had never been over because he never said it was over. And now, it finally was. I didn't have to worry that I would need a fourth surgery because everything was completed. I didn't need to wonder if the doctors had missed something because my healing had been perfected. The seven scars and the seven stitches created a symbol that only God could create. With it, he healed my deepest wound, both physically and spiritually, and he turned it into my biggest weapon. He completed and perfected the work he had begun. It serves as a perfect reminder of his faithfulness, when my fickle flesh so easily forgets, and it will stay with me until the day I die. Whenever I doubt God's goodness or his faithfulness, all I have to do is look down at my right arm.

One of the other things I love about my scar is that it makes me a little bit more like my Savior. After Christ rose from the dead with his body made new, he was perfect in all of his glory, yet he still chose to retain the scars of the nail punctures in his wrists. He could have easily made his body perfect. He just defeated death for crying out loud! Miraculous plastic surgery would have been nothing! Yet he chose to keep his scars. They were a symbol, not to him, but to Peter, the apostles, and everyone else, that he was truly the One who had been nailed to a cross and the One who defeated it. And he will still have those scars as he charges into the final battle against Satan.

The Word says Christ sat down at the right hand of God, scorning the shame of the cross (Hebrews 12:2). It will be just for Christ to wield the scars of the enemy as he wields his final destruction. Final payback. Final retribution. Proof that nothing Satan attempted could destroy the everlasting light of the Savior. What the devil intended to harm Jesus, what he intended to end the promise of God to every person in the future, was the very thing that God used to complete it. Jesus's scars may even be the last things Satan sees before his banishment to the eternal pit of fire.

Just as God turned everything in Christ's life around for good, he wants to do that in our lives today. As much as Satan hates you, God loves you more. And guess what? God wins. He's already won. Time was a convention created by God, and just because we live within its confines doesn't mean that he does! If he lives outside of time, then he has already fought the final battle. He has already defeated Satan. That means we now fight from victory, not for it. Whether you're sitting on your bum watching television or changing the world, Satan will fight you with a tenacity equal to the passion you employ against him. So, if that's the case, rise up and give him a fight worthy of the calling you've received!

I will call Satan out on his schemes, for I am aware of them. I will fight against him with everything I have until the day I die. I don't know if I'll get to fight in the Lord's final battle against Satan and his battalions, but part of me wishes I could. Part of me wishes I could charge into the fray alongside my Savior as he rides with swords flying out of his mouth and tattoos glimmering on his leg as his tunic blows in the wind of his steed's gallop (Revelation 19:11–21).

If I could, I would ride, dressed in a white garment of flowing majesty, completely redeemed in the purity of my Savior's blood that washed me clean. And as I raised my sword high above my head with the very arm that Satan would have had me never lift again, a blood-curdling scream would erupt from my lips. I would relish the moment when I could show my one true enemy how everything he had intended for bad in my life, God turned into good.

Just as Christ kept his scars, I think he will let me keep mine. I believe my scar will shine with radiance on the skin of my new body, and maybe, just maybe, God will let me wear a sleeveless tunic. As I slash down demons and death in victory, the last thing they will see is my scar, glimmering in the light reflected off of the one true source of light in all the universe: Jesus Christ, King of Kings, Lord of Lords, Savior of the world, and warrior to boot.

Grab that scar-torn hand and let him guide you to eternal victory. Let him show you that the cost he paid for your sin is greater than any cost you will ever pay to follow him. Let him show you that with him, you will always fight from victory. In this life, we will bear scars, whether visible or not, but may they always remind us of his faithfulness until the day he takes us home.

17

Never Get over It

Fear not, little flock,
for it is your Father's good pleasure
to give you the kingdom.
−Luke 12:32(ESV)

The trees covered the hills like fall-colored popcorn. Red, yellow, and orange leaves speckled the mountains of the Ozarks, swaying with the wind as their beauty floated down to cover the sidewalks on campus. This was my third time experiencing a true Arkansas fall, and I still couldn't get over its beauty. Back in Austin, Texas, live oaks meandered through fields and creaked ever so slightly as their leaves turned from green to brown, and then they fell. Fall was only a theoretical concept for Texans.

My freshman year of college had been the first time I had ever seen trees change color, and I had been so enamored with the piles of crunchy goodness and the feast for my eyes that spread across the hilltops. Running into my dorm room one day, I had flaunted my prize leaf in the faces of my roommates. The leaf was so big it covered my entire face! Yet the northerners didn't even get out of their chairs, so unimpressed were they with my grand discovery. Now, as I walked up the hill from the training room to my classes, I still smiled at the beauty of God's paintbrush.

I had spent three weeks in a body brace at my grandparents' house, unable to shower or to wash my own hair. Then I transitioned to a sling for six more weeks, and I had just been released to life with an unimpaired arm. We increased my physical therapy exercises for a few weeks, and I was finally able to start lifting my arm above my head about three months after surgery.

Walking up the hill I had trudged up so many times listening to worship songs and begging God to fill me with enough hope to make it through another day, it was as if I was seeing fall for the first time. The fog of chronic pain takes the color out of the world. It focuses your attention inward until the only color you see is the scarlet of wearing pain and the suffocating darkness of depression. After a resurrection, the world blooms again. You start to notice details you haven't seen in years because the lack of pain finally frees you to experience the world with all of your senses again.

I felt like a freshman again, soaking in the colors of the trees, the smells of pumpkin lattes floating down from the Starbucks on campus, and the sounds of the leaves crunching under my sneakers. The world's vibrancy had returned, and I took in all the details my rebirth allowed me to experience.

A leaf fluttered down just above my head. I lunged for it with my right arm, caught it in victory, and twirled it around in my fingers. A childish grin engulfed my face as a giggle escaped my lips. I couldn't help it. I thought some students walking by might think I had gone bonkers, but I didn't really care. This moment was between God and me, and no one could take that away.

Grabbing a leaf was the kind of thing I never would have been able to do before the last surgery. The smallest movement of my arm had caused me agony. Now, even though my arm was so atrophied it could pass as a twig, I could already do things I hadn't been able to do without pain for seven long years.

I stared at that orange leaf like I was holding a winning lottery ticket—because I was. In my mind, life didn't get sweeter than holding proof of God's faithfulness between my fingers. I didn't want to ever lose the feeling of that moment, the feeling of inexpressible gratitude for the life I got to see and live. The feeling of a resurrection.

After the sling finally came off, I began to try new things. Each day, I felt strength returning to my shoulder. Setbacks were common, but every new thing I could do was a new miracle. I found myself wanting to open a door or give someone a high five, though the familiar warning bell sounded in my mind that those actions would hurt. But I did them anyway, and each time I cringed, bracing myself for the pain, I found there was none.

Finally, Dalton told me I could go on a "mini jog," interchanging jogging and walking for one mile. I set out with a giddy trot, nearly bursting with excitement. I smiled as I jogged a small loop around my apartment complex. I casually wondered if the cars passing me on the street wondered why I looked so happy during an activity most coaches used as punishment. The thought made me laugh more, and I had to restrain myself from running at full speed just because I wanted to express the joy I felt. I wanted to run with abandon. Instead, I followed orders, but I jumped more than I jogged my way through that mile.

I crossed the finish line filled with new life and energy. It was the first time I had exercised in more than eight months. The last time I had tried to jog, I had crumpled up in my bed that night, a ball of pain and frustration. Now, I gleefully bounded up the stairs to my second-floor apartment and ran to turn on the radio. Singing praises as I went, I started my normal Sunday routine: cooking, cleaning, and doing laundry. I took my clothes out of the dryer, one by one, folding them and placing them in their appropriate stacks. I hummed along to the song, full of gratitude. And then, as I picked up a blue washcloth, it all hit me. In one stark moment of realization, I fell to my knees as tears streamed down my face.

Not only was I able to exercise for the first time without pain, but I was also doing normal things after exercise: humming, dancing, and singing, and none of it hurt. I could not remember the last time I had exercised without pain. Not walking, not biking, not even activities that only consisted of using legs.

And in that moment, I realized I was going to have a normal life. I realized I was going to be able to exercise without pain. I realized I was going to be able to paint again. I realized I was going to be able to "Call the Hogs" at football games. I realized I was going to be able to worship with my arms in the air, my posture finally matching my heart. I was going to be able to carry a saddle by myself. I was going to be able to pick my kids up one day, and I was going to *throw* my children in the air and catch them, laughing in joy. And I *was* going to swim again, not in mediocrity, but with the resurrection power of my God flowing through my every stroke. My tears turned to sobs. Folding a washcloth became the happiest moment in my life.

From that day forward, I began to jog, and eventually run, every day. With each passing run and with each passing day, I found myself more and more sure of the promise God had given me. He was bringing it to fruition before my very eyes. And after every run, I couldn't help but fall to my knees in gratitude, thanking God for the ability to exercise without pain.

After about three weeks of being able to jog again, I sat blow-drying my hair on my apartment floor.

"Come on, God, this is amazing. I'm a living miracle, and I'm walking in your astounding faithfulness. But seriously, how long is this supposed to last? When I'm back to swimming miles a day and doing weights and a full training load with no pain, what am I supposed to do? Fall on my knees every day in the middle of the locker room and start sobbing from gratitude?" I chuckled.

And his still small voice responded immediately, *Am I not worthy of that?*

I sat, stunned for a moment by my own facetiousness and embarrassed by my words. I swallowed a lump in my throat, and tears filled my eyes once again.

"Yes, you are, God," I whispered. "You are worthy of all of me, of everything I have to give in every situation, in every decision, in every thought, and in every action I have for the rest of my life, because you are my King, my Savior, my friend, my joy, and my love; and I will *never* get over what you have done in my life."

To this day, I still make a point of reaching for objects slightly above my head. I relish the opportunity to use my right arm when a lady asks me to grab a canister for her at the grocery store that she can't reach. I tap the doorframe when I'm walking into my classroom each morning to remind myself of God's faithfulness. I purposely put the dishes that I use most often above my head in the cabinet, so I have to reach higher for them each day. I jump to reach tree branches as I walk through the neighborhood, just to show Satan that I haven't forgotten that what he intended to use for harm, God used for my good. I brush my teeth with my right hand, just so I never forget the miracle. Just so I never get over what God has done in my life.

Don't ever get over it. Regardless of where these pages find you, if you are breathing and you are reading, God isn't finished with you yet. And not only is he not finished with you, but he has already done something in your life that is worthy of more praise than you could give him in a lifetime. If you can't think of anything, start with the cross.

Whether he has given you a miracle, pulled you through

the impossible, or simply given you grace to get through each day, whether he healed you from cancer or whether he gave you fresh energy to get out of bed today, *don't ever get over it*. Find ways to make sure you don't forget God's mercies in your life and make habits to remind yourself of his miracles. Don't ever get over it. He is worthy of all of you, of all you have to give, both now and forevermore.

18

A Closed Door

Conversations of miscommunication were a monthly, if not weekly, occurrence between Blake and me since he had become our head coach. After more than a year of painstakingly attempting to help my coach understand my situation, I felt like we were no further along the spectrum of communication than the first day Blake had walked onto campus. If anything, we had regressed, and he had only convinced others to turn on me in the process.

After the third surgery, Blake never acknowledged what the surgeon found inside my arm because that would have meant that he would have had to admit that he had been wrong. Even though I had apologized to them for my frustration on numerous occasions, neither my coaches nor my athletic trainer ever apologized to me for their harsh words, even after a surgeon had confirmed everything that I had begged them to understand.

Since communication had already been a struggle, my dad thought it would be good to keep the door open to avoid misunderstanding. To be sure we were all on the same page, my dad drove eight hours to Arkansas to help Blake grasp what Dr. Schlegel had discovered from my third surgery.

Blake and my dad sat across from each other at Jason's Deli. My dad explained the discovery from the surgery and what the healing timeline would look like.

Blake said it would take close to a miracle for someone to be able to swim after such a major operation.

"Do you know my daughter?" my dad chuckled.

Blake nodded and restated matter-of-factly that my chances were slim to none.

My dad sat in silence. "You don't know my daughter," he paused. "She'll be back, and when she comes back, I want you to take care of her." My dad wasn't trying to argue; he stated what he knew to be true of me after having known me for twenty years. "Can you do that?"

Blake agreed, realizing how I had become so crazy: my dad was clearly as delusional as I was.

After their conversation, everyone in Arkansas continued with my rehab as planned. Many Division I universities do not use PTs to help their athletes recover from injuries. Normally, there is a PT on staff, but he or she predominately supports football players, or one PT attends to all five hundred student-athletes at the university.

Hiring athletic trainers who studied sports medicine is the less expensive way for universities to support their athletes. At many universities, the athletic trainers are graduate assistants who are still studying while juggling the responsibility of tending to the health of collegiate athletes. In order for an athlete to see any kind of doctor, she has to go through the athletic trainer first. The athletic trainers are the first responders.

Sure, I studied journalism and Spanish rather than sciences, but I was an intelligent person who had only a couple years fewer education than the person to whom I was supposed to entrust my health. I didn't feel comfortable with that, especially after the nightmares I had already endured at the hands of physicians with many more years' experience than my athletic trainer.

So, I continued to pay to see my physical therapist, Dalton Smith, outside of the University of Arkansas because I didn't want to leave my one chance at having a normal life in the hands of those who never believed in me in the first place. Furthermore, my surgeon also wouldn't allow me to undergo physical therapy with someone other than a certified physical therapist; the PT at the Steadman Hawkins clinic in Denver remained in constant communication with Dalton.

Blake made it a requirement that I see my athletic trainer in addition to Dalton in order to be on the team at Arkansas, so I bit my tongue and followed orders . . . until my recovery was at stake. My athletic trainer started stretching my biceps tendon after my surgery, and it flared up badly. I told Dalton about it, who informed me that the stretch she used was only intended to be used for tendonitis in the biceps.

After a surgeon had cut off my biceps tendon and reattached it, my athletic trainer was still treating me and diagnosing me as if I had tendonitis, a common inflammation in the tendon. I didn't blame her; I'd just had a cutting-edge surgery, and I didn't expect a graduate student to know how to rehab an athlete from it. I headed to Blake to see if we could find a better gameplan for recovery. I didn't want to ruin my chance at having a strong shoulder again, much less the opportunity to ever swim again, for not having spoken up over my rehab protocol.

When I expressed my concern to Blake, he lit into me and defended the athletic trainer. I had walked into his office of manipulation again, naively believing that I would walk out with a solution. I had tried to cover for my athletic trainer. After all, she had her own classes to worry about and tended to multiple athletic teams. She had told me that she only had time to meet with me a few times a week, which I totally understood. When I told all of this to Blake, in addition to how she had stretched my biceps, he lambasted me with accusations of arrogance.

Little did Blake know that after Dalton told the PT at Dr. Schlegel's office in Denver that she had stretched my biceps after a tenodesis, Dr. Schlegel's PT had picked up the phone and called my athletic trainer. He gave her a blunt low down of how things were going to progress from now on and told her she was not to lay a hand on me again. She was strictly allowed to give me rehab exercises but never manual therapy.

After cutting out the degenerating tissue from my biceps, Dr. Schlegel had reattached the remaining biceps lower on my arm with anchors. The stretch my athletic trainer had performed could have ripped the anchors from my bone and caused me to have a fourth operation to repair the damage. But according to Blake, a grad student knew more than a top surgeon in the country. Clearly, I was in the wrong because I didn't trust her and couldn't get over my own pride.

I kept chugging along, fighting my way through a broken system run by broken people, all for the chance to chase my dream one more time. Anything was worth it to me to taste that chlorine again, so I swallowed my pride and did what was asked of me. I continued my rehab exercises with my athletic trainer to appease Blake but truly followed orders from Dalton and Dr. Schlegel's PT.

My patience was wearing thin, and I had no idea how frayed the line of tolerance had become until it snapped.

After seven years of torment, three surgeries, and countless injuries, the proof was in: I had a degenerating biceps tendon. Now, I had rehabbed my shoulder to a point where I could get back into the pool. The last time I got out of a pool, I wasn't sure I'd ever get in one again, and I certainly never dreamed I would be jumping into the pool to attempt a third comeback. I had left the pool in agony, but I was returning in triumph. My jubilation was unquenchable. I woke up at four o'clock in the morning, skipped to my car, and annoyed my teammates with jittery joy. I was only allowed to kick six laps (150 yards) with a snorkel and arms at my side, but that didn't matter. I was returning to the chlorinated, frothy waters of my natural habitat after eight months on dry land. I was going home.

I had texted Blake the night before that Dalton and Dr. Schlegel had released me to start kicking, and he told me I could come in for morning practice. Kicking six laps takes about two minutes, so I knew I could get in the allotted allowance a few minutes early and finish before my teammates needed to start practice. I skipped around the locker room and pool deck, stoked to be back alongside my swimming family after coming back from my third and final surgery.

Once Blake arrived at practice, I frolicked over to him—certain he would give me a high five, a hug, or the words of affirmation that I had sought from him for so long. With a cheek-to-cheek grin, I asked him in which lane I could complete my six laps. With a bemused expression, he told me I could kick the 150 in the end lane. Since it would take me about two minutes to complete, I wouldn't get in anyone's way. I smiled in acquiescence, but just before I could trot to my assigned lane, he stopped me. With a small smirk of victory, he told me I couldn't swim with the team after that morning. Instead, he said I'd have to practice during the pool's recreational hours and train by myself until I could keep up with the team.

Jeff had welcomed me with open arms after my first surgery and encouraged me to come early to the university *in order to* train with the team while I recovered. While I didn't understand the disparity in treatment between my two head coaches, all I wanted to do was swim. So what if it wasn't the same as how Jeff had handled it? I could do what Blake asked of me. I knew I would do whatever it took to swim again, so my authority-pleasing nature took over.

"Okay!" I immediately responded. I told him I would do just that and that I would be back with the team soon.

A small smirk crossed his face, so small the unobservant eye might have missed its implication. He seemed genuinely amused that I had agreed so easily to his degradation. To ensure I understood what he meant, he added that I'd have to train by myself until I could complete an entire 5,000 to 6,000-yard practice at normal speed and be able to keep up with the team. What had been a nearly unnoticeable smirk twisted into a self-satisfied smile. He had finally forced me into accepting what he considered the reality of my situation.

I agreed to his request and left to kick my 150 yards in the end lane. As I took out my snorkel and pulled the strap around my head, my mind swirled in shock. I couldn't grasp what had just happened.

I jumped carefully into the water, letting my right arm hang limp at my side as I shot to the surface, pulling with my left arm and dolphin kicking to break the water. Instead of celebrating the moment I had imagined for so long, questions bombarded my mind. I had to complete an entire practice before he would even let me train with the team? Having been through two prior surgeries, I was well acquainted with the progression of returning to swimming after an operation. I blew the water out of my snorkel and kicked, quickly doing the math in my head. At the soonest, I wouldn't be at full speed for another six months. He intended to ostracize me to recreational hours for six months!

I finished my bewildered exercise and paddled to the ladder with my left hand. I got out of the pool, careful to use only my left arm to leverage my body out of the water. Some of my best friends on the team enveloped me in hugs, congratulating me on my return. But as they hugged me, the truth of what he had said sank in. On my way to the locker room, I shared the news with one of my best friends, and she was just as confused as I was. Instead of marching triumphantly into the rest of my day like I had imagined, I picked up my wet bag and trudged through the locker room door.

Training during recreational hours meant that I had to figure out when I could come to the pool on my own in order to practice between my classes. Since student-athletes' schedules are designed around their practice schedule, my classes were already made to allow me to swim with the team. Now that I couldn't swim at those times, I was going to have to find a different time to come to practice.

Furthermore, rec hours were when all University of Arkansas students could swim, and more commonly, they were when the retirees came to swim. Blake was asking me to swim with sixty-year-olds trying to stay in shape when I was a scholarship student-athlete for an SEC program.

Blake had just given me the biggest middle finger a coach could possibly give his swimmer. His real motive behind banishing me from the team was too clear: "I know you can't come back from that surgery, so don't even waste my time." Though he didn't say those words, his actions communicated them.

No sane person would train on her own for six months coming back from such a grueling surgery. In his mind, Blake believed he had won. He had accomplished his goal from the start, which was to put me in my place and show me the real world. In that moment, I think he believed he had forced me to quit.

I grabbed my shampoo and headed to the shower, my mind still reeling with the shock. What was supposed to have been one of the best days of my life swiftly turned into a nightmare. Couldn't he at least have said he was happy for me? Or, "Forget the sport of swimming. Your being here this morning shows that you are going to live a happy life free of pain." Something, anything, would have been better than zero acknowledgment of how hard I had worked and how far I had come.

Hot water poured over my head and washed away all indecision. For two years, I had fought vehemently for the approval of a man who never wanted me on his team in the first place. And after fighting for him and fighting for my team and giving him chance after chance after chance to prove himself, something in my heart snapped. During that shower, it was as if all my desire to earn Blake's approval came crashing down in a violent avalanche. I felt lighter. Then resolve replaced rejection.

I could never swim for him, I thought. *Even if I come back like I hope, even if I make it all the way to the Olympics, I could never swim for that man.* I could never stand to have him get any credit for my success after how he had shunned and humiliated me. He had abandoned me in my toughest trial. It is those who stand by you in your trials who will be able to fully celebrate with you in your victories. I did not care to celebrate with those who believed in me *after* I came back and proved myself but with those who had believed in me *before* I had accomplished the impossible.

I barely heard the little whisper of the Holy Spirit over my emotions: *Go to Texas A&M.*

I'm sorry, God, I didn't quite catch that . . . A&M? I debated if water stuck in my ears could alter how well I heard the voice of God.

The Arkansas women's swim team, at its best under Jeff Poppell, ranked seventeenth in the nation. Texas A&M currently ranked fourth, competed for the SEC Championship every year, and was on its way to contending for a National Championship.

The coach of a team no longer in the Top 20 had just confirmed I was such a lost cause that I was not even worthy of training with his team, and God expected me to try to swim for one of the best teams in the nation? If my current coach didn't believe I'd ever swim again, why on earth would Steve Bultman, a previous *Olympic* coach, believe I could swim again?

Texas A&M, God whispered again. In that shower, I realized one thing for certain—I didn't know if I was ever going to swim for Texas A&M, but I sure knew I was finished swimming for Arkansas.

19

Resurrection

If you saw the size of the blessing coming,
you'd understand the magnitude of the battle you're facing.
—Anonymous

Throughout the fall of 2013, I spent so many hours in physical therapy trying to recover from my third surgery that I created a routine. In November, I sat on my usual table in Dalton's physical therapy office, surrounded by the elderly and the youthful, all dutifully completing their exercises. Even three months after my surgery, all I knew about the operation was that Dr. Schlegel had found severe trauma in my shoulder, which had been the source of my pain.

After seven years of torment, that explanation satisfied me. For months I hadn't questioned it because I didn't feel more explanation was necessary. After listening to medical jargon for the majority of my life, "severe trauma" sounded serious enough to give me hope that its removal would be enough for me to regain health. But that day in the physical therapy office was different. Beaten down, frustrated, and believing myself psychotic, I had only made it halfway through my exercises when tears began to roll down my cheeks.

"Dalton, why am I doing this? Who in their right mind would ever believe she could come back from this surgery and swim again, much less at a national level?" I paused. "I really am insane."

Not wanting to see whatever reaction Dalton had, I waded through my misery without looking up. "I can't swim five laps without elevating a rib. I'm swimming ten laps when a normal practice would be three hundred and twenty laps. I have so much pain just moving my arm in a circle that the thought of swimming butterfly makes me cringe. Plus, my arm still looks like it belongs to a skeleton dummy dangling from someone's door on Halloween."

The negativity ran loose in my mind like a rabid coyote eating away my purpose and willpower. The thoughts that normally sat stationary on the "excuse" shelf of my brain suddenly seemed accurate—even reasonable.

"I have my life back. Maybe I should be happy with that. No one would judge me. They would all say it made sense. God healed me, and now I'm risking my quality of life on an unreachable dream. I'm the only one who believes in me anyway. What's the point? Why am I pushing myself to accomplish something that was impossible before I began?"

The coyote in my mind quieted when it discovered that final nugget to gnaw on, and Dalton and I sat in silence for a few moments. A pensive look and a crease in his forehead replaced his usual comedic demeanor. Resolution settled in his brow as he looked up, having made the decision to share what he had been keeping a secret.

"Tera, there is something we didn't tell you because we didn't think you were at a good enough place mentally after your surgery to handle this information," he began. "When Dr. Schlegel cut off your bicep, it wasn't just trauma he found underneath. Your bicep was *necrotic*."[1] He stressed the final word as if its significance was unmistakable. I sat dumbfounded.

Recognizing the lack of comprehension on my face, Dalton explained, "It means your arm was degenerating, Tera. Your arm was dying."

I began to grasp the gravity of the situation. My determination began to rise.

"Tera," Dalton's voice refocused my train of thought, "let me explain what you're trying to do. You had the biggest surgery you can have on an arm. If there is one thing that would be the hardest to accomplish after that surgery, it would be returning to competitive sports. Of all the sports that would be the hardest to endure with your specific injury, it would be an overhead sport. Of all the overhead sports, swimming is the most strenuous on your repair. Of all the events in your sport, you are trying to come back to compete in the biggest endurance event that swimming has to offer. In that event, you are trying to return to the national and global scene. You want to compete against girls who have whole arms, while you're racing despite missing part of your biceps tendon and with three-fourths of your shoulder capsule rebuilt."

He paused to let the incredulity of the situation from an outsider's perspective sink in. What seemed like an obvious return to competition to me was every bit as impossible as I had suggested moments earlier. In fact, it was even *more* impossible than I realized. *And I loved it.* Resolution fluttered back into my heart. What seemed ludicrous to the world made perfect sense to me.

---

1 After interviewing my surgeon while writing this book, he reported that my biceps tendon was not specifically necrotic, but rather it was a different type of degenerative tissue. Before surgery, my immune system showed many signs of deterioration, but we don't know what the specific causes were nor what would have happened without surgical intervention. I have retained the dialogue of this conversation as I remember it happening at the time.

God would turn the least likely person and the most impossible circumstances into the most unlikely of victories. If I could have accomplished it on my own, then it wouldn't have been a miracle. God wanted the greatest glory, and the best way to receive the most glory would be to use someone facing the most impossible odds. I wanted to be that person. I wanted to be a part of that story.

"Tera," Dalton's eyes locked onto mine. "You are attempting one of the biggest comebacks the world has ever seen."

Everyone wants a miracle, but no one wants to be in a situation that necessitates one. Everyone wants a great comeback, but few recognize the opportunities that setbacks often create in order *to* come back. We want a resurrection without a crucifixion. We love the stories about Jesus healing paralytics and blind men and mutes. We imagine the healed running through the streets, praising God for their miracles, and a sense of awe mingles in our hearts with a slight hint of jealousy. We want that story; we want that kind of miracle; we want that kind of testimony. But we don't want cancer, we don't want to be disabled, and we don't want a life-threatening injury.

Too often, we are unwilling to allow ourselves to be in situations that require God's intervention. We settle for a life in the boat when we were meant to walk on water. We have enough faith to ask God to prevent things but not to reverse them. When we feel God has not protected us from a situation, we infer he is powerless to change it. But this is contrary to the gospel through which Christians claim to live their lives, for Jesus's resurrection was the most powerful reversal of all time.

As Jesus's body sat wrapped in Jewish burial cloths behind the door of a closed tomb, his body started to decompose. According to the rules of this world, the story ended. But then God raised him from the dead. He appeared to hundreds of disciples, frightening many of them, and the situation seemed so absurd, so mind-blowingly ridiculous, that eleven of the twelve disciples gave their lives for their belief in Jesus's resurrection. They were burned to death, crucified, stoned, clubbed, impaled with spears, and beheaded for the sake of one man who had reversed the laws of physics. That reversal was something worth dying for; that reversal forever changed the Christian walk from fighting *for* victory to fighting *from* victory. Rather than the trepid walk of preventative faith, this side of the tomb offers us the victorious walk of resurrection faith! On the other side of degeneration is resurrection.

Like Jesus's body had begun to degenerate in the tomb, my biceps had begun to degenerate in my arm. By the world's standards, both stories were over, but God doesn't have to abide by the laws of the universe that he created. What the world sees as a nail in a coffin is only the takeoff signal for God. What we think is the end of our story is often God getting to the end of *us* so that he can show up in divine intervention. This is the joy of serving a resurrected Savior. Once you accept Christ into your life, the same power that resurrected Christ from the dead, the same power that reversed decomposition and defied all things possible in the physical realm, *lives in you*. And when that power lives inside of you, there is no circumstance, no diagnosis, and no proclamation that can hold power over you.

God did not create us to live a preventative life. He created us to live a resurrected life. It's never over until God says it's over. If he hasn't told you it's over, then it's not. God resurrected Christ. He resurrected my arm. He resurrected my life. And he can resurrect you today.

20

An Indomitable Will

A champion becomes a champion
because he believes in himself
when no one else will.
—Anonymous

Swimming is the most isolating sport that exists. Few actvities are so solitary as following a black line hundreds of times up and down a pool, surrounded by nothing except the rush of water past your ears and with nothing except your own thoughts for company. You might be able to cheer on your teammates as you gasp for air on the wall during a set, but most of the time, it's just you and the water. No one is there to give you a high five, pull you up when you fall, or help force your muscles do what they need to do.

Your one saving grace is that other teammates surround you. You may not be able to talk to them, but their presence is felt in front of you, behind you, and across the lane line. Without words, all of you know that you are there for the same reason. You all get up at four o'clock in the morning with the same purpose, and you are all forced to inflict the same punishment on your bodies. With teammates, swimming is a brutal mind game. Without teammates, it's an island of isolation.

After Blake told me I couldn't train with the team, I trained by myself for six months. I drove twenty miles to see my physical therapist, Dalton, two or three times a week, I made my own game plan, and I found a way to get to the pool between my classes at the university. I was attempting to recover and return to national competition after one of the most invasive surgeries a human shoulder can undergo. The comeback would have been challenging enough if I had had a team supporting me, but I had no one. My only companions were the clock and my will.

Dalton became my substitute coach, but even his pump-up speeches in the therapy room and his helping me decipher how much yardage I could increase couldn't alleviate the brutality of solitary training. Dalton couldn't do the work for me, even though he believed in me. Each day, I had to go to the pool, train by myself, and have the self-discipline to only do the maximum distance allotted in my rehab program for that day. I had never been the sole person in charge of my training and my recovery, and now the responsibility of protecting my health fell on my shoulders—pun intended.

At first, I could only kick with a snorkel and with my arms at my side. Then I started swimming but only a few laps at a time. My arm had atrophied so much that when I first got out of the sling, Dalton could fit his entire hand around my biceps—the thickest part of my arm—and close it with his thumb overlapping the fingernail of his middle finger, my stick of an arm encompassed by his grip. As I built more and more muscle, his middle finger withdrew further and further from his thumb. I have many freckles on my arms, and Dalton would judge my muscle growth by which freckle his fingers reached as he wrapped his hand around my biceps. His little games helped me see minute improvements and preserve my sanity on the days when I couldn't convince myself that my goal was anything short of insanity.

Having been banished from training with the team was in some ways a blessing in disguise, as I wasn't tempted to come back faster than I should in order to keep up with my teammates. For the first month, I came in and swam fewer than 500 yards. I bided my time, knowing I had to allow myself to fully recover in order to swim at the elite level that I wanted to attain in the future. No matter how impatient I was, I couldn't rush the healing process. For the first time, I allowed my body to heal on its own timeline, rather than on mine.

But in other ways, training alone was a nightmare. Recovering from a major surgery to play sports at a competitive level is an entirely different ball game than returning from a major surgery to attain the capability of participating in everyday life. I essentially had a new arm, and I had to teach it how to do everything all over again. I had to learn how to eat, how to write, how to move, and, eventually, how to swim.

For competitive swimmers, propelling themselves through the water sometimes comes more naturally than walking on land. In fact, at the level of collegiate and professional swimming, swimmers walk fewer miles a day than they swim. On a solid day with two swim practices, mid-distance or distance swimmers can train between eight and ten miles, more than even the aggressive power-walker might attain. So, for me, having to teach my arm to swim again was the equivalent of learning to walk again. Even with a task as second nature to me as swimming, my arm seemed unwilling to bend to the forces my mind exerted upon it.

As I recovered, I had seven years of awful habits in all of my strokes. My body had created exaggerated compensations to avoid pain, and those compensations produced inefficient movements through the water. To have a brand-new chance to teach my body how to do things the right way was a miracle! I was ready to write all over the blank slate of my new arm with proper movements and technique that would enable me to be better than ever. Except there was a problem: while my surgery left me with a miraculous lack of pain outside the pool, I still had substantial pain trying to swim. I figured this pain would eventually go away once I strengthened my muscles, since the source of pain had finally been found and fixed in the operation. But in the meantime, I had to fight my own subconscious to swim correctly.

While the human body loses its muscle memory quickly, it also regains its memory rather rapidly. This process is worse when the cause of the movement, in this case my pain, is still alive and active, both subconsciously and consciously. I needed a pair of outside eyes, someone who could look at my strokes and tell me which movements were incorrect, even if I couldn't feel it. I needed someone to watch me and remind me when I stopped catching water with my arm or started to swing it around without bending my elbow. These habits were so ingrained in my mind that without someone analyzing and critiquing my strokes, it was guaranteed I would revert to my old habits, sacrificing the beautiful opportunity I had to start afresh. I needed a coach.

Training by myself during this essential, pivotal time in my recovery meant that I was missing the single most important element of my return to the sport: objective support and guidance. But that wasn't going to stop me. Never daunted by a challenge, I bought an app called "Coach's Eye" and asked a friend to come to the pool with me once a week to film my strokes.

Afterward, I watched the videos and analyzed them, drawing arrows and circles on the footage to show myself where my right arm lacked efficiency. I did the same for my left arm. While I didn't know everything, I had swum under the instruction of top-tier coaches my entire life. I was an athlete and a student of the sport, and I possessed enough knowledge to identify compensations. I analyzed the footage and then replayed it before swimming the next day to fix my errors.

Gradually, I progressed, comparing my progress from month to month, rather than from day to day. After an operation as gargantuan as mine, setbacks and roller-coaster drops were never lacking. Sometimes my body acted like it had a mind of its own, and sometimes I could correlate increased pain to something I had attempted. Other times, a flare-up had no rhyme or reason whatsoever. But if my shoulder was stronger and experienced less pain compared to the month prior, I knew I was on the right track.

I tried to make the training fun for myself, working out with my church friends or athletes of other sports. I invited a friend with me to run "birthday bleachers," where we ran up and down the Arkansas stadium for an hour on my birthday. I took yoga classes, planked on my Bosu ball in my room, and did one-legged squats with my foot elevated on the living room sofa. I ran up the hills on campus and supplemented as much as I could while I continued to wait for my shoulder to heal.

But none of those friends could partner with me in the pool. I alone could monotonously drag my rebuilt arm up to my head to begin yet another stroke on the days when I didn't think I could even get in the pool. No one gave me a high five when I had a good practice, and no one was there to pick me up when I had a bad one. I lived in the dichotomy between self-motivation and self-doubt, letting anger fuel the difficult days. Sometimes, I would get into bed at night and wonder if I had completely lost my mind.

I had to make a decision. But before that, I had to talk to Blake. I scheduled a meeting with Todd and him, and I planned the entire conversation in my head. I would present the option to Blake to fight for me. I would explain that my academic scholarship didn't carry over to grad school and that I couldn't afford out-of-state tuition without a scholarship. I had done meticulous research over the past few weeks. I had also spoken to program advisors at the U of A, who told me they thought it would be too difficult to continue with a master's degree in Spanish while also pursuing an athletic career.

God had whispered Texas A&M to me in that fateful shower so many months ago, but my logic had continued to reign over my faith. I lacked the fervor to take a leap of faith big enough to believe I could swim for one of the top teams in the nation—at least before exhausting my options. Plus, I loved Arkansas. I had no intention of ever leaving. I had a nice life plan of finding a down-to-earth cowboy, living on acreage with horses, and staying in Arkansas forever. The whole idea in my head created a pretty package, and I didn't like that God had started to untie the bow that held it all together.

As hurt as I felt by Blake, I was a big believer in second chances, and I thought maybe I just didn't understand the man. Maybe he really *did* believe in me, and I simply didn't understand how he expressed himself to his athletes. With this hope, I walked into my coach's office, where Blake and Todd sat awaiting my arrival. As I made my way over to a chair, I struggled to suppress my emotions as I realized the full-fledged reality of what I was about to do. Sure, I was mad at my coach. Irate, even. I could not bear that he had given up on me. I had tried to salvage that relationship for nearly two years, truly believing it would all work out and life would continue in Arkansas, just as it always had. Until God told me something different.

I loved this institution with all my heart. My spirits leapt with joy at the sight of Old Main when I rounded the final hill coming home to Arkansas. My body flooded with childlike glee as I stomped on leaves bigger than my head in the fall. I treasured so many memories, like making snow angels with my teammate in our apartment complex in the winter. Nothing enthralled me more than the atmosphere before an Arkansas football game—the anticipation building and the adrenaline pumping as the huge hog snout began to smoke with dry ice. I hadn't even realized that when I had "Called the Hogs" in the fall that it was going to be the last time I ever sat in the student section at a football game. I didn't even get to take one last photo in the cardinal-colored grandstands with a hog tattoo plastered proudly on my cheek. I hadn't known it would be needed. I never dreamed I would leave.

Now, I was going to relinquish all of it with one simple conversation because my God had spoken. I tried to focus my thoughts as my coaches cordially asked me how my independent training was going.

"I'm kicking a 500 per practice now," I told them, feeling pretty good about the fact that I had made so much progress from a body brace. Blake resisted a snicker. Five hundred yards was still about one-fourth of warm-up for any Division I swim team. Their team was swimming 16,000 yards a day, and I couldn't even use my arms to hold a kickboard.

Determined, I continued, "I'm going to come back, but I want to make sure I take it slow and recover properly." I don't know why I wanted to justify myself. A small part of me clung to a shred of hope that Blake might still be in my corner. I barreled ahead, explaining my situation and detailing my research into grad programs before ending my speech with my lack of funds to continue at Arkansas without their help.

Todd sat pensively. Blake rocked back and forth in his chair, bemused by my resilience to continue my folly of attempting to swim at a competitive level again. I read sheer incredulity in his raised eyebrows and crossed arms, but my goal held fast in my mind. Blake's disbelief angered me, but I stifled it and reminded myself that I was here for a purpose. If he didn't want me, then I was going to swim for someone who did.

"So," I got to the point, "I was wondering if you all would release me to swim for a program in Texas. I have three years of eligibility left, and I'm planning on recovering from this surgery. When I do, I want to continue swimming but in a way that keeps my tuition in-state and affordable."

Blake shrugged his shoulders, saying he didn't know why they wouldn't do that for me. Then he asked me where I planned on going.

I was stunned that he gave it so little thought. My last shred of hope that he believed in me vanished, so I responded with equal frankness.

"Texas A&M," I said. "They have the grad program I want to pursue, and they are the least expensive school in Texas," I said. "And they have a great swim team," I added.

Blake's eyebrows shot to the sky. An amused smile pulled at the corners of his mouth. If nothing else, I never ceased to surprise him. He confirmed he'd heard me correctly by sardonically repeating my plans aloud.

I looked him in the eyes, my belly full of anger, my heart full of resolve, and my mind filled with a new faith I didn't realize had grown in me.

"If they will consider me, yes," I stated.

Blake immediately burst out laughing, and Todd spoke up.

"You know you'd have to sit out a year," Todd warned, wanting to be helpful. "Now that they're in the SEC, we're in the same conference." There was a rule banning athletes from transferring within the same NCAA conference without becoming ineligible for a year.

"I know," I said, a plan already forming in the back of my mind.

I appreciated Todd's response. The fact that he reminded me

that I'd have to sit out a year meant that he at least believed I could make the Aggie team.

After Todd's comment, a small silence spoke its piece. Hurt brewed behind what I hoped was my calm exterior. I sat in undisputed silence, realizing that Blake had so little faith in me that he could not even contain his laughter. Couldn't he at least have waited until I left the room? His reaction left no room for doubt. The man didn't believe I could ever swim again. On some level, I knew he believed that all along, but to have it confirmed in the form of laughter lit a fire so deep in my gut that I knew it would last a lifetime. I would never forget his laughter.

"Well, thank you, guys," I said as I fought the urge to tear up from anger and humiliation.

"Of course," they said. Relieved at the outcome of the conversation, yet hurt by the ease of procuring a solution, I wrestled with my emotions as I gave each coach a hug. I thanked Todd with genuine gratitude for the many good things he had done for me.

As I turned around to leave their office, I turned my back on that chapter of my life. I walked into the fresh air and inhaled. I had been right about all of it. I now faced my future, and with each step, my determination and anger intensified. My pace quickened. Motivation tingled in my fingertips. Resilience abounded in my heart, and the desire to prove Blake wrong reigned wildly in my mind. No more tears. No more conflict. Only unparalleled resolve.

How dare he underestimate me, I fumed. *I'll show him.* My vision blurred red from rage. I had given Blake a chance to reveal his true character, and he had. Now, it was time to show him mine. I found my feet marching straight to the compliance office on campus. I walked in and asked for a release form to be sent to Blake immediately.

"He said he would release me," I told the compliance officer. "I want him to sign the form. Today."

Blake wasn't going to get out of this by waiting to see if I *could* come back. If he was convinced that I couldn't recover, then I wanted him to prove it in writing. That way, he wouldn't be able to change his mind like he had so many times before. In a matter of twenty minutes, I had gone from believing I might have misjudged my coach to a full attack of vengeance on account of his disbelief. The new plan took shape in my mind.

Texas A&M, God? Fine. Let's go to Texas A&M, I thought.

After the compliance officer sent the release form to Blake, he backtracked and said he thought we had all agreed to wait and see if I could come back. My confidence may have made his ego waver, but I told the compliance officer to send the release form to Blake again; I wasn't getting sucked into the manipulation. He signed the release form, and with his signature, I was free to talk to other coaches and be recruited to swim for their programs.

I continued to train on my own. Most of the time, I swam right after the Arkansas team did, awkwardly grabbing my wet bag from the locker room and passing my former teammates as I headed in for my own workout. Blake, too, would be there as he often did his personal workout on the pool deck after the girls finished swimming. Nothing fueled my dedication like seeing the cause of my isolation at the other end of the pool as I swam lap after lap by myself.

At first, I could understand where Blake was coming from when he told me to train on my own. Since I could only kick, I knew I would get in the way of my teammates who were swimming much faster than I was. However, Title IX legislation states that women's athletics teams had to receive the same amount of funding as men's teams, and the University of Arkansas didn't have a men's swimming team. That meant the women's team had an entire Olympic-sized pool to themselves. And during the short course season (the course of the NCAA competition), a bulkhead divided the pool into two halves. The girls swam two to a lane, which left empty lanes at practice. I could have easily swum in an end lane without getting in their way.

What would it have hurt Blake to have given me a chance? So what if I fell on my face and became the laughing stock of the sport? What would it hurt him? If that happened, then he could have humbly rested in the knowledge that he had been correct. We could have shaken hands and parted ways, and that would have been the end of it. But instead, he did the one thing that motivated me above all else: he told me I couldn't do something. His conclusion wasn't entirely incorrect; he knew that few people could come back from the surgery I had undergone and compete at any kind of collegiate level again. Ninety-nine percent of people in his situation would have agreed with him. But even if he thought the feat I was attempting was impossible, he didn't have to treat me the way that he did. His disbelief was justified, but his disrespect was not.

As he sought to put me in my place, he only threw logs onto my fire of revenge. More than a few times, I made my planned intervals faster when he was at the pool to prove myself. He probably never paid attention, but I imagined that he did in order to challenge myself further. Every time I saw him, it renewed my belief in my ability to come back.

As I progressed to where I could truly attempt some real practices, my club coach, Terry, started emailing me the practices he did with his team. I edited them to make certain sections more appropriate for my capabilities, but I used them to test myself with genuine intervals and sets. I printed the practices out, splashed water on the pages, and stuck them on the wall in my lane to see the sets during my workout.

One day, Blake and Todd came to the pool and watched me get up on the blocks to swim 50-meter repeats without breathing. Normally, a coach would tell a swimmer when to go, and then he would call out her time at the end of the 50. They both stood against the wall with their arms crossed, talking to each other as they watched the times I was putting up.

"Tera, I really think you should consider Rice University," Todd told me later. "I'd be more than willing to put in a good word for you to the coach." He wanted to help me, and Rice was a top academic school in Texas and had a decent swimming program. It would have been a step down in terms of swimming caliber from Arkansas, but I probably could have gotten a hefty scholarship for that reason.

"Thanks, Todd. I appreciate it, but I still want to talk to Steve and see if Texas A&M is an option. I'm waiting for the season to end so he is less busy, and then I'll see what he says." Steve Bultman was the head coach of Texas A&M's women's swimming team.

Todd shrugged his shoulders. "Just remember, I'm more than willing to talk to the Rice coach for you."

"Got it," I replied.

The only thing I "got" was that Blake watched me come back before his very eyes, training by myself for months, and still did not believe that I could swim for Texas A&M. Todd believed it possible that I might make it onto the Aggie team, but he also thought I wouldn't want to be at the bottom of their totem pole. But I wanted to compete with the best of the best. I may have occasionally doubted myself, but I never doubted what my God could do.

I did not fault my coaches for not believing I could come back. Knowing the severity of my prognosis and experiencing the excruciating measures of what it took to bring a recovery to completion, I am aware of how impossible it seemed. It was absolutely, undeniably, inescapably impossible . . . in *this* reality. Impossible has always been and always will be God's starting point. You can't defeat someone who refuses to give up, and you can't force someone to quit, especially when that person's purpose for continuing is greater than the forces of our physical world. I didn't believe I could come back any more than my coaches did, but I believed God could—and would—bring me back.

No Plan B

Don't downsize your dream to fit your reality;
upgrade your conviction to match your destiny.
—Stuart Scott

"I would have ten knee surgeries again before I'd ever endure another shoulder surgery," my teammate told me one day. She had undergone both a knee and a shoulder operation. Comparing the pain and the difficulty of both surgeries, she said a knee surgery couldn't begin to compare to the excruciating pain of a shoulder surgery.

According to human anatomy, there is logical basis for her assertion. Of all the joints in the body, there are only four ball and socket joints: two hips and two shoulders. This means these are the only joints in the human body capable of moving 360 degrees since the ball of one bone fits nicely into the groove of the other bone. The rest of the joints in the body belong to categories like hinge joints or pivot joints. Hinge joints, like the knees, the elbows, and the fingers, all enable back-and-forth movement in one direction.

To gain range of motion back in the knee, one has to devote

her effort to recovering movement in a single direction. To gain range of motion back in the shoulder, one has to approach recovery from all angles and perspectives. Thus, shoulder surgeries are arguably the most difficult from which to come back. In my case, I had endured not one, not two, but *three* surgeries on the most complicated capsule in the human body.

As a comparison for what I was attempting, let's discuss baseball pitchers. Pitchers commonly tear their labrums, like I originally did when I tore my shoulder on the wall finishing the 50 Free at age twelve. Since pitchers throw balls between ninety and one hundred miles per hour, they put tremendous strain on their shoulders, and these tears are rather common for the position. Major League Baseball even has rules to regulate pitchers in order to keep them from severely injuring their arms. For example, a starting pitcher in the MLB is often pulled from the game after one hundred pitches. That's roughly the maximum number of balls a pitcher should throw if he wants to be able to throw again four days later.

Like baseball, many sports are limited by impact. Division I cross country runners must limit their training to between sixty and seventy miles per week because of the pounding stress each stride places on their ankle, knee, and hip joints. Football players take rest days in season to heal from the impact of tackles. Divers only train from the ten-meter platform a few times a week because the impact of their wrists hitting the water at nearly thirty-five miles per hour can lead to serious injuries if they overtrain.

Swimming, however, is not limited by impact. Pulling a body through water does not require a collision of joints with a reciprocating force, and swimmers are not limited to certain training distances. In fact, the buoyancy of water is so supportive that swimming is often recommended for recovery training and for pregnant women. Since swimmers are not hitting concrete with each stroke or crashing their bodies up against other 250-pound linebackers in a game, the common trend of the sport is to believe swimmers can handle as much mileage as their time and their mindsets will allow. But what many people often do not consider are the injuries created by repetition and lack of recovery.

The average Division I swimming program trains nine two-hour swimming practices, two one-hour conditioning workouts running stadiums or pushing sleds with weights around a field, and three one-hour weight-lifting workouts—all in one week. Their only day off is Sunday. In my practices, we swam between 6,000 and 8,000 yards per practice. Using the higher estimate, this means that on days when we had two swim practices (doubles), I swam 16,000 yards, or around nine miles, plus a weight-lifting session, each day.

My freestyle stroke count per lap was thirteen to fourteen strokes. That means I took 8,960 strokes on doubles days, or about 4,480 strokes with my right arm. On single-practice days, each arm still pulled through the water about 2,240 times. That number of rotations is about twenty-five times more than the maximum allowance on professional baseball pitcher, and while the rotations are completed with less force than a pitch, they are performed in water that's 1000 times more dense than the air through which pitchers throw their arms! Even with that amount of stress, I didn't get four days off like a pitcher would. I showed up the next day and did it all again, and then I did it the next day, and the next, with a shoulder that had been cut open and reconstructed three times.

The mathematical odds of my comeback were next to impossible. Not only did I have three surgeries on the most complicated joint in the human body, and not only did I have one of the most excruciating surgeries possible to have on that joint, and not only was I attempting to come back to the national level of a sport, but

I was also trying to return to the very sport that was the most difficult to endure after my specific injury.

God is honored by prayers so big that only he can accomplish them, because then he gets the glory instead of allowing us to convince our small minds that we had anything to do with our own success. It is only once we can imagine something beyond the periphery of our reality that we begin to step into a fraction of the miraculous life that God has for us.

Math certainly wasn't a problem for God when he multiplied five loaves into enough bread to feed five thousand people. Chemistry wasn't a problem for God when he turned water into wine. Physics wasn't a problem for God when he walked on water, calmed the storm, or parted the sea. Why would a few thousand rotations per day on an arm missing part of the biceps and held together by surgical anchors be a problem for the God of the universe?

Mathematically, realistically, physically, mentally, and emotionally, my comeback was impossible. Only God could accomplish something so outrageous. And he would do so in style.

Now that I was free to restart the recruiting process and talk to other coaches, I had to put myself back on their radar and ask if I could visit their schools. Not many coaches would recruit a swimmer who could barely paddle or who had endured three shoulder surgeries, which left me tempted to take Todd up on his offer and visit schools like Rice. A smaller school with great academics would certainly fit part of my lifestyle. But that wasn't the dream. If God told me he was going to accomplish something in me, then I wanted to believe it wholeheartedly. I didn't want to be a big fish in a small pond, but I wanted to be an ankle-biting piranha in the ocean of Olympic-caliber athletes. I wanted to swim for Texas A&M.

At first, I didn't call Steve Bultman, the coach at Texas A&M. I talked to Terry, and he took over the recruiting process for me—just like he had when I was in high school. Terry talked to Steve at a couple of swim meets, and Steve agreed to let me take an unofficial visit to Texas A&M. Since the visit was unofficial, I was financially in charge of the visit, including lodging and transportation to get to College Station. More importantly, Steve Bultman had offered me his time and his attention, which was all I could have hoped for.

I didn't think a coach like Steve Bultman would let me swim for him when I could only swim 3,000 yards, but I had enough confidence to think I could make a deal with him. I had heard that in the past, he had offered spots on his team to girls if they could compete at a specific time standard. For example, he might tell someone they could walk on to the team if she could swim, a 1:02.86 in a 100-yard Breast.

I applied to the Master's of Education program at A&M but figured it would take me a year to hit the times Steve would require for me to be on his swimming team. I wasn't keen on delaying grad school a year, but anything was worth it to have an opportunity to swim for Texas A&M. I hadn't come back from a rebuilt arm to let the hurdles of circumstance or time stop me. The time would pass regardless of what I was doing; I may as well fight for my dream rather than live the rest of my life wondering what would have happened if I had matched my faith with action.

I took action. Or rather in faith, I didn't take action. I only applied to the grad program at Texas A&M. I had no plan B. I would either make the Texas A&M team or I would be forced to move back to Austin and train with Terry for a year until I could make the team, but I would not settle for less than what God had for me. If I had to, I would move in with my parents in Austin, substitute teach during the day to save money for grad school, and then train with Terry at night.

It was everything or nothing. It would appear I had nothing to offer and everything to gain, but through faith, I had everything to offer and nothing to lose. When I prayed, God whispered, *If you keep taking steps of faith, I will keep meeting you there in power.* All I had to do was surrender to God to get me through each day.

Revelation 3:8 says, "See, I have placed before you an open door that no one can shut. I know that you have little strength, yet you have kept my word and have not denied my name." What God opens no man can shut, and what God shuts no man can open. If God has opened a door in your life, no one can keep you from walking through that door except yourself. Many times, we beat down a closed door because it is easier than facing the uncertainty behind the door God has already opened for us. If God has called you to something, if he has opened the door, then all you have to do is grab his hand and let him walk you through it.

The journey will not be easy, and sometimes the door will seem so small you don't know if you'll fit. Or the entryway is so full of darkness that you can barely see the light shining on the other side. But as long as your hand is in God's, he will guide you through it. He will shrink you to fit through the small door; he will enlarge your heart to battle the darkness victoriously, and he will hold each door open with a bloody cross until you have the faith to live in the power of its shadow.

If God has opened a door, you don't need a plan B. If that door is God's plan A, then he will take you through it. It may not be what you expect, and it may not happen how you expect it to, but the journey will be worth it. God is not a god of confusion. If it seems impossible to even turn the handle of your door, it might just be that you are meant to walk through it behind God instead of without him. Drop the handle and grab his hand. Seek plan A. Have faith to cross out plan B. Who knows? Maybe you'll get to swim for a Top-4 program even though you're missing part of your arm.

22

An Open Door

Fall seven times, stand up eight.
—Chinese proverb

In 2014, there were 165,799 American female high school swimmers. Out of those, 13,769 went on to compete in collegiate swimming. On average, 8.3 percent of female high school swimmers go on to swim in college, and 3.3 percent of them compete at the Division I level.[2] There are 132 Division I women's swimming programs.[3] If each team carries approximately twenty-five swimmers, about thirty-three hundred female swimmers compete in the top tier of the NCAA.

To put it into perspective, Texas A&M consistently ranked in the top four teams in the country. Stellar swimmers compete for a number of teams across the country, not just for the highest-ranked teams, but at the risk of oversimplifying, this meant that

---

2   High school data is from the *2013-14 High School Athletics Participation Survey* conducted by the National Federation of State High School Associations. This data is based on competition at the High School Level during the 2013-14 School Year.
3   Collegeswimming.com

my asking to swim for Texas A&M was the mathematical equivalent of asking to be a part of the top 0.0065 percent of women's collegiate swimming.

A few weeks before attempting to convince the coach of the Aggies to let me swim for their prestigious program, I swam my first race since my third surgery. I had upped my training regimen, and I finally got the go-ahead from my physical therapist to enter one event at a swim meet. I chose the 100-meter Backstroke, and I could not have been more excited to prove the world wrong. I knew that even if my time wasn't great, it would still be a monumental milestone to compete again.

As I jumped into the pool at the Arkansas natatorium, my heart giggled with joy, but it couldn't overpower the intensity of my mind. I was racing again! Backstroke races start in the pool by using your arms to pull up on the handles of the starting blocks. I tuck jumped into the pool and swam back to the wall.

"Swimmers, take your mark," the official's voice commanded from the speaker.

I wrapped my fingers around the bar, planted my feet on the wall, and used a rebuilt arm to pull my entire body weight up for the start. *Never get over it*, I thought.

Beep.

I pushed up and back with my legs to shoot my body backwards in an arch. Kicking like a dolphin underwater, I broke the surface and took my first strokes of freedom. I had little strategy but so much passion.

Racing girls half my age from the end lane, I knew it was just the clock and me. I sped across the pool, flipped, and raced for home. My arms and legs started to go numb around the seventy-meter mark because I was asking my fast-twitch muscles to work in a way I hadn't asked them to in more than a year. *Never get over it*, I thought.

I saw the line hanging above my head signaling there were fifteen meters left in the race. I saw the flags. One, two, three strokes, and a dive for the wall.

No applause. No high fives. No coach to slap me on the back and tell me I had just accomplished the impossible. But I knew there was applause in heaven. I knew the cloud of witnesses were cheering me on in an eternal race and an earthly marathon that had only just begun. The eyes of countless Christians who had fought the fight burned with pride because one young woman was willing to fight for the destiny God had placed on her life.

To the seen world, that race meant a solid one minute, twelve seconds of swimming on my back at a small-time Arkansas club meet. To the unseen world, that race meant more than an Olympic gold medal. *Never get over it.* I climbed out of the pool, went home, and fell on my knees, thanking God for the miracle.

The next day, I ran into Blake on the pool deck. Still giddy from the accomplishment and half-proud of the time I swam, I told him that I had competed in the club meet. He feigned exaggerated surprise that I had swam all the way down the pool *and* all the way back. He meant it as a joke, but jokes of this kind derive their irony from a smidgen of truth.

I squinted, my pleasure disintegrated by the insult. "Yes," I stated. "I even went a 1:12." I turned my nose up, protecting myself from further slight.

Even though I don't think Blake meant the joke to diminish what I had worked so hard to accomplish, I tucked the nugget away for a needed shot in the arm during a future practice when I would need motivation to push through. He probably made an inappropriate comment because he truly had no idea how terrible my journey had been. He hadn't seen the ups and the downs. He hadn't been there for any of it. And that in itself was motivation enough.

Then, in June of 2014, I drove from Fayetteville, Arkansas,

to College Station, Texas, ready to make my case to Steve Bultman to be part of that distinguished 0.0065 percent. Combine the probability of me swimming for a top-four program in the nation with the probability of me returning to legitimate competition after my surgical history, and my trip to College Station appeared to be an ill-fated mission of deliberate humiliation.

As far as coaches go, Steve Bultman was a legend. Before he became the head coach of the Texas A&M Women's Swimming team, the Aggies had never placed higher than fourth at their conference championships or higher than tenth at the national championships. Ever since Steve has held the reins, the Aggies have never finished lower than second at a conference championship, even after Texas A&M moved into the formidable SEC conference in 2012. Furthermore, they have finished in the top ten at the national championships for eleven consecutive years at the time of this writing.

Steve didn't always get the fastest recruits, but he had an incredible improvement rate on the team. Steve loved finding talented, undeveloped swimmers and pigeonholing their talent until they achieved success. Giving people chances fed his inner coach's desire to partner with swimmers and help them become all they could be, and he had a heart for the underdog. But he was also the coach of the number four team in the country, and he didn't simply hand chances out. He didn't have to take on anyone he didn't want to, and oftentimes, he didn't.

I knew all this about Steve before I met him, and I knew what I was going up against. Terry had told Steve about my character and how I would give him a 4.0 GPA every semester. He promised that no one would work harder than me, and I would only add to the team morale. Now, it was my turn to do the convincing. I had to convince him I could handle his training, that I wanted this opportunity more than I wanted to breathe, and that I believed in myself.

I placed my confidence in God above all else. I had to believe in myself, and that had to be apparent. Because I believed in what God could do, I also believed in what I could do through him.

After I arrived on campus, I first met with Tanica Jamison, the assistant coach of the Aggies. Seeing her made life twist back on itself like a pretzel; Tanica and I had swum together under Randy Reese when I was part of his National Group, prior to his move to Florida. I was her little ten-year-old twerp of a teammate who was now a twenty-one-year-old woman asking her to be my coach.

After she showed me a little of the academic center, we met up with the famous Steve Bultman. Although he garnered an underappreciated yet still iconic status in the swimming world, Steve was gentle, unassuming, kind, and humble. He walked the pool deck with an air of authority, which came from his willingness to serve rather than his ability to wield power. He was the kind of coach swimmers wanted to make proud, not for fear of his wrath but gratitude for his generosity.

Steve could often be found reading up on the latest technique changes in the sport, sitting on the edge of his seat to see the Aggie Band at the football game, or challenging his swimmers to suck it up with his silent old-man pull-ups that outdid the pull-ups of some elite athletes. And when the normal calm in his eye transformed to a mischievous glint, you knew you were about to hear an unabashed dad joke so cheesy it could overflow a Wisconsin cheese hat with queso. Steve Bultman was a man whom all others respected, and he was the man for whom I wanted to swim.

After some small talk and driving around campus, the two coaches and I sat down at a mahogany table. I knew what was coming next, and butterflies quivered in my stomach. Steve wasted no time in bringing up my swimming situation.

"Well, Tera, I appreciate you coming down here, and I think you can come back. But in reality, you still aren't very far out from an intensive surgery, and I'm just not sure we could get you back to performing at a national scoring level in the next year, which would be the only logical reason to let you on the team. I only have so many spots, and while I think you will improve, I don't think your recovery will be fast enough for you to contribute significantly to our team in the next year."

In a brief instant, I saw the door that God had opened begin to close. My options flashed before my eyes. I hadn't applied anywhere else. I was all in, no turning back. No plan B, right? I had jumped off the skyscraper, and I was about to splat on the pavement. Tears burned behind my eyes, but I had to defend myself one more time.

"Okay," I said. "But just so you know, I have three years of eligibility left, not one." Steve's eyebrows lifted to the top of his forehead in slow motion. He asked me if I was sure I would have three years of eligibility. I responded affirmatively, laying out my collegiate swimming journey and how I had only competed for one of my three years at Arkansas. Steve pursed his lips and nodded up and down.

"Now that's a horse of a different color," he said decidedly. Hope sucked in a sharp breath of anticipation. Suddenly, a trampoline appeared at the bottom of my fall.

Steve continued to nod. "We'll get our compliance team to make sure you'll really have three years of eligibility. If you do, that's another story. We can do something in three years."

I could have kissed his hand for reconsidering. Instead, I simply thanked him. The next morning, I went to Saturday morning practice and watched some of the best swimmers in the nation post faster times in practice than most people could post at a meet. I watched Sarah Henry train in beast mode. Sarah had already won high point at the US Open, placed in the top seven at Olympic Trials, and nearly won a national title. She would be my captain, and I would train with her in the IM group—if Steve let me onto the team.

Well, might as well set the bar at the top, I thought. If I trained next to the best in the country, I would always know how much I needed to improve to get where I wanted to be. There was no room on this team to convince myself I was better than I actually was.

The girls finished their final set and started to warm down. I turned to Steve, nerves clenching my chest. He had given me hope, but I still didn't have a final answer as to whether I could swim for Texas A&M.

"So, Steve," I started, "I was wondering if you could tell me whether or not I have a legitimate chance to swim for you in the fall. I mean, I need to decide if I'm going to move to College Station or move back to Austin to train with Terry. Since it's already June, people are finding roommates fast, and I just want to know if I should start looking for an apartment or not . . ." I trailed off, hoping he would pick up on what I was asking amidst my rambling.

Steve responded in genuine shock, "Oh, you mean whether or not you can swim is going to determine if you come to College Station or not?"

I nodded.

"I had no idea," he said. "I thought you were already accepted into grad school and wanted to see if you could swim too."

I swallowed hard. "No, I want to swim for you. I am accepted into the grad program here, but I enrolled so I could swim. If I'm not where I need to be yet, I understand, and I will delay my acceptance while I train with Terry until I'm fast enough to be on your team. I'm here to swim, Steve," I repeated.

Surprising people seemed to be my forte. For the third time that weekend, Steve's eyebrows lifted in acknowledgment of my goal and then furrowed as he thought about my question. His seconds lasted an eternity as I awaited the final verdict.

"Well," he paused, "if you're healthy and improving, you can come try out in the fall."

My mind reeled. Instead of reeling in the confusion of someone betraying me or in the ire of someone not believing in me, for once it reeled from the utter shock that someone would give me a chance. Steve saw something in me that he thought he could develop. He saw my heart and my motivation and didn't ask me to hit a certain time. Missing parts of my shoulder and all, he was giving me a chance to try out for his team.

"Really?" I asked. Between the shock and excitement, my voice almost cracked.

"Really," he said, chuckling. He patted my back in that first, awkward swimmer-coach interaction kind of way. I was really going to have a chance to swim for Steve Bultman.

"Oh, thank you, Steve. Thank you," I said. Words couldn't sufficiently express my gratitude.

I could barely believe it. But then, I could. Hadn't I believed God would do exactly that before I had driven to College Station? My actions reflected my faith, even as my thoughts threatened to drown it in doubt. Regardless of my emotion, I had chosen to believe God. And God had chosen to open a door I could have never opened on my own.

It was a hot July morning and my last in Arkansas before I moved to Texas. I was at the pool doing my independent recreational practice and ran into Blake, which happened sometimes. He usually seemed to do his best to avoid the nuisance who was lapping the other rec swimmers, but this particular morning, he did something different. He sat on the bench and talked on his phone, but his eyes followed me up and down the pool for twenty minutes. I immediately changed the technique-driven set I had been practicing to sprints and pace sets from the blocks. He watched as I swam until the lifeguards made me stop so that they could change the pool from long course to short course.

Blake had seen me practicing alone, of my own volition, without requirements by coaches, and without suggestions by friends for the last six months. Was he finally asking himself what it was that made a person train by herself for six months without scholarship, reward, or recognition?

The reality is that I will never know what thoughts flowed through his head as he scowled those twenty minutes, but I like to think that maybe he finally admitted to himself that he had misjudged me. Maybe he finally saw that I had the heart of a champion. That I was someone who believed in her God and herself more than her circumstances or the proclamations with which others tried to define her. I was someone who was moving to College Station without the safety net of other options; I was someone who would redefine the meaning of a comeback.

23

More Than a Sticky Note

Enthusiasm is common.
Endurance is rare.
–Angela Duckworth

Everything was beige. The grass was beige, the trees were beige, and even the starched uniforms of the corps were beige. Everything was severe. The buildings were rigid, with sharp corners and small windows. The land was flat with the only curves in its design emanating from the low, twisted, beige Texas Live Oaks. The campus was uniform, as if a building with an arch would have somehow disrupted the monopoly of lines and rectangles.

Instead of a rolling sidewalk with names carved aesthetically into the pavement, a stadium cut straight into the sky. Instead of a Greek theater with its romantic colonnade, a domed fortress astutely named the Academic Building stood. Instead of a snorting hog being wheeled into Razorback Stadium, a prim and proper First Lady barked to release students from the confines of their university classes. I had traded in the rolling hills of the Natural State for a man-made conjuncture of rules and respect. I had traded in cheerleaders and hog-wild fans for yell leaders and an iconic Aggie ring. I had traded in cardinal Nikes for maroon Adidas. I had traded in my heart's love for my heart's goal. I had left my future in Arkansas to chase my dream at Texas A&M.

A tremendous respect pervaded Texas A&M, but I was determined not to betray my alma mater by giving undue merit to a school with which I had just become acquainted. The deep friendships I had forged at Arkansas were not easily replaced, and as I acclimated to my new home, I left the pool each day to arrive back at my condo with a lonely heart. Even though I was surrounded by sixty thousand Aggies who welcomed me with a warm howdy on every corner and even though I was welcomed onto a team I didn't even know, a huge Arkansas-shaped hole remained in my heart. I would be finished with grad school in two years, so what was the point of trying to make real friendships?

I knew my friends were just a phone call away, but a phone call had never seemed so far. Part of my isolation stemmed not from a lack of kindness from others or the impossibility of making new friends. I had found a new church immediately and was trying out for a new team, throwing myself into getting connected. Rather, my gloom stemmed from the fact that no one in my new home could truly understand my pain or my story, not because they didn't want to but because they simply had not experienced that gut-wrenching season of life with me.

The Aggie swimmers, who I hoped to soon call teammates, didn't know my hopes, my dreams, or my quirks. Some of them had grown up in Texas and knew of Tera the Terror, having raced me when we were younger, but no one had a clue as to what had become of me once I dropped off the radar of the swimming world. All they knew was that I had had a simple shoulder surgery, but the reality was so much more than that. I had now undergone eight years of tormenting trial, multiple surgeries, anguished betrayal, and an incomprehensible miracle. They saw the last stitch in a blanket of miracles, but they couldn't appreciate the warmth of the blanket when they had never endured the storm of the blizzard.

No one had any clue what I had endured, and how could they? I longed to enjoy each stroke of my newfound miracle with people who knew what I had overcome in order to take that stroke. My heart pounded with excitement when the Aggie girls saw me as worthy competition, for I knew how unthinkable it had been for me to be able to push such impregnable competitors just weeks before. But my teammates saw the power battle as just another day at the pool; they expected me to compete with them. They couldn't give me a celebratory high five for God having delivered me from the realm of the dead because they didn't know that he had.

Since I had moved to College Station in July, I had a few weeks of extra training before the whole team arrived on campus. I was able to train with about ten members of the Aggie squad, and immediately, my casual, self-controlled workouts escalated to elite-level racing in the warm-up and diehard competition in the sets. I showed up to each workout with the knowledge that even though I had been given the chance of a lifetime, I was still a tryout who had to prove herself. Restraining my killer instinct was hard enough when I was training by myself, but with so much on the line, the bloodlust became insatiable.

While I strove to demonstrate my value to the team, my new teammates strove to prove the new girl wasn't capable of beating them. One Saturday, Tanica gave us a set where we were supposed to descend our times down to a 200 pace on a 50. I raced a team-mate down to a quick twenty-four seconds on the last 50, a pace neither of us could dream of holding in a real 200-Yard Freestyle race. I knew she wasn't a freestyler, but to me, it didn't matter. If I could show that I could compete with some girls on the team, and if I could train well enough to ankle bite the rest of them, I thought I stood a fair chance of making the cut.

Nevertheless, I wouldn't believe that I had secured a spot on the team until Steve told me I had, and I discovered with shock that my training buddies didn't think of me as a tryout; they regarded me as a teammate. I wasn't truly aware of this until I walked into the locker room, and the captain of the team, Sarah Henry, was scribbling on a sticky note with a metallic Sharpie. She peeled the note from the pad and stuck it on an empty locker. The note read, "Tera."

"I'm sorry we don't have a name plate for you," she said, "but we can use this until it comes in." She strode off acting like her action was the simplest gesture in the world, but I stood in the empty locker room staring at that sticky note long after the door closed behind her. Tears of gratitude welled up in my eyes, and I melted onto my knees on the cold tile.

"Thank you, God. Thank you for this chance. Help me make you proud."

I wasn't officially part of the team yet, but my teammates were treating me as if I were, and that meant just as much. To Sarah Henry, that sticky note was a symbol of respect written at the whim of a captain who sought camaraderie. To me, that sticky note was freedom. It was the embodiment of others' acknowledgment that I could make the team. In that moment, I realized I was no longer the only one who believed in me.

Fall arrived, and the campus buzzed to life in a way that the ghost town summer did not imply possible. And as the student body returned, so did the rest of the swim team, and with them came a new challenge: making myself worthy to not just some of the team but to all of its thirty members.

During my first few months in College Station, I sorted through feelings of excitement, gratitude, frustration, loneliness, and determination as grad school commenced and as I dedicated myself to an intense physical therapy program. Unlike Arkansas, Texas A&M hired a fully certified athletic trainer who focused solely on the swimming and diving programs without having to juggle her own university classes. This allowed me to spend a much-needed three to four hours in the athletic training room each day, where I would undergo treatments on my shoulder and complete physical therapy exercises. Although I was still technically trying out for the team, I had talked to the coaches, and I was able to work with the team's staff until we decided if I had made the team or not.

I started and ended my days doing rehab. When my classes hindered my ability to receive treatment after night practice, I threw my leg over my bike and pedaled as fast as I could to Harrington Tower. I showed up to class with my to-go box of dining hall food and loudly tore the plastic wrap from my shoulder to free the ice pinned underneath. I only went to night classes three times a week, and most of my days were free between practices. This allowed me to sink my metaphorical teeth into the new challenge of expedited rehab and sink my literal teeth into towels, as some treatments on a rebuilt arm proved insufferable.

Physically, I recovered more with each passing day. Academically, I discovered how to balance the responsibilities of pursuing a master's degree while remaining a student-athlete. And spiritually, I dove into a new church and faced my fear of being misunderstood by forming lasting friendships. Although I had to adjust, one beige brick at a time, College Station began to build a home in my heart.

Transitioning to Steve's workouts was an adjustment all of its own. Although I was the grandma of the team since I was the age of a traditional senior, I still fell into the freshman group of newbies because I had no idea what was going on. I had to memorize Steve's warm-ups, learn his sense of humor, and adjust to how his training system worked.

Once everyone was back, Steve eased us into practice with two weeks of technique training. Then it was full throttle ahead for the season. Before College Station, I was swimming about 3,000 yards on my own each day. This was a modest amount of yardage—a great amount after coming back from a rebuilt arm—but still barely more than a warm-up for college swimmers. It had taken me more than a year to progress from the operating table to 3,000 yards a practice, and then, in a matter of a month of training with Steve, I leapt from 3,000 yards a day to 7,000. I shifted from a steady cruise control to slam-the-pedal speed racing in order to keep up with the team.

The leap in yardage was astounding. Through the disguised blessing of training on my own, it appeared I had finally done what I needed to do. My body had healed on its own clock, and now I was able to push it back to the top tier of competition. But getting to a respectable quantity of yardage wasn't the only goal; I had to raise my quality of swimming to match a higher level than any I had trained with in my life.

The depth was obscene. Not the depth of the Texas A&M pool, but the depth of the roster of swimmers who practiced in it each day. The breaststroke group I walked into consisted of Bethany Galat, who placed at NCAAs as a freshman and who would go on to finish third at Olympic Trials in the 400 IM; Jorie Caneta, a recent transfer and a Junior Pan Pacific member in the 100 Breast; Sycerika McMahon, an Irish breaststroke Olympian; Franko Jonker, a sub-minute 100-Breaststroker who represented South Africa at the Pan Pacific Games; Esther Gonzalez, the Mexican record-holder in the 200-meter Breast at the time; Ashley McGregor, a Canadian who went on to swim the 200-meter Breast semifinal at World Championships, and Breeja Larson, an Olympic gold medalist for her 100 Breast split in the 400-meter Medley Relay, with the occasional additions of Sarah Henry, a national champion in the 400 IM, and Sydney Pickrem, who would go on to become an Olympian and multi-SEC Champion. And then there was me, the transfer who recently had her shoulder reconstructed and tried not to get lapped by the rest of them.

The contrast between my teammates and myself was stunning, not only externally but also internally. My teammates didn't notice the mundane black lines covered in familiar aqueous chlorine as they practiced each day. But every day I came to practice, my vision renewed to see the miracle: vivid aqua water overlapping the lines that led to my dream.

Outmatched in stamina, body structure, and talent, I took a deep breath and started making targets. I placed a small target on the feet of one of my teammates until I kept up with her consistently. Then, I moved the target to her torso, then her fingertips, and then, the target moved to a faster fish to chase. One by one, I inched my way onto the team.

I not only kept up, but I also started to challenge some of my teammates. One day, on an IM practice, I took off after a teammate who I knew was a world-class breaststroker. She took a lead on the fly, I caught back up on the back, she extended her lead again on the breast, and then I gunned her down on the free. We kept that pattern up all night. Near the end of practice, I jumped out of the pool ten minutes early to get to my night class. Steve stopped my traipse to the locker room and raised his eyebrows.

"That was a nice set, Tera." He nodded his approval.

As my bike rattled over the cement campus, those five words rattled around my head all the way to class.

Though the sticky note denoted that I had been given a chance, it was also an adhesive easily removed from its place. It was placed on my locker, but I was not officially on the team yet. But if Steve had noticed my work ethic, it meant I had a chance. It meant I was slowly proving myself. It meant I was fighting again.

It meant that although I knew I could come back, more and more people were starting to believe it too.

Steve had an uncanny way of shrugging his lips and his shoulders at the same time, as if to acquiesce to your assertion while at the same time processing what was being asked. It was this lip-shoulder shrug I received when I asked him if I had made it past a tryout. To Steve, my need to know if I had made the team seemed pressured; he didn't know why I needed a definite answer when I was already training with his team and still recovering from surgery.

On paper, I was a tryout, but in Steve's mind, I was an experiment. As long as I had a good attitude and could prove the mettle in my heart outweighed the anchors in my shoulder, he would keep me. My haste ended up having its desired effect, and Steve made his decision official. My name and picture appeared on the Texas A&M roster. I received t-shirts, gear, an embroidered, maroon towel, training suits, caps, the athlete dining hall plan, and, of course, a nameplate for my locker.

As I stood with my new nameplate in hand, I reached up with the other and took the sticky note off my locker. Splotches of chlorine drops discolored my metallic Sharpie name, and salty drops threatened to ruin it again as they welled up behind my eyes. In one hand, I held the sticky note that symbolized when the captain of the team had given me a chance; in the other, I held the nameplate that sealed my team membership. I stuck the sticky note in my backpack and set the nameplate at the top of my locker. I was officially a part of the Texas A&M swimming team.

24

Remember Whom You're Fighting

The essence of forgiveness
is absorbing pain instead of giving it.
—Timothy Keller

slowly read over the words that haunted the past nine months of
my life:

> Stop living in the past.
> You can't handle your fall from fame.
> I think you should see a sports psychologist.
> This. Is. In. Your. Head!
> You need to train on your own until you can
> keep up with the team.

I had a picture of Blake Johnson, with every word or action
he had spoken or committed against me, taped to my bathroom
mirror. For three months, every morning when I woke up, I saw
those words before practice. Every day as I brushed my teeth, ire

boiled in my stomach. Every night as I went to bed, I left the words at the top of my mind, ready for immediate recollection when my alarm sounded the next morning at 4:00 a.m.

I let each word roll around my mind, savoring each insult as I transformed it into motivation. I heard his voice in the exact tone he had used. I felt the same rage that had been born when he originally mocked me. Then my eyes drifted down to the numbers I had meticulously calculated:

29 weeks
203 days
244 hours of rehab
148 swim practices
58 hours of dry land

The numbers quantified all of the independent training I'd done from the time Blake banished me from swimming with the Arkansas team to my move to Texas. I wanted nothing more than to prove Blake wrong and show him that he had misjudged me. Yet as I read those words over again, I felt triumphant because I had already proven him wrong. Steve gave me a chance. I swam for one of the best teams in the nation. I trained with thirty of the fastest women in the country.

The director of compliance for Texas A&M Swimming and Diving brought me into his office one day to share devastating news. "I thought it was a shoo-in," he started, dejection flooding his face. "It seemed like a no-brainer that of course the SEC would allow an exemption for an athlete who graduated from her previous university and transferred for monetary reasons."

Within the NCAA, there is a rule that athletes are not allowed to transfer to another institution within the same conference without sitting out for a year. It is mainly to prevent athletes from the big three (football, baseball, and basketball) from making deals with coaches, transferring to a school in the same conference, and getting to compete the next year against their previous institution. While this rule applies to all sports, it was not an issue commonly experienced in swimming when compared to the "moneymaker" sports.

Still, none of this mattered in my situation because the rule applied to *all* NCAA athletes. "Your Arkansas coach refused to write the recommendation," the officer continued, "so the request was declined. I'm so sorry. I gave you hope because I thought there was no way it wouldn't be approved."

Blake had found another way to keep me from competing and pursuing my dream.

"Is there anything we can do?" I knew the answer before I inquired.

He looked at his lap. "No, Tera. You're ineligible for another year."

The Texas A&M compliance office was known for their conservatism, and if they said something would happen, it almost always did. Almost. Why was my situation different?

I replayed his words in my head: *Your Arkansas coach refused to write the recommendation. He released you, but he wouldn't write the recommendation.* I would sit out from competing in collegiate athletics for a third year. I would watch the bus pull away with all my teammates for two more semesters. I would compete in club meets alone for another year. Because of one man.

I stared at my reflection in my bathroom. Eyes, once full of so much passion and determination, stared back at me blankly in defeat. They began to lower in shame when an abnormality in my reflection caught their gaze on the way down: a jagged outline of a promise etched in my skin. My left hand instinctively reached to touch my shoulder. I watched my fingers trace the outline of my scar, and its message carved itself into my heart. Tears started to blur my vision as I looked away from my arm's reflection in the mirror and down at my actual arm. *Haven't I had enough trials already, God?* I thought. *Wasn't this enough?*

My thumb rubbed the scar back and forth. Pity ceased. Determination resurfaced. Conviction turned my eyes back to the mirror. Blake could keep me from competing, but he could not keep me from coming back. He did not deserve to occupy space in my mind. I wasn't doing this for him; I was doing it for God, and I was doing it for myself. Yet somehow, I couldn't let it go.

That week, Texas A&M had raced Arkansas in the first dual meet of the season. During warm-up, one of my teammates overheard Steve's conversation with Blake. According to her, Steve had asked Blake why he seemed to be preventing me from swimming, knowing that my shoulder could go out on me at any minute. Apparently, Blake's retort was that I had graduated from the University of Arkansas but never contributed to the team, and he wasn't going to make it easy for me.

My new Aggie teammates walked out of the locker room for the meet, and about one third of them sported a new decal written "#forTera" in Sharpie on their arms. They had asked me beforehand if I was okay with them doing so, and in my bitterness, I agreed. Tanica, our assistant coach, told them to wash it off. She loved their support for me but thought it lacked sportsmanship. In hindsight, Tanica was right. Most of them obeyed orders but not before Blake saw the logo during warm-up.

The meet began, and A&M destroyed Arkansas. The Aggies shut the Razorbacks out, winning every event. The Aggies were so far ahead that Steve had some of the best swimmers swim exhibition, meaning their points didn't count toward the overall score, and the Aggies still won. Needless to say, it was not a good day for Blake Johnson. While part of me felt guilty for not taking the high road and for allowing my teammates to write my name on their arms, I still couldn't believe that teammates who had only known me for three months would fight for me like that. They cared enough to defend me on a national stage. They had my back. The victors returned to College Station, but I remained ineligible to compete.

As I looked at Blake's face on my mirror, I relished the humiliation he must have felt at the dual meet. Sweet revenge. Other than getting to swim in front of him, having other people support me was the best revenge I could imagine. Victory was sweet and simultaneously bitter. It didn't satisfy.

The Holy Spirit whispered to me, *Tera, remember whom you're fighting.* It was a simple whisper, but it shot an arrow into the core of my vengeance. *Remember whom you're fighting.* There is a very real enemy in this world, and his name is Lucifer. He is already defeated, but God has given him a short time to reign on this side of heaven. *He* was worthy of my anger and my hatred and my vengeance, for *his* purpose is to steal, kill, and destroy. If he cannot steal your joy, he will try to kill it. If he cannot kill it, he will seek to destroy it. He never ceases his pursuit. He knows you so well that he designs custom weapons for your downfall.

Satan was whom I fought, not Blake Johnson. Ephesians 6:12 says, "For our struggle is not against flesh and blood, but against the rulers, against the authorities, against the powers of this dark world and against the spiritual forces in the heavenly realms." A very real enemy exists, and he was trying to aim my anger in the wrong direction. Blake may have wronged me, but the only person I hurt holding onto bitterness was myself. Satan knows how bitterness works. It eats you alive. It starts as a tiny parasite, worming its way through your heart at a microscopic level that you can barely detect. But after a few months, you develop holes in your heart and eventually, the bitterness will saw your heart in two.

Satan also understands forgiveness, and he never wants you

to understand the freedom it brings. Forgiveness is a double death; not only do you have to die to the pain of the original injury, but you also die to your ability to inflict injury in retribution. You die to your right of ever leveling the scale. You surrender justice to God and choose to have faith, for God will make all things right in the end.

Forgiveness isn't an emotion; it is a choice. Long before you feel like you've forgiven someone, you have to *choose* to forgive them. Forgiveness isn't a flesh wound; it strikes the core of your soul, and it can feel so painful that it makes you wonder why on earth God would create such an action. How can you pardon the unpardonable? How are you supposed to let someone walk away without getting what he deserves?

Those are the wrong questions. It is not how you forgive; it is *why* you forgive. If your *why* is strong enough, your *how* will find a way. And the *why* is because Jesus Christ forgave you. When his blood covered the wood of a cross on Cavalry, he died as much for your perpetrator as he died for you. Your sins nailed him to that cross. Exodus 14:14 says, "The LORD will fight for you; you need only to be still." When you become a Christian, you surrender your right to vengeance. You accept that sin has made the world unjust, but you will leave righting the scales to the one who created them.

I pulled Blake's picture from my mirror. Before I let it drop into the trashcan, I looked at the face of the man who changed my life. And instead of anger, I felt compassion. I saw a broken and hurting man. I was no better than he was. I had retaliated and felt good about it, but I was someone who strove to live for God. With a different set of circumstances, I might not know God. I may be like Blake Johnson. The blood of my Savior poured out just as much for Blake as it did for me. If Blake was the only person on earth, Christ would have died for him too. Who was I to judge? *Remember whom you're fighting.* I threw the picture in the trashcan. The cross was enough, the enemy was real, and the freedom was mine.

25

Tougher than Tebow

Never be mad at someone for doing
what you said could never be done.
—Anonymous

Anyone who says swimming is not a contact sport has clearly never been hit by an oncoming butterflyer. At a mid-season club meet in high school, I was warming up for my race when one of the guys on my team started swimming butterfly in my direction. He came gliding through the water with his enormous wingspan. Absorbed in my own little world, as swimmers often are, I was completely unaware of him moving rapidly toward me until his hand collided, quite ungracefully, with my face. Pain shot through my nose as an expanding red cloud spread through the water.

Certain he had broken my nose, I recovered from my momentary discombobulation and resurfaced with blood pouring down my chin. I swam back to the wall and got out of the pool, cupping both hands under my face to create a makeshift reservoir to catch the blood and keep it from flowing onto the pool deck.

I walked over to my coach, who had his back towards me as he talked to one of my teammates.

"Uh, Terry?" I tentatively questioned. He turned around and took in the sight of my blood-smeared face as my cupped hands quickly filled to their capacity. Eyes bulging, he grabbed my arm and dragged me to the first aid room. My race was in three heats, so I didn't have time to truly stop the bleeding; we just tried to keep the torrential floodgate at bay.

Terry asked me if I was still going to swim my event. I nodded and gave him a befuddled look that asked, "Why wouldn't I?" As soon as we staunched the river enough for me to walk without blood running down my face, I headed to the starting blocks. I swam the 200 Butterfly with blood leaking the whole way, and the swim was fast enough to make it to the final.

I got out of the pool, warmed down with some Backstroke to keep the nosebleed draining in the right direction, and then casually returned to talk to Terry about my race as if nothing had happened.

"So how was it?" I asked.

Arms crossed, without even turning to look at me, he said, "Well, that was very Tebowesque of you."

The analogy was not a new one. My dad graduated from the University of Florida, and I grew up a diehard Gator fan. In second grade, I donned a Florida Gators cheerleader costume for Halloween. By middle school, I yelled at the TV alongside my dad for every bad call, fumble, or interception, and by the time I met my high school club coach, Terry Olson, who graduated from the University of Georgia, I could hold my own talking smack. Every year I swam under Terry, we made a bet on the Florida-Georgia football game, and the loser had to wear the other team's T-shirt for an entire day. In all three years that I swam for Terry, Florida beat Georgia. I think the orange and blue suited him well.

When I had my first surgery in the spring of my senior year of high school, I concocted a devious plan. As soon as the doctor cleared me to drive, I headed to the pool with my father's "Florida Alumni" license plate frame in tow. With my right arm in a sling and only my non-dominant arm available, I set to work unscrewing Terry's "Georgia Alumni" license plate. I replaced his car's attire more appropriately and drove off, grinning in victory. I'll never forget the voicemail I received from Terry about his car being "corroded." Then, the week before I left for college, Terry left the pool deck for about ten minutes during practice. I didn't think anything of it until I left for school and noticed a strange glint to my license plate frame: Terry had replaced my red Arkansas Razorbacks license frame with his Georgia one.

Even through all the good-natured rivalries, Terry always admitted that he held Tim Tebow in high regard. Tebow's drive, passion, and intensity were second to none, and sports fanatics like us felt pure joy when watching him play. But more than his boldness displayed on the field, Tim Tebow was the epitome of a man on fire for the Lord, boldly proclaiming his faith every opportunity he received. Terry saw the same competitive drive, dedication to faith, and obscene resolve in me, and he would say that Tebow and I must have been long lost twins who were separated at birth.

It wasn't long before the nickname "Tebow" attached itself to me, although Terry made sure to only bestow the compliment on special occasions so as not to diminish its significance. After a particularly good set or practice, where I had raced to the death or pushed beyond myself, Terry would give me a high five on the way out and say, "Nice job, Tebow." Occasionally, we would be in the middle of a high-intensity set, Terry shouting our pace times as we gasped for air on the wall. Between breaths he would yell out, "Last one! Finish strong, Tebow!" Every time Terry caught me consoling a teammate or encouraging a younger swimmer on the team, he would smile as he walked by and comment, "How ya doin', Tebow?" And my favorite, when I pushed myself beyond the limits we thought possible during practice, Terry would shake his head and exclaim, "Tough as Tebow!"

Although the nickname was infrequently used, my coach utilized it in specific scenarios to catch me by surprise, motivate me, or make me laugh. Tebow was a role model for every Christian athlete, and deep down, Terry knew that the comparison to the Heisman winner was the highest compliment I could receive.

When I told him over the phone that I was ineligible for another year, his papa-bear instincts came out in full force: "So, are you ready to fight this thing?"

"I'm not going to fight it, Terry," I replied.

"What?! Are you kidding?!" I smiled at the shock in his voice as he gawked at the idea of Tera Bradham giving up on something.

"No," I remained calm. "The NCAA procedure is so messy that I probably wouldn't get the SEC exemption even if we had Blake's recommendation. He won this battle, and I don't think there's anything we can do."

Terry thought of every possibility, churning out ideas as quickly as he could think of them. He told me it wouldn't hurt to at least try to get the recommendation and resubmit the SEC exemption for another consideration.

"No," I said. "Why would I give Blake that satisfaction? I can sit out another year. I've done it twice already. What's one more year? I'm still working out with the best team and the best coaches in the country. I've already proven him wrong just by walking onto the team. Plus, it's a great opportunity to serve my teammates from a humble position and let my body continue to heal for a year. He can keep me from competing, but he can't keep me from coming back. Blake doesn't know who I am, and he has never understood that the harder he makes it for me, the more I like it. He's not going to make me quit, Terry. I will sit out another year, I will work harder than anyone has ever worked, and when I see him a year from now, he will know he could not break me. Everything he's doing is just going to make the comeback that much sweeter."

There was silence at the other end of the line. "Wow," Terry said. "Well, I'm still going to call him to see what he says about it all."

I laughed, grateful he wanted to defend me.

"One more thing," he said before he hung up.

"What?"

"T, you're officially tougher than Tebow," then Terry hung up.

Terry called Blake the next day, and within about thirty seconds, the conversation turned uncomfortable. Blake asked Terry if I knew how much the Razorbacks had done for me.

"I'm sorry," Terry said. "Did I hear this wrong, or did Tera *not* swim by herself for six months because she wasn't allowed to train with the team?"

Blake said that had been my choice. I certainly didn't remember it that way.

"Well, will you write the recommendation?" Terry asked.

Blake refused, saying I could knock one of his swimmers out of an SEC final.

"If you believed that, then why did you sign a release form and let her go?"

Silence.

"Here's the thing," Terry started, "whether or not Tera Bradham is on the Texas A&M swim team has no effect whatsoever on whether A&M would beat you in a dual meet or at a competition like SECs. Texas A&M would destroy Arkansas either way. This means that your decision is a personal vendetta against Tera Bradham to keep her from competing. I don't know how anyone could hate Tera Bradham, so that leaves me to conclude that what she's told me over the past two years is a mild version of how you've actually treated her. I'm sorry, Blake, but I don't know how I could recommend any of my swimmers to swim on your team after the way you've treated Tera."

After their talk, Terry called me and said it had been the most uncomfortable conversation he had ever had with anyone in his life. He finally understood what I had dealt with for two years, and he told me that I was right; I should move on. That battle was futile, and it was over. My jaw clenched as I listened to more of Blake's condescending words. I wanted to put his picture right back up on my mirror and add every new quote to my list of motivation.

But I heard that small voice whisper, *Remember whom you're fighting, Tera.*

The desire for vengeance was a battle I would continue to fight for the rest of my career; forgiveness was never a one-and-done deal. Besides, I was not fighting Blake Johnson. I was fighting for freedom. Freedom from the constraints of this world and freedom from every boundary that people like Blake had tried to place on me throughout my entire life. I was fighting for a story that brought God glory and inspired others to fight for their own freedom. I wasn't swimming for revenge or to prove someone wrong. I was swimming for freedom.

26

A Boxed Promise

Cherish the bad days.
It confuses the devil.
—Dalton Smith

Doubt creased his forehead, and cynicism twisted his lips. Defensiveness straightened my shoulders, and confidence steadied my stare. A new place and a new campus meant a new doctor. He looked up from his clipboard and extended his hand to introduce himself.

"I spent quite a while looking over your medical history," he started with raised eyebrows and a slow exhale, almost whistling at the extent of damaged goods sitting on the table in front of him. I tried not to tune him out. I needed to endure this meeting so that he would clear me to swim for the Aggies.

"I know you're quite aware of what it says in here," he waved the clipboard flippantly, "and we need to talk about what will happen if you can't swim anymore."

I grimaced and bit my tongue. He hadn't even examined my shoulder yet.

"According to the notes Dr. Schlegel wrote about what he did in Denver, this surgery was extensive," he explained. I nodded like a compliant athlete would. "And the chances of you being able to return to the same level of competition you had before are slim. You probably won't be able to compete in the same events, and when you decide you're in too much pain, we're going to need to reevaluate if you should continue swimming."

"When?" I asked. I couldn't bite my tongue any longer. Since I was twelve years old, my life had consisted of sitting on doctors' tables and hearing the presiding authorities project their personal skepticism onto my life. My propriety towards doctors had been removed alongside the stitches from my third surgery.

"I came back from the first surgery, I came back from the second surgery, and I scored at SECs with a rotting arm," I stressed. "You cannot convince me that I will not come back from this surgery. I know what I'm capable of."

"Well, you may be able to come back," he countered, "but you won't be able to swim the 400 IM."

My eyes locked onto his with swelling confidence. "Watch me," I quipped.

Shocked by my bluntness, he didn't fight the girl inundated with idealistic ignorance. Instead, he came to the side of the table and started testing the strength of my shoulder.

"Wow, this is strong," he said. He shuffled around the table, testing my shoulder in all directions. He didn't find an outstanding weakness in any area and finally leaned back against the table next to mine.

"Your shoulder certainly is stronger than I thought it could be," he rubbed his chin in disbelief. "Well, we'll see how it goes," he said as he signed the clipboard.

His skepticism had been challenged but not nullified. I walked out with determination in my step and a goal accomplished in my head; the doctor had medically permitted me to swim for Texas A&M, so swim I would.

Walking in the wake of a miracle, there was nothing I believed God could not do. His hand of provision had not only granted me the fulfillment of his promise, but it had also given me the opportunity to walk onto one of the best teams in the country. I was finally going to be able to train up to my potential and compete the way I did before tearing my shoulder.

After seven years of misdiagnoses and confusion, I had been right. After clinging to a promise for the last four of those seven years, I felt confident I knew God's voice. I had clung to God's Word against all odds, and he had proven himself faithful. I felt with confidence, like I had after my first surgery, that I could finally be who God made me to be. I could reclaim my destiny from the foes who had sought to rip it from me, and it would all be for God's glory. The next Olympics were in two years. Sure, that goal was impossible, but I had already lived the impossible countless times. What could bring God more glory than a full resurrection and an Olympic feat?

I had always been a dreamer, but this time around I sought God's heart, and I wanted to be fully healed because I believed that returning to *my* former glory would bring *him* the most glory. After all, they had truly found the cause of all the madness in my third surgery, so what could keep me from coming back now that it had finally been fixed? But God's definition of glory is often far different than our own, and I had no idea just how different God's trajectory would be from mine.

About one month had passed after I obtained approval to swim for Texas A&M, and to my dismay, my shoulder was not fully healed like I thought it would be. Outside of the pool, I was in very little pain, less pain than I had been in for as long as I could remember, and I praised God for it. But inside the pool, my pain seemed worse than it had been before surgery. The original plan had been to slowly increase yardage until I could return to two practices a day. But as I increased yardage, I discovered that my arm couldn't withstand what I assumed in faith that it would. And God was not intervening. I couldn't reconcile the miracle in my everyday life with the pain I still endured in swimming.

Then, after one week of trying two practices a day, my body rebelled. In the middle of the pool, a bloodcurdling torrent of pain ran through my shoulder. The jolt shocked me as if lightning had hit the pool, and I immediately curled into the fetal position. I nearly choked as I screamed underwater. Hoping this was an isolated incident, I kept trying to swim a second practice in one day, but without fail, unfathomable pain shot so powerfully through my shoulder that I was forced to stop in the middle of the pool, paddling to the wall with my left arm and clenching my right arm tightly to my side until I could begin my walk of shame to the locker room. The great Tera who could suppress all pain could not suppress this. It was beyond my control.

After multiple conversations and many tears with Steve, my athletic trainer and I decided that we had increased my yardage too quickly, and since I had to sit out my first year at Texas A&M anyway, I needed to continue to swim just one practice a day. Even so, I couldn't allow myself to just skip the afternoon practice; I needed to make up for it somehow, so I wouldn't lose the respect of my teammates, my coaches, or myself. I knew I could still use my lower body, and running seemed like the perfect alternative to get a cardio workout. I began to replace the second swim practice of the day with a run.

During one of my new afternoon runs, I had felt minor ankle pain. The next day, I had asked a chiropractor if he could adjust my ankle since it had been bugging me. As he jerked my foot one way, I felt pain but not enough to give me concern. The next morning, I woke up unable to walk. I couldn't put pressure on my foot without stifling a scream. My ankle had disappeared in a mass of swelling, and my calf appeared to merge with my foot without contour or shape. I had never experienced a stress fracture before, but I figured I had to have one in my ankle. When I was younger, I had rolled my ankle and sprained it, but nothing had produced this shade of purple or this amount of internal pain.

The next morning, I showed up to practice hobbling like a raccoon with its foot caught in a trap. I thanked God that I competed in the one sport that didn't require walking. As the student athletic trainer taped my purple cankle, I rationalized my pain. Surely, I would get over this hiccup in a few days; I just had to make it through practices until then. I tested the tape. It prevented me from flexing my foot for a flutter kick, and hopefully, it would stabilize my ankle enough to allow me to complete practice that morning.

I jumped in the pool, and after twenty failed attempts, I realized I couldn't finish four laps without tears flooding my goggles. I had underestimated the need to be able to push off a wall every twenty-five yards, and clenching my jaw with each flip turn did nothing to alleviate the pain. After a fourth of warm-up, I got out of the pool, hopping on one leg. I tried to look my coaches in the eyes without dissolving into a puddle of humiliation. It was bad enough that I had been given the chance of a lifetime to be on this team after a massive shoulder surgery even though I was unable to swim the same amount as my teammates, but now I couldn't swim because of an ankle injury.

I was a walk-on. The coaches could cut me from the team at any point. When it didn't even make sense for them to give me a chance in the first place, what would motivate them to keep a girl who could only use one arm and one leg? If another girl injured her upper body, she could kick the rest of practice. If she injured part of her lower body, then she could use a pull buoy and pull the rest of the workout. I could do neither because pulling an entire workout would make my shoulder flare up so badly that I wouldn't be able to use it the rest of the week. I was a sitting duck. A sitting, humiliated duck. I wilted with the guilt of being finished with my practice while my teammates still had ninety minutes left.

Just one day before, I had swum four miles in the morning practice, lifted weights for an hour, spent two hours in the athletic training room doing physical therapy and treatments, and ran four miles. Now, I felt like the most pathetic athlete to have ever graced the pool deck of Texas A&M. My ankle had started hurting while running two days prior, but I was well versed in injuries and knew the difference between tendonitis pain and the sharp, searing pain of a tear or a sprain. Most of the time, tendonitis pain got better as I kept exercising and warmed up the muscles. As the run continued, my logic proved correct as my ankle followed the laws of physics. The pain decreased, and I was able to complete my workout. The run had only lasted thirty minutes.

What gives, God? I thought. *I'm swimming for your glory now. Shouldn't I be steadily progressing every day? Instead, I'm decreasing in value to the team, proving my naysayers right, and humiliating myself of my own volition. I'm starting to think that following you is code for things never turning out the way I want.*

God whispered to my spirit, *What if what you think will bring me the most glory isn't what will actually bring me the most glory?*

Internally, I retorted, *Well, what if I don't like your plan for glory? And isn't that a bit arrogant, always wanting glory for yourself?*

Don't ever get over the miracle, dear one. I am the only thing worthy of worship. Didn't you say I was worth it all?

I crinkled my nose and considered sticking my tongue out at the wall. *Yeah, well, I'm not feeling like you are right now.*

God and I argued daily as I fought to understand why he would lead me through the biggest miracle of my life just to have it end in more frustration. I ended up having to wear a boot for the next six weeks. I received a diagnosis not of a fractured bone, which would have healed faster than my injury, but a torn posterior tibial tendon. Of course, the tendon I tore was on the inside of the ankle, which was notorious for taking longer to heal compared to tendons on the outside. I never thought that pushing through some minor pain on a run would result in an inability to jump or run for an entire year. The grand plan to supplement exercise had not only failed to help my swimming, but it had also backfired and hindered swimming even further.

More than just my ankle began to struggle. My body started to crumble like Humpty Dumpty's. At twenty-two years old, I wasn't quite old enough to be suffering from a different injury every other week, but that's what happened. Just like my body had compensated and made my legs an inch different in circumference during high school, now the pain was so intense that I started to compensate even more, and my body let me know. I pulled my groin on a consistent basis, I strained a nerve in my back, and I tore my ankle all within a few months of receiving a chance to swim for the Aggies. Each injury set me back at least a week, and I had to constantly substitute different modifications to be able to complete workouts.

One day, I jumped into the pool a little too enthusiastically, arching my back with arms outstretched for the joy of entering the pool in style. My abs were tight from the previous day's workout, and the abrupt stretch in my fancy jump resulted in a pulled abdominal muscle. Since every part of every stroke ties together through a swimmer's core, a sprained ab made swimming nearly impossible. The next time you go to the pool, try to do a flip turn without using your abdominal muscles. Talk about a flailing nightmare.

As I grappled with my newfound reality, God provided exciting, wonderful opportunities for me to talk to my teammates about who he was and to show them love. The amount of pressure that athletes at a Top-4 program put on themselves was obscene, and it felt good to suggest that there was more to live for between their ears than there was between two walls in a pool. Did the joy I felt from sharing God with others mean that was I supposed to lay down my dream to go to the Olympics and live in agony just to serve my teammates? Did God really bring me this far to experience no athletic comeback whatsoever?

I had fashioned God's miracle into the box that I wanted it to fit. I had unwrapped the present and seen the gift of a new shoulder, but now that I had started to play with it, I realized its limitations. I had assumed I knew what the gift was for, but each day, I realized more and more how wrong I had been. God wasn't the one putting limitations on his gift—I was. He had never meant for me to confine his miracle to the boundaries of my own imagination.

27

A Different Kind of Miracle

People of mediocre ability sometimes achieve outstanding success
because they don't know when to quit.
Most men succeed because they are determined to.
—George E. Allen

Spring of 2015 came, and needles protruded from my groin as the box next to me pounded an electrical current into my body. The electricity traveled the full length of the needles, which poked through my skin and deep into my muscle. My groin contracted in a three-second spasm from the electric wave. The box continued to shock my leg into submission, and after a few minutes, the knots in my groin released, bringing relief to my overworked legs.

As the sensitive muscles in my upper leg flared their frustrations, I sat with my back against a wedged maroon pillow, my upper body encapsulated in a black, Michelin Man contraption called a NormaTec. Air pumped into adjacent capsules of the machine as they contracted in succession from my fingers, to my forearms, to my biceps, to my pectoral muscles, to my lat muscles. The compression pumped toxins and lactic acid out of my shoulder and back to my heart, where my body could more easily rid itself of the enemies in my bloodstream.

At my ankle, a student athletic trainer used lotioned fingers to massage my injured tissue and begin a flush. She pressed her thumbs up my ankle towards my heart, stimulating the release of fluids that had caused my ankle to swell. It was already my fourth time in the athletic training room that day, and as people and machines attempted to remedy the effects of swimming with a reconstructed arm, I read my language textbook before class that night. To me, it was just another day living my miracle.

I found humor in the day-to-day ridiculousness of what I was trying to accomplish. Everything was a balance, and I had to figure out how far I could push my body before I passed the point of no return. One wrong move or exercise could set me back a week or more. I could only ask so much of my shoulder each day before the pain thermometer exploded. I couldn't even kick with a kickboard most days; putting my shoulder in such a vulnerable position out-stretched in front of me immediately skyrocketed my pain dial, and I didn't want half of my physical capacity for the day taken from me before we finished the first thirty minutes of practice.

A forced compromise included in the "denying myself bundle" was to no longer use a kickboard at all in warm-up and only occasionally in sets. This decision killed me because kicking during warm-up was the only time during practice when we could socialize and talk. But I couldn't sacrifice my shoulder to foster friendships. If I lost my shoulder, then I wouldn't be on the team to enjoy those friendships. Instead, I used a snorkel and kicked with my arms at my side. It was a much slower way to kick due to the less streamlined position of my body. I had to work harder to make the intervals, but it was worth it if it could help me live to swim another day.

I affectionately named my snorkeled worm undulations "Nessie" after the Loch Ness Monster. I had a lot in common with the rarely sighted, misunderstood, gimpy-finned lake creature. If I had to put up my kickboard for the day, my teammates would cheer, "Go, Nessie! You can do it!"

In fact, my therapy routine caused me to appear like more than one sea creature. I had started a therapy called cupping, which derives from Chinese medicine. Glass cups suction to an area of skin to break up scar tissue or adhesions in the muscle underneath and pull toxins to the surface of the skin. The process leaves noticeable, purplish-black circles on the skin.

"You look like you got attacked by a giant squid," Steve chuckled as I walked onto the pool deck with my colorful marks, and he wasn't wrong.

While I could usually make light of my circumstances, the amount of pain management that my body required to simply endure what my teammates did day in and day out wore on me at times.

High-performance athletes become desensitized in a variety of ways, punishing their bodies to daily extremes most people couldn't fathom on the hardest workout day of their lives. Yet even among the most desensitized of top-tier athletes, my comfort with the bizarre took desensitization to a whole new level. The general public wouldn't like the idea of a stranger digging his fingers into an area as sensitive as their groin, much less sticking needles in it. My reality was that I had pulled muscles in awkward places for so long that propriety no longer fazed me. I fell asleep during the ear-splitting thump of CT scans. I read books for homework while I took ice baths to manage my time efficiently. Ultrasound gel was rubbed not on my belly to assess the health of a growing baby but on my shoulder to reduce inflammation.

A few of my friends had started getting married and having kids. They used Dixie cups for their children's snacks each day; I used them to freeze water and rub my shoulder down with an ice-cup massage each night. I had to wake up thirty minutes before the rest of my teammates to get to the athletic training room and heat my shoulder each morning before practice. I had to stay thirty minutes after practice to receive treatment on my shoulder. On average, I spent one to two hours per day managing pain rather than progressing past it.

Because I was an athlete at Texas A&M, I received free chiropractic care. It was a tremendous blessing because I probably wouldn't have been able to swim without it. Every week, the chiropractor had to reposition at least one rib that had elevated itself into a ferocious knot of bone and stretched tissue to the right of my neck.

I had a knot the size of a ping-pong ball in the belly of my biceps muscle. I named it Victor due to its constant presence in my arm and used it as a tool to give me a positive frame of mind: I would be victorious, and I was a victor! Each day, my athletic trainer used a metal, gun-like contraption to hammer the knot into submission. Finally, Victor would concede and flatten out to rejoin the rest of the biceps muscle in normalcy, but by the time afternoon practice ended, he had taken up residence as my friendly biceps bulge yet again.

Probably my least favorite technique in reality, but perhaps my most favorite because it made me feel the toughest, was scraping. After so many years with an unseen injury, I always liked when there was something to show for the pain, and the scraping process produced eye-catching bruises. Imagine a plastic spackling knife grinding into your tissue, scraping back and forth against the tendons and muscles to break up inflammation and scar tissue. If normal scraping didn't do the trick, there was an even more grotesque version of the technique: cupping combined with scraping. An athletic trainer suctioned a portion of my skin and muscle into a glass cup and then dragged the cup up and down across my biceps to break up adhesions. I always had a towel on hand to bite to suppress my screams.

Sometimes treatments were more therapeutic, like the HivaMat, which created an electrostatic field between the athletic trainer and me to accelerate tissue regeneration. Just imagine the sound of a fly buzzing in your ear and the feeling of a vibrating medical glove stroking your arm. The humming nearly put me to sleep.

Other times, I rocked the Kinesio tape to help my shoulder stay stabilized for a distance practice. Unfortunately, I had an allergic reaction to the adhesive, so I broke out in a rash each time I used it. Sometimes I decided the hives were worth the support to my shoulder capsule, but other times I decided the tape didn't help enough to merit self-inflicted poison ivy on my arm for the next four days.

One of the most effective devices we used to promote healing was the laser: a machine that costs up to tens of thousands of dollars. I thought the whole nitrous oxide release thing was cool, and the machine seemed to have legitimate alleviating effects rather than the placebo effect I felt from most things we did. But really, I just liked the fact that I got to wear green sunglasses to prevent my retinas from being fried by the power of the laser if I accidentally looked at it. Plus, it was cool when we accidentally hit a sensitive nerve and my arm would flop involuntarily like a spastic fish out of water. The fact that light could make my nerves react in lunacy intrigued me.

After a year at Texas A&M, we discovered my shoulder blade had adhered to my rib cage. Because I had sat stationary in a body brace for three weeks and then remained a combined sixteen weeks in a sling from my three surgeries, my muscles had affixed themselves to my back, substantially hindering my range of motion. If you were to reach behind your back and try to reach up towards your neck with the same arm, your shoulder blade would pop out like a wing. For swimmers, this wing can be raised up to three inches from their backs. Mine could not lift enough to create a dent of a millimeter, giving me almost zero percent of the range of motion a swimmer should have in that area. After months of manual therapy, with my athletic trainer digging her fingers into my shoulder blade, she was able to break up the scar tissue and allow my arm to move more fully than it had in years.

Beyond all these devices, the most unique part of my injury was my nerve damage. If someone touched my arm with vibration, hit a sensitive part, or even used compression, my arm would involuntarily fly up and down or side to side. I could force the spasms to stop by holding my breath, but a lot of the time, I was so tired that the effort wasn't worth it.

I embraced my freak-show of a life, and my teammates played along. They found it so humorous that they would start humming the tune to the chicken dance as they flapped their wings and mocked my poor little arm.

One day, some folks from NASA came to our athletic training room to try out a machine on Texas A&M athletes. The PEMFT machine—Pulsed Electro-Magnetic Field Therapy—had long, white tubes that were placed around the injury site, and magnetic pulses were sent through them into the body. When I heard the machine was originally used to heal broken legs of racehorses, my interest was piqued. I shared my backstory, and instead of placing the tube around my arm, the professional decided to place the tubes around my head. When you live through trauma, whether physical, emotional, or mental, the brain blocks passageways to protect you from pain. This is why some people suffer memory loss or forget entire periods of their lives.

Because I had endured chronic pain for so long, my brain had blocked passageways to protect itself from more pain than necessary. The PEMFT machine was supposed to open up these neural pathways and tell my brain that it was okay to use these communication roads again, since doctors had removed the source of pain (the degenerating biceps) from my body. Immediately after targeting the areas of my brain that controlled the right side of my body, my entire arm swung back and forth across the table, like a maniac. I didn't know if I should try to stop it or let it continue to flail. The NASA man's eyebrows rose in shock and then furrowed, trying to solve the mystery.

We finished the treatment, and I sat up slowly. I felt dizzy, and I had to take slow breaths for fifteen minutes before the nausea calmed enough that I didn't think I would get to have a second helping of my protein recovery drink.

The technician sighed. "I've been working with machines like this for twenty years, and I've never seen anything close to that kind of nerve damage," he said. "You are really something else."

If I hadn't been suppressing the urge to vomit, I may have accepted his comment as a compliment. Instead, I headed home, where I discovered my arm refused to stop its spastic thrashing. Normally, the nerve spasms started with contact of a machine or person and stopped when the treatment stopped. But this time, I couldn't stop the shaking or the spasms.

Three hours later, my shoulder still involuntarily tried to slap me, and I couldn't fall asleep because my arm wouldn't stop moving of its own accord. I feared I would walk around with an uncontrollable arm permanently. Had we pushed my nervous system too far? But after eighteen hours, the spasms finally calmed down and reduced to their normal contact-induced state.

All of this treatment was my normal. *This* was my miracle. It was not the miracle I had thought it would be when I woke up in a body brace, convinced I would recover completely. Without knowing anyone in the sport who had tried to come back from my specific surgery, I had no precedent to follow. Others presented their doubts and their beliefs in me, and reality proved to be somewhere in the middle. I could do more than many dreamed possible, but my body put limitations on me that I was stunned to find I could not overcome through sheer willpower.

Miracles don't always look the way we expect. People often think that miracles are grand acts of God or displays where reality is suspended for a brief moment and the laws of science are reversed to produce an effect that is physiologically impossible. The miracle is instantaneous, and then the healed person is free to dance down the streets in victory. Many of these stories appear in the Bible, and I do not deny that God sometimes displays his will and his heart by healing people in this manner. However, I am convinced that far more often, miracles don't look like that. More common than the grandiose, sweeping display of God's healing hand in one act are the other miracles God works in our lives—miracles that require our cooperation.

God is after our hearts, not our bodies, and he is going to heal us in whatever way brings him the most glory. Many people miss the reality of a miracle in their lives because they are not willing to surrender their comfort, and they are not willing to practice the self-discipline necessary to live in the miraculous. God gave me a miracle. I was swimming miles after having been completely incapable of turning off a light switch. Every stroke of every practice was my living rebellion against everything that Satan had tried to do to destroy my life. You'd better believe I lived my miracle every day, and I lived it to the fullest.

But living a miracle is not always easy. Sometimes you have to spend two hours in a training room every day. Sometimes you have to commit to getting up at 4:00 a.m. instead of 5:00 a.m. because if you can get up at five o'clock for your sport, then you can get up at four o'clock for your king. Sometimes a miracle looks like a dance of two steps forward and twenty steps back. Sometimes, you have to grab God's hand while you bite a towel. And sometimes, the miracle looks so different from what you expected that you sacrifice the life you imagined for yourself before ever giving God a chance to partner with you to enact the impossible. Some miracles take a lot more surrender and a lot more dependence on God than people are willing to offer, but if we would hang on a little longer, give God all the trust that he deserves, and believe that we will see the goodness of God in the land of the living, then we would start to live the kinds of lives in which others discover much-needed inspiration.

Miracles are simply another demonstration of the gospel. The great mystery of the universe is that God could do it all on his own, but he chooses not to. He chooses to use us to impact this world and to display the mighty ways he can work in our lives if we just *let* him. We have to give up our control to display his greatness. You cannot force God to make your miracle what you want it to be. Instead of healing, sometimes our greatest witness is the testimony of loving God amidst terrible pain. Instead of deliverance, sometimes we need to see that God is worth crucifying our desires to break an addiction. Instead of immediate success, sometimes the world needs a healthy dose of work ethic to realize that they will only walk on water after they are willing to get out of the boat. It's never too late to join the greater story of God at work in the universe. He is more than willing. Are you?

28

Flying Again

The difficult is that which can be done immediately;
the impossible, that which takes a little longer.
—Anonymous

Back in 2007, during my freshman year of college at Arkansas, I sat trying to listen to God at a prayer meeting. My friend from church had invited me to the intimate gathering at her house, and we sought to pray intentionally one night during the week. The worship music had only been playing for a couple minutes when the host tiptoed over to my corner of the room.

"I was praying for you," she started, "and I got this picture in my head."

With almost no exposure to the gifts of the Spirit during high school, this introduction spooked me a little, but I wanted to hear her out.

"I don't know if this means anything to you, but I just saw a picture of a gorgeous bird flying over the water of a huge pool. It was free, in no pain, and others couldn't help but stop to look at it. They gawked at its beauty, and the bird kept flying, soaking in the glory of its flight. I just felt like God was telling me to tell you that he knows you're in a lot of pain right now, but you're going to fly again."

I sat there stunned. My friend left me as stealthily as she had arrived, and I was left to ponder her image. Immediately, I knew what she did not: flying had more significance to me than simply relating to winged creatures. Even after only having endured the first of my three surgeries at the time, fly, or butterfly, was the one stroke I could never swim without severe pain. Fly put the most strain on my shoulder and was the hardest for me to execute. It made succeeding in my best event, the Individual Medley, nearly impossible.

When she told me I would fly again, I saw myself through the bird's eyes. I was the bird. I soared above the pain, wings outstretched to their full capacity as I hurtled above the pool. And I knew instantaneously that I would compete in the IM again. God would bring me back to fly again.

Mark Spitz won seven gold medals in the 1972 Olympics in Munich. He achieved an unprecedented level of success by increasing his training from one swim practice per day to two. More and more swimmers began to emulate the icon, and the sport of swimming was forever changed. Since then, swimmers and their coaches have fallen prey to the belief that more is always better. Michael Phelps augmented this claim when he became one of the most decorated athletes of all time by increasing his training from two swim practices a day to three.

Nowadays, science is beginning to disprove the more-is-better mindset. True, incredible endurance develops through the intense distance workouts that have epitomized the sport of swimming for more than four decades. And beyond that endurance, the keenest advantage to training so extensively is the invincible mental toughness that brutal training develops. After swimming eight to ten miles per day, a two-minute race seems trivial. Some are starting to believe the pendulum swung too far in one direction, and the swimming world's elites are beginning to realize they can only push the human body to a certain extreme before lack of recovery negates endurance gained. Some of swimming's best are proving that, to an extent, quality could be more important than quantity.

The new generation of coaches who were discovering that a one-training-fits-all mold did not work for all swimmers had only just been born at the end of my career. It was nearly impossible to convince myself that I could succeed on less training rather than more, but that's what my body was telling me I had to do. After my operations, I could not train the way old schoolers told me to succeed. My body simply would not allow it. So, I had two choices: quit or innovate. I chose the latter.

At the beginning of the 2015–2016 athletic season—my second year at A&M—I worked with my swimming coaches, my strength and conditioning coaches, and my athletic trainers to develop a workout regimen that would allow me to become the best I could be, given the parameters of my new miracle arm. Even though I felt comfortable with the new plan, the imaginary blinders I placed around my eyes could never fully block my view of how different my teammates' training was than mine.

And beyond the pitfall of comparison, I had my own inner critic to deal with. I had always prided myself on being able to push myself further than other competitors, to train more than others, and to finish the strongest. I lived to push the boundaries of everything. If a coach didn't count my reps, I did extra in the weight room. I had a thing against even numbers in general, yet I liked the number eight, and I preferred numbers like sevens, threes, and multiples of eleven (We're all a little quirky, right?). I would convince myself that instead of doing twenty-five crunches, I could do twenty-eight. And once I got to twenty-eight, I knew I could push myself to thirty-three. After that, surely, I could make it to forty-four, and so on. The mental game I played with myself had no limits. Once, I completed 228 reps on a round of twenty sit-ups before I forced myself to stop. I believed I could always do more to succeed. And worse, I saw it being done by my teammates on a daily basis.

Now that same girl, the girl who would run an extra lap after stadiums, the girl who always made sure she did eleven underwater kicks off the last turn in warm down, the girl who would sneak heavier weights than what was written on her weight sheet, had to convince herself that *less was more*. But after almost nine years of trial and error with my injury, deep down, I knew I had only one chance to succeed with my injury. If God was not going to miraculously heal me, my only option was to decrease quantity and increase quality.

I had to come to terms with the fact that I wasn't going to be able to compete in my best event, the 400 IM, by swimming fewer practices. I would not have enough endurance to compete with the likes of swimmers who were training five hours a day when I was only training three. I also realized that sacrificing a traditional training style was probably sacrificing whatever chance I might have to come back to qualify for the Olympics. But as it was, I certainly wasn't going to have a chance if I was clenching my arm at my side, trying not to choke on water as I screamed from pain.

My promise from God seemed validated by the way he had given back my day-to-day life. I knew I would live a fulfilling life after my swimming career ended, which was a certainty I didn't enjoy until my third surgery. But what happened to "every nation will tremble and fear and be in awe" of what God did in my life? What else could that life verse have meant except that I was destined to make it to the Olympics? I knew reality did not match up with the dream that had propelled me through so much pain, but

I never stopped believing that God would make it possible if he wanted to. But he wasn't choosing that reality.

With the amount of pain I faced daily and the loss of being able to fully recover, I debated giving up swimming entirely. It seemed so futile, and I could be doing so many other productive things with my life. But to give up would not be to give up on swimming; it would be to give up on what God was trying to teach me through this—that I couldn't do everything on my own out of sheer willpower, that I had to surrender, that I had to be humble, that I was made to be different, and that it was okay. I didn't understand God's lack of intervention, but I had walked with him long enough to believe that whatever he was doing, it was for my good. Whatever he had up his sleeve, he would make it better than anything I had imagined.

In the meantime, all I knew was that I was going to finish my swimming career to the best of my ability. And right now, that meant swimming only one practice a day. If all I could accomplish was making Olympic Trials, then so be it, but I would know that I had done everything I could have done to give my very best. It took me a year to continue to heal and build up strength, but during my second year at Texas A&M, I started to see vast improvement. I trained with incredible swimmers each day, and I gave them a swim for their money on plenty of occasions.

All the while, Steve relentlessly helped me with my strokes despite the fact that I was a non-scholarship athlete. Changing a habit is difficult for most people, but for me, it was a nightmare. I wanted so badly to please Steve by fixing the areas that he was helping me with, but if I stopped thinking about the technique even for a second, my body reverted to my old form, even if I had been working on it for weeks. With as much pain as my shoulder caused me, my body would automatically and subconsciously betray me without focused concentration, and I'd start all over each day. If

Steve gave me something else to fix, the other technique tip I had just mastered would fall prey to pain while I focused on the new suggestion.

Before swimming for Steve, I had seen swimming as a time for me to use my body and let my mind zone out. Once I started swimming under the genius technician, Steve Bultman, I fell into bed completely spent; I pushed both my mind and body beyond their limits each day. However, during my second year as an Aggie, the hard foundation I had dug up and laid afresh began to pay off. I started to get lifetime best times, and my times dropped to the national level again. Even still, the beauty of swimming for Texas A&M was that I would always be a small fish in a big pool. No matter how good I got, there was always someone on the team to chase.

And I loved a good chase. Swimming beside big fish can inspire a small fish to reach new heights. For example, one practice started out like any other. Nothing was different except that my shoulder seemed to be having a good day. Additionally, not as many people were at practice because it was finals week, the only time of the year the NCAA could not force us to be at practice. Because fewer people were at practice, I got the chance to lead my lane, which meant I was swimming first in the lane rather than behind others—an opportunity one never took for granted while training with elite Aggies. As we started the set, I realized I was hanging with the other two lane leaders, Béryl Gastaldello and Sarah Henry.

Béryl has since competed in the Olympics for France, broke the French record in the 50-meter Backstroke, and signed a sponsorship with swimming brand TYR. She was a multiple-time SEC champion and consistently ranked in the top twenty-five in the world for her best events. Sarah Henry, whose stats I mentioned previously, was a beast of a swimmer with hopes of an Olympic berth.

At the end of each round, we descended a set of 50s, getting faster on each one until the last one was an all-out race. On the first round, I pushed them both and hung tough until the finish. Not used to competing with two of the fastest girls on the team, I figured I must have caught them off guard, and they'd try harder the next time so I couldn't keep up.

But then on the second round I continued fighting the whole set and still raced them down to the wire on the last fifty. At that point, I started justifying my success, wondering if they weren't trying as hard as they could for some reason.

Finally, the last round came. By the third round, I believed I had earned the right to duke out the finish, and the three of us gave it everything we had left for the last fifty meters. Every breath, I was stroke for stroke with them both. The final fifteen meters, I buried my head and charged for the wall. I hit the wall and looked to my right. The race was close enough that I couldn't tell who had won.

Sarah yelled across the lane line, "Awesome set, Tera!"

And with her comment, I realized, in shock, that she had given me her best. They both had. She wouldn't have told me good job unless I had truly kept up with her; if she could have, she would have destroyed me. It was a pretty common occurrence. We warmed down, and I got out of the pool to head to the locker room. Steve sat on a starting block, wheels turning behind his brooding exterior.

"*Very* nice practice today, Tera," he said, nodding his approval in slow motion.

As I drove home that night, I couldn't help but wonder, *Who am I? I mean, truly?* If I could compete with and beat two of the best swimmers in the country (I like to think I out-touched them on the final wall) on a day when my shoulder was in slightly less pain, who on earth could I be without this injury? I pondered these questions in my heart but had to let them go. Those thoughts held no place in reality. The fact was that I could never go back and change the second that I flew into a wall and tore my shoulder from the bone. I could never change the fact that I swam every day on a reconstructed arm and that some days I curled up in a ball in the middle of the pool in agony, while other days I challenged the best in the sport.

That practice gave me a taste of who I used to be. Moments like those made me question what could have been if I had not torn my labrum and biceps nine years prior. Could I have contended with the best in the world? I would never know what kind of a swimmer I could have been without my debilitating injury. But now, I was someone better. Given the chance, I wouldn't change what happened during the 50 Free at the state championship that fateful day. My trial had made me who I was, and I didn't want to know the kind of a person I would have been had I not faced nine years of God's humbling grace. What I did know was this: after all I had endured, I was flying again.

One of my favorite hobbies throughout my undergrad years was painting. I felt like covering a canvas with colored acrylic was a form of worship. It was one of the only times I could escape into my own little world and forget about the pain, stress, and pressure of life. It was just God and me, an almost ethereal experience where I felt like we were together; neither of us had to say a word, but we enjoyed each other's presence.

During my sophomore year, I started painting a rainbow phoenix rising from the ashes. I loved the idea of a bird rebirthed from the ashes of defeat, and I felt that the mythical creature paralleled my journey thus far in life. But after I completed half the painting, my shoulder deteriorated to the point that I could no longer lift my arm. The pain had started to interfere with my relaxation hobby for many months, until I finally had to put the paint-brush down. I grappled with what life would look like without the use of my right arm, and the canvas sat on the easel for months, untouched, mocking me. How could I paint such an inspirational picture of a persevering, rebirthed creature when all I seemed to do was rise from the ashes only to be set ablaze again?

Three months after I stopped painting, I received my miracle. Six months after my third surgery, I picked up the paintbrush again. I finished the painting, emblazoning the words *Beauty from Ashes* at the top and bottom of the canvas. The words stemmed from Isaiah 61:1–3:

> The Spirit of the Sovereign LORD is on me,
> because the LORD has anointed me to
> proclaim good news to the poor.
> He has sent me to bind up the brokenhearted,
> to proclaim freedom for the captives
> and release from darkness for the prisoners,
> to proclaim the year of the LORD's favor
> and the day of vengeance for our God,
> to comfort all who mourn,
> and to provide for those who grieve in Zion—
> to bestow on them a crown of beauty
> instead of ashes,
> the oil of joy instead of mourning,
> and a garment of praise
> instead of a spirit of despair.
> They will be called oaks of righteousness,
> a planting of the LORD
> for the display of his splendor.

Over the years, the image of a bird soaring over a pool kept resurfacing in my mind. The snapshot pushed me forward after my second surgery, and it gave me enough hope to attempt butterfly after my third surgery.

Now, I realize something more about the word my friend spoke over me. The bird was more than just a prophecy that God would bring me full recovery. After my swimming career ended, I envisioned the bird another time, and I realized that it was the phoenix I had painted from the ashes. I completed half of the painting as I entered the darkest season of my life and half of it after God had resurrected my life. The very painting he had put in my heart to demonstrate his truth, the very painting that had bookended my miracle, was the same bird he had shown me four years prior before I weathered the storm of all that was to come.

Now I see the bird flying, its rainbow feathers blowing in the wind as it soars over a pool. Except the pool is an ocean. I didn't reach the end of the pool when I quit swimming. Rather, the great deep beckons to me, and the air calls me further; its blue horizon stretches out before me. My wings strengthened, now I stretch them out wide, spindrift flying up in my face as I fly. Undeterred, my eyes are fixed ahead on one thing: Jesus.

Most people see their lives as a marathon that they run for God, for Paul wrote that he wanted to finish the race of life he had run well. But I see life as an open water swim; only I'm not a fish, I'm a phoenix. I soar every day, taking the waves head on, stopping to land on the branch of a friend when I need to but all the while aiming ahead to the One who made me fly, the King of kings, whom I will reach one day when my journey transitions from this world to the next.

29

The Beginning

There are only two kinds of people in the end:
those who say to God, "Thy will be done,"
and those to whom God says, "Thy will be done."
—C. S. Lewis

"It's my Olympic Trials suit, Steve!" I said as Steve shook his head and suppressed a grin that would give me the satisfaction that I had indeed humored him. I wore my red, white, and blue Speedo as I warmed up at the meet that I had waited for since I woke up in a body brace—the meet where I would qualify for Olympic Trials.

After two years of grueling recovery, I had trained, I had tapered, and I was ready. This was my night. I could feel it in every fiber of my being. The scene was set: my home pool, my Aggie teammates, and a swim at night that I had qualified for earlier that morning. I was seeded in lane four of the B final, an optimum position. My parents, faithful to come to every meet since I had moved back to Texas, sat in the stands. And to top it all off, my club coach, Terry, who had endured the pit of hell with me and fought for me through it all, was there. He would be on the sideline, cheering with my club team. After all we had gone through together, having him there made me sure it was my destiny to qualify that night. It was all simply perfect.

During warm-up, Steve timed a 200-pace 50 and a build 50, where I increased speed until the end of the effort. I hit lightning times on both with energy to spare. I was swimming both the 100-meter Breast and the 200-meter IM finals. I had a chance to make the Olympic Trials cut in both events, but the events were back to back, which meant I would get as few as ten minutes to rest between my two races. With the lineup in the back of my mind, I knew the 100 Breast was my best shot to prove to the world that I had overcome.

Steve and I had a strategy: in reality, I was more of a mid-distance swimmer, but since my third surgery, I had been forced to turn to shorter events. Thus, my second 50 in a 100 was always much stronger than my first 50 and not how a typical 100 Breast-stroker would swim the event. Steve told me to save some energy going out and bring that sucker home with everything I had in me on the second half. I felt confident in our plan because it catered to my strength—finishing strong.

I changed into my fastest racing suit, my Speedo Lazr, and my fingers tingled with excitement. Lyrics from "Awake and Alive" by the band Skillet screamed in my ears as I threw my jacket over my suit and danced around: this was my time.

Adrenaline coursed through my body, just like it used to when I was young. I bought in. I believed in myself. I was no longer numb to the result of my race. I cared, and my body responded. I drank in the feeling of nervous energy; I thrived on the advantage it gave me.

My heat was up in two minutes. I looked to the stands to find my parents seated with some of my dearest friends from church.

They all grinned in excitement, waving at me. I threw my jacket in the bin beside the timer's chair, walked up to my block, and lifted my goggles onto my eyes. Game time.

The announcer ran through the line up, adding extra pressure before an event, which I loved. I never got tired of hearing my name over the speaker; somehow, it made me want to swim better, as if the stands knowing my identity meant I had to defend my reputation.

One long whistle sounded. I stepped up onto the block, clapped, and waited.

"Swimmers, take your mark."

Beep.

I flew into the water and patiently waited to start my pull out. I counted, timed the technique, and then shot forth from the water to begin my strokes. Breaststroke challenged my trust in Steve, for we had decreased my stroke count by increasing my glide time. This technique was faster than my previous stroke, even though it was counterintuitive to believe that waiting could make me swim more quickly. I fought the temptation to spin into a faster stroke, and I held the glide, taking half the number of strokes of the girls to my right and left. As I approached the turn, I barely felt winded. I knew I had enough in the tank to qualify for Olympic Trials.

This is mine, I thought.

I hit the wall, patiently timed my second pull out, and charged for home. I was building speed, and I could feel the water flying past me. By mid-pool, I was a body length ahead of the rest of my heat. The crowd cheered excitedly, and I knew I was on track to make Olympic Trials. The crowd knew it. I knew it. I lunged harder.

On the right sideline, Steve watched my stroke, flicking his heat sheet as if it would propel me forward. Next to him, my teammates jumped up and down, screaming until they were hoarse. In the stands, my mom grabbed my dad's arm. At the end of the pool, a teammate stood behind my block, cheering me on as she prepared to race in the next heat. On the left sideline, my club teammates waved their arms like fanatics. And amidst it all, Terry stood with his arms crossed, tears filling his eyes.

With fifteen meters left, I counted my strokes to time the finish. My arms and legs were numb, but I could still hear the crowd, which meant I knew I was on track for the qualification time. I willed myself forward and plunged my head beneath my arms in a final streamline. My hands collided with the wall, and I gasped for air.

Silence.

In the millisecond it took me to turn around, I realized the crowd had stopped cheering. My eyes flew to the scoreboard, and I squinted to see the time through the faint fog in my goggles.

The minute was correct. The seconds were correct: 1:11. Had I done it? Then my eyes reached the decimals: *.86.* The cut was a 1:11.49. I had missed Olympic Trials by thirty-seven one-hundredths of a second.

My head fell back against the wall behind me as reality sank in. I closed my eyes behind my goggles in devastation. How could I have missed it? I knew I had it. *I knew it.*

My teammates deflated, some with jaws slightly parted, some slumped with empathy, knowing the pain tenths of a second could bring in our sport. My parents and friends sat dumbfounded in the stands, wanting to comfort me but knowing they couldn't.

The rest of the girls in my heat finished, and the music started playing for the next final. I turned around and grabbed the handlebars on the block to pull myself out of the water. In shock, I stumbled to the diving well to warm down.

I knew I had another race in a few minutes, but the disappointment was almost more than I could stomach. After two laps, Terry stopped me. I lifted my goggles and tears began to pour.

"That was incredible," he told me.

"It doesn't matter," I groaned.

"You listen to me, Tera. I don't care what the time was. I don't care what the cut was. That race was incredible. Now you have one more race left. You can qualify for trials in this one. Warm down and go get 'em in the IM!"

I did my best to let anger overwhelm me. Anger was my best shot to propel me to the IM cut. But after the first half of the 200 IM, I felt the exhaustion in my muscles. I just didn't have it in me after such a short break. I touched the wall and didn't even look at the time, knowing I didn't make the cut.

I plodded to the diving well one more time. Now that my racing was over for the night, I let the emotion overwhelm me. Tears filled my goggles, like they had so many times before. I wanted to wait to cry until I got home, but I needed to let out the emotions a little before I washed the tears off and tried to talk to Steve.

A kickboard hitting me on the legs broke me out of my melancholy. It was Terry.

"Listen," he said. "Four tenths does not define whether or not you came back. Don't let a fraction of a second define who you are and whether or not you overcame. Tera, I almost cried the whole last fifteen meters, and you know I don't cry. I couldn't help it because in those last fifteen meters, I saw a girl who took on the world *win*."

He was right. I knew he was. My head knew that four tenths of a second did not define whether I had come back. In fact, Olympic Trials time standards lowered in certain events every four years, meaning the qualification times were always getting faster. If I had simply swum the same time four years prior, I would have qualified. But not in 2016.

My head heard Terry, but my heart didn't. The Olympic Trials were my last saving grace, my one goal after realizing my shoulder would not allow the training I desired. I thought if I could just finish my career at trials, then no one could ever take that away from me. For the rest of my life, I could say I ended my career with Olympians.

Of course, I wasn't going to quit that easily. There was another meet in two months in Georgia. I entered the meet, booked a flight, trained for another six weeks, tapered again, and flew to Atlanta for another shot. In order to compete in the May meet, I had to miss the graduation ceremony for my master's degree, but it was worth it to me. I had already bought the cap and gown, so I packed them in my bag. Before the meet, my teammates and Steve threw me a mock ceremony. I put on the scholarly garb over my Speedo, Steve handed me a heat sheet as a diploma, and a teammate snapped a photo for the history books.

At the meet, I competed in the 100 Breast and the 200 IM. I missed both cuts again, coming within 0.56 of a second on the 100 Breast yet again. I was crushed, but the race didn't feel as good as the first one at my home pool at the end of February. And besides, I had one final chance. This one really would be the last one, for I had run out of time. Then again, I had always been a pressure performer.

What happened to the girl who cried herself to sleep because she got second at the state championship? What happened to the girl who trained by herself for six months because she believed she could come back when no one else did? What happened to the girl who inspired a standing ovation from a crowd of hundreds when she demolished a twenty-year-old state record? What happened to the girl who hit the wall so hard at the end of a race that she tore her shoulder from the bone? What happened to the girl who swam for seven years with a degenerating biceps? What happened to her? Where is she?

These thoughts bombarded my mind throughout the last week of my career. I wanted so badly to force myself to believe that my last chance was a do-or-die moment. Surely that kind of pressure would fuel me with enough adrenaline to make the time standard that I needed. After missing Olympic Trials again by half a second in Atlanta, my very last chance to make the cut came two weeks later in Dallas.

You have worked your entire life for this one moment to show the world what God can do with a life surrendered to him, I told myself. *Hundreds of hours of rehab, hundreds of people laughing at you, thousands of strokes a day. All to get to this moment.*

I was closest to making the cut in the 100-meter Breaststroke. To give myself two chances at the qualification, Steve and I decided to go for the 100 Breast split time during the 200 Breast. That way, if I didn't make the cut, I could swim the actual 100 Breast event the next day as well. You can swim an event of the same stroke that is longer than your event in order to qualify for a meet. If you earn the time standard, then you must finish the race legally in order for your split time to count. I planned to get Olympic Trials in the 100 Breast and then swim the last 100 Breast easy to avoid disqualification.

It was not a championship meet, which meant I had no walkout music, no pump-up when my name was announced, and no one to compete with. Everyone else was swimming a 200-meter race. I thrived off the adrenaline of a night swim, but this race was in the middle of the morning with no one except my coaches, teammates, and parents who understood what I was attempting. I had done this before, four years earlier after my first surgery, where I missed the 400 IM Olympic Trials cut by a couple seconds at a small club meet in Arkansas. I knew how to fake myself out and rise to the occasion; the best swimmers knew how to overcome the time of day, the setting of the meet, and any other factors to keep nothing on their minds but their goal and their ability to manipulate water to their advantage.

In one minute and eleven seconds, I would know if I made Olympic Trials and if my comeback would have a triumphant ending. I could feel the adrenaline in my body, but I also sensed peace in the recesses of my mind that I'd never known before. I didn't admit it to myself for fear of not racing as hard as I could, but somewhere deep in my spirit, I finally understood that this race did not define me. I figured this was simply a test between God and me. He knew I had grown, and now he would give me the ending to my career for which I had strove. Or so I hoped.

I stood on the blocks, curled the toes of my right foot over the edge, and everything around me faded to await the sound of the buzzer. The shrill beep pierced the stillness of the auditorium, and I lunged forward into the water. I tried to take the first 50 meters out faster than I had in previous attempts as I kept having too much reserve in the tank at the end. My stroke felt smooth and powerful until about ten strokes into the race, when I felt the all-too-familiar pop of a muscle pushed beyond its limits. Pain shot through my groin. Immediately, my focus switched from pacing to preventing pain by making my kick smaller. Breaststroke is a leg-propelled technique, and I didn't have a chance at the cut without good kicks.

As I turned at the 50, I gunned it for home. I could tell my kicks were small, and the pain continued to radiate with every kick I enforced upon my leg. My body subconsciously rebelled, but I had conquered my body my whole life. This was my last chance. In the top of the periphery of my goggles, I saw the wall inching closer and closer. I gave everything I had with no regrets. My body passed under the flags, and I whipped my feet to lunge forward in one final surge of pain, propelling my hands towards the wall. My fingers felt the touchpad, and I turned around to look at the clock at the other end of the natatorium. Once again, I had missed Olympic Trials by less than a second.

Swimming the next 100 was pointless since I didn't make the cut, so I hopped out of the pool. I hardly noticed the official raise his hand to disqualify me. It didn't matter. As I limped over to my coach, I tried to swallow the reality of what just happened. Not only had I missed the cut, but I could also barely walk, much less swim another 100 Breaststroke.

Still, there was the 200 IM the next day, and my mind rapidly calculated my chances of qualifying for Olympic Trials in that event. The problem was that one-fourth of the IM was breaststroke. I headed back to my teammate's house, where I was staying, and the pain worsened. My leg stiffened, and I realized the severity of the injury. As gutsy as I was, I didn't think I could make one of the fastest meets in the world without being able to use my leg for a fourth of the race. My career was over.

Yes, I cried. And yes, I was deeply upset. To overcome a degenerating biceps, three surgeries, a near lung collapse, and countless compensation injuries along the way for ten years only to end my career four-tenths away from the ultimate competition in a swimmer's life absolutely *sucked*. But instead of beating myself up for failing, I beat myself up with guilt. I didn't feel guilty for feeling like I could have done more; I knew beyond a shadow of a doubt that I did everything I possibly could have done with the hand I was dealt. My true source of guilt was that I felt relief. As reality settled in, I was relieved that it was finally over. I was relieved to no longer have to question my sanity, and I was relieved to no longer experience such physical pain.

Don't get me wrong, I knew I would miss my sport tremendously, but living my miracle on a daily basis exhausted me. I berated myself because I thought that if I could have found the girl I used to be, if I could have forced myself to care about the sport like I used to, if I could have pushed through the pain a moment longer, then I could have written the perfect ending to an epic story.

But I wasn't that girl anymore, and I never will be. Because somewhere along the way, I lost her. I lost her at the feet of a Savior who is more entrancing than any gold medal ever could be. I lost her in the extravagance of a romance filled with more adrenaline than any race. I lost her in the plot of the story of my life, which was so much better than what I could have written for myself. I was trying so hard to hold onto a girl who I just wasn't anymore. I couldn't convince myself that that race was an ultimatum because it wasn't. I couldn't convince myself that the end of my competing meant the end of my life because it didn't. Somewhere along the way of finding God, I lost myself. And I'm okay with that.

That fearless little girl who thrived off of intimidating her competitors was still in me, but I had found a much more important battle to wage than the one in the swimming pool. I didn't live for the applause of the crowd in a natatorium but for the applause of the crowd of witnesses who had persevered through faith and now stood on the other side of heaven, cheering me on in the battle that was yet to be won. I didn't live for the domination of my competitors but for God's love to be known and shown through the story of my life. My heart broke more for the girls on my team who did not know my Savior than it did when I didn't get a best time. God had rebirthed me, and a phoenix could never become a pigeon again, no matter how hard I tried.

Even still, we keep some parts of our personality because they make us who we are. I figured finishing well was a characteristic of mine that would glorify God and leave me without regrets. No sane person would have swum another race, but even if my groin was pulled, I certainly wasn't going to end my career with a race in which I had injured myself. I decided to swim the 200 IM one last time and give it everything I had, knowing I wouldn't make

Olympic Trials. As I stood on the block one last time, I stood with a smile on my face, for I knew that the end was only the beginning.

Of course, I was determined to go out in style. Diving in for the 200 IM, I had every intention of kicking butterfly on the breaststroke leg of the race, which would have been an automatic disqualification. I knew kicking on a pulled muscle wasn't worth the risk of worsening the injury or creating more permanent damage, but I would go down fighting. However, when I turned into the third leg of the race and did my pull out, a breaststroke kick magically escaped from my legs. Halfway down the pool, my legs were still flailing in narrow little frog kicks, avoiding the pain, and I told myself I had to start kicking butterfly. Then classic, carnal Tera instinct took over. I decided to kick the whole lap breaststroke anyway. I turned, raced freestyle home, and touched the wall one last time.

I looked up to see that I had swum the fastest 200 IM since my third surgery. I still missed Olympic Trials by a little, but that didn't matter. My teammates enveloped me in a hug, the Aggie parents cheered from the stands, and I passed from being a swimmer to being a swammer. I warmed down, changed, and walked over to Steve before leaving the pool as his swimmer for the last time. He gave me a hug.

"I wish I could have coached a healthy Tera Bradham," he said.

"Me too, Steve. Me too," I replied. As a swimmer, I did wish that. But as a person, I knew that a healthy Tera Bradham would have been different from the person I had become.

The athlete in me still wished I could have implemented the wisdom of a coach like Steve Bultman but with a body that would actually accept his guidance. But the deeper part of my heart spoke a greater truth: I knew that the audacious, no-comprehension-of-pain little girl I began my swimming journey with was still in me, even if she showed her stubbornness less frequently than before, and I had no doubt that God would use her in the future. But after a trial of ten years, she now found herself inside of a woman who planned to take the kingdom of darkness by force and use everything the enemy meant for bad for the glory of the One who was and is and is to come. And that was a much greater destiny than any platform, medal, or healthy body could have ever given her.

I have been the fastest swimmer my age in the country, and I have begged God to let me die. I have leapt on the mountaintops of all that swimming has to offer, and I have trudged through the trenches of the worst agony a sport can inflict. And through it all, swimming was simply the tool God used to show me more of himself. I wasn't upset at leaving it all behind; it was all for him anyway. No matter where I go or where life takes me, God will continue to complete the work he began in me. Now, he uses different things to mold me and shape me than he did while I journeyed through swimming.

I asked God for an impossible life: to live in the miraculous became my utmost goal, more prized in my prayer life than anything else. It became the prayer that defined all others. God has answered my prayer. He has given me an impossible life. I came four-tenths of a second away from qualifying for Olympic Trials with part of my arm missing and three-fourths of it rebuilt with anchors. But living an impossible life isn't my ultimate prayer anymore. Now my prayer is simply, *God, let me be faithful to you until the day you take me home.* That's it. Nothing dramatic. Nothing awe-inspiring. Because that's all we really need.

If I am faithful to my King until the end, then he will lead me into the impossible in every aspect of my life. I will impossibly forgive people, I will impossibly challenge the constraints of this reality, and I will witness impossible miracles. But most importantly, I will get to know the heart of the King of the impossible, the One who defeated death and makes all things possible for us: Jesus. If I am faithful to him until the end, then I know the journey of finding his heart will always be my reward.

Epilogue

was not born to prove people wrong. I was born to be set free and to set others free in the process. I didn't get my horse after all. I never made the Olympic team; by swimming's standards, I didn't even come close. I don't ride Freedom through the fields of Texas. Instead, I live my freedom. What started as an Olympic dream ended in the discovery of the truest freedom: the ability to live above the expectations and realities of the world in the way that God originally intended. I can watch every Olympics with joy, enjoying the success of others, because I know I have a freedom that isn't found on a podium. It isn't found in sports, hobbies, or even relationships. True freedom is found in Christ alone.

You were not meant to live an ordinary life. You were made to shake the foundations of the kingdom of hell as you fight for your God-ordained destiny. You were created to live in freedom. I don't know what freedom looks like for you. Maybe freedom for you is forgiveness. Maybe it looks like serving underprivileged children in your neighborhood. Maybe your freedom is humility, or maybe it looks like moving to a foreign country to bring love to a hurting world. Maybe freedom for you is courage.

Whatever freedom looks like for you, I can assure you of this: it is yours in Jesus Christ. Galatians 5:1 says, "It is for freedom that

Christ has set us free. Stand firm, then, and do not let yourselves be burdened again by a yoke of slavery." Jesus died so you could live in freedom. You may as well take him up on the offer of a lifetime. True freedom comes with elbow-grinding work and knee-jerking sacrifice, but you will never outgive God. Whatever you lay down for him, he will return to you tenfold in ways you never expected.

Since I finished my swimming career, I have lived my miracle all over the world. Sometimes I have pain, and I still have quite a bit of nerve damage, but I wake up every morning knowing that I am free. Part of me believes that God will not take all the pain from my shoulder until heaven. If he did, I might forget the journey. I might forget the power of the miracle and everything he saved me from. But I will never quit asking God to take the pain from me. I believe that one day I might wake up, and my nerve dissonance will have disappeared. After all God has done, why not? But either way, I am *free*.

My miracle came in a different form than instantaneous, physical healing. It came in the form of doing headstands for children, in sharing my testimony in prisons, in writing above my head on the whiteboard in my classroom, and in finishing third in my first triathlon. It comes in the everyday realization that I am living a second chance at life, and I don't intend to waste it. I know that one day, I will lift my children in the air and laugh with joy. I will do everything the world told me would be impossible because I serve a God of the impossible.

And God doesn't just work in the miracle industry; he is also in the business of making good on his promises. Nothing he says will ever return void. God told me that nations would "tremble and fear and be in awe" of all the good things he would do in my life. I thought that meant he would take me to the Olympics. But as you are reading this book, I want to thank you for taking part in the true completion of that promise. The very words you're reading are God's completion and perfection of my redeemed life. Not the Olympics but *this story* was what God intended to use to bring glory to his name. It may not look like what we think, but God is always, always faithful in doing what he said he would do.

May you grab his hand and hang on until you see his goodness come to your life in such a way. I look forward to dancing on the streets of gold with you in freedom.

Living My Miracle... as Told in Photos

‿‿‿‿‿

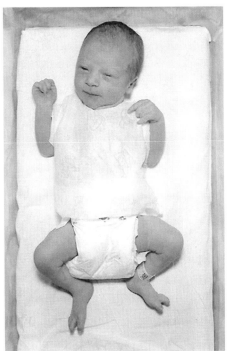

Already defying expectations at seven hours old.

I started swimming because I wanted to be like my big brother, Taylor.

TERA BRADHAM SHOWS off her impressive collection of five gold medals.

Cradling Lexi, the dachshund my brother and I earned for achieving goals that our parents had set and believed insurmountable.

A newspaper clipping highlighting my qualifying for the South Texas Age Group Championships at age seven, making me the youngest competitor in the meet's history.

Bradham sets new standard at Junior Olympics Meet

By DOUG DODSON

Just when you thought it was safe to go back into the water, you dive in and find yourself face-to-face with the threat of your life.

At least, it must have seemed that way to swimmers who had to face Georgetown's Tera Bradham last month at the Junior Olympics Swimming Championships held in McAllen, Texas.

Bradham, who is the daughter of Charlie and Krista Bradham of Georgetown, and a second grader at Frost Elementary School, shocked her coaches and her competition at the Junior Olympic meet by devastating the field, capturing a total of five gold medals on the day.

Bradham collected all of her hardware despite being seeded first in just one of the five events.

Competing in the 8-and-under division, Bradham demolished her challengers by taking top honors in the 50-yard freestyle, 100 freestyle, 50 backstroke, the 50 breaststroke and the 100 individual medley.

Not only did she roll up five wins in as many attempts, Bradham also distinguished herself by being just one of two 7 year olds who achieved new qualifying times for the 8-and-under division while dominating her older competitors.

In an even more impressive feat, Bradham was the sole 7 year old in the state who qualified for the South Texas Championships, which will be held in Corpus Christi.

Bradham qualified in the 10-and-under freestyle, and the 10-and-under breaststroke.

According to the Junior Olympic meet officials, Bradham is believed to be the youngest competitor in the history of the championships.

Eight years old and enjoying my chlorinated habitat.

My brother and I looked up to Josh Davis, a multi-time Olympic gold medalist, as our role model.

Getting a pep talk from my dad.

My teammate congratulating me at ten years old after breaking a twenty-year-old Texas state record in the 200 Freestyle.

Swimming for Freedom

My swim cap came off in the final race of the 200 IM at the state championship, but I still won!

Round Rock swimmer could challenge Spitz, Phelps at 2008 Beijing Olympics

By PATRICK DANIEL
Leader Sports Editor

Tuesday, August 24, 2004

Eleven-year-old Tera Bradham is not in Greece competing for gold this year, but Mark Spitz's record of seven gold medals could be in trouble in 2008.

Bradham of Cedar Valley Middle School has been demolishing state swimming records for the past two years.

At the Texas Age Group Swimming state championships in July, Bradham won three indi-vidual gold medals. She won the 50-meter, 100 and 200 breast-stroke races. All three races were in Top 16 National times.

The 200 breastsroke was a South Texas record. She also won gold medals in four relays.

In early August, the young swimmer attempted open water swimming for the first time in Fort Lauderdale, Fla. While swim-ming a 3000-meter race in the Atlantic Ocean, Bradham posted a time of 45:30, the second fastest among girls her age.

"I was just proud to finish the race, and I was grateful I didn't learn the media had announced that a 10-foot manta ray was fol-lowing us for the whole race, until I was on dry land."

As a swimmer in the 10 & under category, Bradham raced to three state records, four South Texas records and finished her career in the age group as the No.1-ranked swimmer in the 200 freestyle, 100 individual medley and 200 individual medley. She was ranked second in both the 50-meter and 100 freestyle events and the 50 and 100 breaststroke events.

She is the state record holder in the 200 freestyle event for the 10 & under age group. She shat-tered the record from 1994 by 2.2 seconds in her final meet as a 10-year-old.

At the same meet, Bradham won six other gold medals. During the 200 individual med-ley, Bradham lost her swim cap, but still finished before the field.

Bradham swims for Longhorn Aquatics and hopes to swim for the University of Texas one day and says she wants to finish her age group career undefeated in the 50 breaststroke. She has won the event at five consecutive TAGS state championship meets.

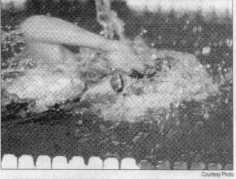

Courtesy Photo

Tera Bradham breaks the 200m freestyle state record in March for the 10 & under age group at the TAGS state championships.

This newspaper article covered my performance at the Texas Age Group Swimming state championships in 2004, where I won seven gold medals.

274

An article from *Swimming World Magazine* covering the tie between Maya DiRado and me for the high-point award at Far Westerns.

Photo by Guy Miller

CALIFORNIA Maya DiRado (left) of Santa Rosa Neptune and **Tera Bradham** of Longhorn (Texas) shared high-point honors among 10-and-unders at Far Westerns in April. DiRado won the 100 yard free (57.64) and 500 free (5:26.63, a Pacific LSC record). Bradham took the 100 IM (1:04.96) and 200 IM (2:19.49, a Texas state record). Both girls swam national Top 16 reportable times in each of their seven individual events.

My mission trip to Guatemala in high school radically changed my perspective on what mattered most in life.

Signing my letter of intent to swim for the University of Arkansas.

My mom and me at an Arkansas baseball game. Woo Pig Sooie!

During my three years at the University of Arkansas, I spent hundreds of hours doing rehabilitative exercises in the athletic training room.

It was such a gift to be in the pool again after my second surgery.

Inside the hyperbaric oxygen therapy chamber. From the outside, I looked like an astronaut!

A couple of days after my third surgery. Excited to be on the road to recovery!

My covenant scar! Count the stitches.

You can take the girl out of the competition, but you can't take the competition out of the girl! #NeverYield

With Dalton Smith, my physical therapist, and my "Eye of the Tiger" K-tape.

At one point, I had to stop painting this due to shoulder pain. I finished it after I rose from the ashes myself.

A screenshot of the Coach's Eye App, which I used to film myself in order to catch compensations in my technique.

Graduation from the U of A with my good friend, Paige, who would later be a bridesmaid in my wedding!

I realized how far I had come once I earned my Texas A&M nameplate.

My athletic trainer, Stacy Germany, and me while I underwent a cupping treatment.

Doing squats in the Aggie weight room. I often did extra leg exercises to avoid shoulder exercises. Photo courtesy of Bailee Starr Photography, LLC.

Backstroke became one of my better strokes, as I compensated for pain.

Me coming through the tunnel of my Aggie teammates during my senior meet, which was my last collegiate home meet as an Aggie.

My friend using her finger to provide scale for my lead during the race in which I came closest to qualifying for Olympic Trials after my third surgery.

My coach, Steve Bultman, holding a faux graduation ceremony for me at a swim meet, since I had to miss the university's ceremony for my master's degree.

I'd just finished my career with a pulled groin and a smile on my face.

I had the opportunity to swim the final race of my career with Bethany Galat, my teammate and good friend.

Sharing my story with athletes at Texas A&M's Fellowship of Christian Athletes. Such a privilege! Photo courtesy of Bailee Starr Photography, LLC.

Finishing strong at the 2019 Life Time CapTex Triathlon. I remain physically active even post-retirement!

When your friend gives you a wetsuit, you do a triathlon in Montana!

I never imagined that lifting a bouquet in the air would be a part of my miracle, but it proved to be one of the best ways of living my miracle yet! Photo courtesy of Ingrid Svare Photography.

How do you live your miracle? Share your miraculous life with me @terabradham by using #liveyourmiracle in your post.

Begin Your Life in Christ

If you're wondering how to begin a relationship with Christ, all you have to do is confess with your mouth and believe with your heart that Jesus died for your sins and was raised from the dead (Romans 10:9), and you will be saved. If you believe it, pray this prayer out loud, or rephrase it in a way that comes from your own heart:

> Lord, I want true freedom. I believe you are the way, the truth, and the life, and no one comes to the Father except through your Son, Jesus Christ.
>
> I believe Jesus died for my sins on the cross and that he was raised to life again. Please forgive me of the wrongs I have committed. I invite you into my life to make me whole, resurrect my ashes, and help me live in true freedom. The truth has set me free, and I am free indeed.
>
> Help me understand your grace, your peace, and your will for me. Thank you, God. In Jesus' name, amen.

Acknowledgments

To my Lord and Savior Jesus Christ: Thank you for giving me this beautiful adventure called life. Thank you for healing me, and thank you for making every day worth living. You are my everything.

To my parents: Thank you for praying for me before I ever entered the world. Thank you for loving me through every aspect of my life and for being the best example of redemption and truth God could have given me. Thank you for fighting for me when the world gave up and for driving across the country for a miracle. God knew what he was doing when he made you my parents, and I'm forever grateful.

To my husband, Jacob: Thank you for believing in my story and the calling God has placed upon my life from our first conversation. Thank you for loving me unconditionally, for challenging me to be all God created me to be, and for leading me to greater heights than I ever could have reached alone.

To Steve Bultman: Thank you for giving me a chance when you had every right not to. Thank you for treating me like gold even when I never won you a gold. This book would have had a very different ending without you.

To my agent, Julie Gwinn: Thank you for believing in my potential. Thank you for seeing the fingerprints of God at work in my story as an unpublished author. And thank you for dreaming big with me. This book would not be where or what it is without your countless hours of work and encouragement.

To my team at BroadStreet Publishing: Thank you for making me a published author. Thank you for valuing my story and my heart while helping make this book as relatable and powerful as it could be. I am grateful to each of you for your support, areas of expertise, and your passion for making Jesus known through the power of writing. I know God led me to the exact publisher he wanted me to have.

To every person who has spoken an encouraging or timely word to me: Life is not made up of the grandiose, sweeping moments of victory but of all the little moments of encouragement in between. I cannot count the number of people whose smile, whose simple word, and whose sincerity gave me just enough grace to keep fighting. You helped write this story in more ways than you know.

To you: Thank you for taking the time to read my story. I pray that you trust God to lead you into the miraculous, that you don't take any moment for granted, that you fight for your destiny, and that you have faith to walk into the impossible life you were meant to live.

About the Author

Tera Bradham is an author, speaker, podcast host, and fitness coach, but she has also been a Spanish teacher, a swimming coach, a journalist, and a travel vlogger. After growing up in Round Rock, Texas, she swam for the University of Arkansas and for Texas A&M University before heading to South America on a year of missions with the World Race. God added another plot twist to her life when she met the man of her dreams, who happened to be from Montana. She now relishes the beauty of Bozeman's mountains each day with her husband, Jacob. Her heart's deepest passion is for others to know her extraordinary God who makes every day a miraculous adventure.